ACCOUNTING CLASSICS SERIES

Editor

ROBERT R. STERLING
University of Kansas

Publication of this Classic was made possible by a
grant from the PRICE WATERHOUSE FOUNDATION

Suggestions of titles to be included in the Series
are solicited and should be addressed to the Editor.

Publications of SCHOLARS BOOK CO.

FINANCIAL ACCOUNTING

A Distillation of Experience

FINANCIAL ACCOUNTING

A Distillation of Experience

by

GEORGE O. MAY

Formerly senior Partner, Price, Waterhouse & Co.,
Certified Public Accountants; lecturer at the
Graduate School of Business Administration,
Harvard University

SCHOLARS BOOK CO.
BOX 3344
LAWRENCE, KANSAS 66044

This edition is reprinted by arrangement
with The Macmillan Company.

REPRINTED 1972 BY
SCHOLARS BOOK CO.

In this volume the American Institute of Accountants is commonly referred to as "the Institute," the American Accounting Association as "the Association," and the National Association of Railroad and Utilities Commissioners as "the NARUC."

Foreword

FINANCIAL ACCOUNTING is now generally recognized as being primarily historical in character and as having for its most important function the extraction and presentation of the essence of the financial experience of businesses, so that decisions affecting the present and the future may be taken in the light of the past. The rules of accounting, even more than those of law, are the product of experience rather than of logic.

Similarly, this book is an attempt to extract and present the essence of an experience in financial accounting in the hope that it may be helpful to those called upon to deal with the problems of the future. It is not the result of a study and appraisal of authorities, and the views that are expressed are those of its author alone—indeed, publication has been delayed until formal ties and official positions which might have been deemed to imply more than a personal responsibility for them have been relinquished. In part, it is based on lectures delivered at the Graduate School of Business Administration of Harvard University and papers written for other purposes since 1936. A few passages have been reproduced from the volume which those who were then partners, with generous insight, prepared in that year to mark the twenty-fifth anniversary of the author's assumption of senior partnership.

The writing of such a book seemed to be justified by the fact that the experience on which it is based extended over a period of exceptional interest and was enriched by close association with men of eminence here and abroad, not only in accounting but in government, business, finance, law, and economics. The obligation owed to those who have contributed to that experience is great, but can be expressed to them here only collectively. Grateful recognition must, however, be given to the guidance, friendship, and inspiration of Arthur Lowes Dickinson, who by his abilities, his writings, and above all, by his example, earned an outstanding place among the independent accountants of America, to whom this book is gratefully dedicated.

Contents

FINANCIAL ACCOUNTING

A Distillation of Experience

CHAPTER I

The Nature of Financial Accounting

The conventional boundaries which we have drawn
between things human and things divine are after all
only the expedients of convenience.
—LORD MACMILLAN, *Law and Other Things*, page 74

ACCOUNTING HAS BEEN defined by a committee of the
American Institute of Accountants as "the art of recording,
classifying and summarizing in a significant manner and in
terms of money, transactions and events which are, in part
at least, of a financial character, and interpreting the results
thereof." [1] It is an art, not a science, but an art of wide and
varied usefulness. The purely recording function of accounting, though indispensable, concerns only technicians. Its
analytical and interpretive functions are of two kinds: one
type of analysis is intended to afford aid to management in
the conduct of business and is of interest mainly to executives; the other type leads to the presentation of statements
relating to the financial position and results of operations
of a business for the guidance of directors, stockholders,
credit grantors, and others. This process of financial accounting, therefore, possesses a wide importance for persons who
are neither accountants nor executives.

The forms of financial accounts generally regarded as
most useful are the balance sheet and the income account.
Other forms of statement may be and sometimes are adopted,

---

[1] Accounting Research Bulletin No. 7, p. 58.

such as those prepared under the Double Account system employed by English railways. But for the present it will be convenient to consider the standard forms of presentation. It will also be assumed that these statements should be harmonized; hence the problems of the two accounts are interrelated. Difficult questions arise in determining what shall be included in assets and liabilities and how the amounts at which they are to be stated shall be arrived at; also, in deciding what constitutes income; and, most difficult of all, when income shall be deemed to emerge or arise.

The purpose of this volume is to discuss and illustrate the nature of the process of financial accounting which produces such statements, in the light of fifty years of accounting experience in the United States, England, and elsewhere. In 1926, when I was completing twenty-five years of active partnership, I decided to relinquish my administrative duties and devote a large part of my time to consideration of the broader aspects of accounting. As a result of that study I became convinced that a sound accounting structure could not be built until misconceptions had been cleared away, and the nature of the accounting process and the limitations on the significance of the financial statements which it produced were more frankly recognized.

It became clear to me that general acceptance of the fact that accounting was utilitarian and based on conventions (some of which were necessarily of doubtful correspondence with fact) was an indispensable preliminary to real progress. A statement of these fundamental characteristics of accounting was embodied in the first bulletin issued by the Research Department of the American Institute of Accountants in September, 1939, and has not been seriously questioned. I shall discuss later other statements relating to accounting principles or procedures, such as those of the American Accounting Association.

Many accountants were reluctant to admit that accounting

was based on nothing of a higher order of sanctity than conventions. However, it is apparent that this is necessarily true of accounting as it is, for instance, of business law. In these fields there are no principles, in the more fundamental sense of that word, on which we can build; and the distinctions between laws, rules, standards, and conventions lie not in their nature but in the kind of sanctions by which they are enforced. Accounting procedures have in the main been the result of common agreement between accountants, though they have to some extent, and particularly in recent years, been influenced by laws or regulations.

Conventions, to have authority, must be well conceived. Accounting conventions should be well conceived in relation to at least three things: first, the uses of accounts; second, the social and economic concepts of the time and place, and, third, the modes of thought of the people. It follows that as economic and social concepts or modes of thought change, accounting concepts may have to change with them.

The first point for consideration is, therefore, what are the major uses of financial accounts. We can recognize at least ten distinguishable uses:

1. As a report of stewardship;
2. As a basis for fiscal policy;
3. To determine the legality of dividends;
4. As a guide to wise dividend action;
5. As a basis for the granting of credit;
6. As information for prospective investors in an enterprise;
7. As a guide to the value of investments already made;
8. As an aid to Government supervision;
9. As a basis for price or rate regulation;
10. As a basis for taxation.

General purpose accounts are not suitable in all of these cases; in some instances, special purpose accounts are called for. This has become increasingly recognized in respect of rate or price control and taxation, and it should also be recognized, for reasons which will be indicated later, in respect of information for new investors—or, in other words, for the prospectus—and also in some cases for the determination of the legality of a dividend. But even if these purposes are eliminated there remain at least six which are expected to be served by general purpose accounts.

It is immediately apparent that any general purpose accounts cannot be expected to serve all the purposes equally well—indeed, if they are to be appropriate for the major use it is likely that they will not serve some other purposes even reasonably well. It becomes necessary to consider which are to be regarded as the controlling objectives, and the possibility of changes therein.

Accounting conventions must take cognizance of the social and economic concepts of the time and place. Conventions which are acceptable in a pioneer, free-enterprise economy may not be equally appropriate in a more mature, free-enterprise economy, and may lose their validity in a controlled economy. Some existing accounting conventions seem to assume implicitly the existence of laissez-faire and may require reconsideration as prices, interest rates, and other vital elements become the subject of conscious Government control. Under this head must be considered, also, the forms of business organization and changes either in the character of the dominant type or types or in the laws governing them. Systems of taxation and legal decisions growing out of them also influence accounting concepts.

The third and last consideration which has been mentioned as affecting accounting conventions is the modes of thought of the people. The extent of legal influence in business affairs will affect the conventions and those developed in the atmosphere of the common law will differ from those evolved under a civil code system. So, too, a people who think in terms of capital value and a people who think in terms of annual value will naturally reach different conclusions on some points, as is evidenced by the American and British attitudes towards capital gains and losses in taxation and accounting.

The relevance and importance of such considerations as these have been borne in on me by the events of the forty-five years of my experience in American accounting. Within this time we have moved from what might be called the last days of a pioneer, free-enterprise economy to a period in which a large and growing segment of enterprise is under a substantial measure of Government control. The major part of the development of the corporation as the typical form of business organization has occurred within it; this is even more true of the separation of beneficial ownership from management.

Beginning with the control over railroad accounting given to the Interstate Commerce Commission in 1906, we have seen a steady growth of accounting by prescription and a shift from the common-law mode of thought towards that of the civil code.

The laxness of our corporation laws and the ease of reincorporation have impaired the significance of the corporation as an accounting unit. The extension of intercorporate holdings has increased the importance of accounting for interest, dividends, and other forms of transferred income; manifestly, such accounting involves different problems from those encountered in dealing with primary income, such as that from manufacturing. The creation of a wide variety of forms of capital obligations has raised questions as to the accounting significance of legal distinctions, often highly artificial, between bonds and stocks and between interest and dividends.

Perhaps the most significant change of all is the shift of emphasis from the balance sheet to the income account, and particularly to the income account as a guide to earning capacity rather than as an indication of accretions to disposable income.

It is appropriate, next, to consider what alternative approaches to the problem of formulating or revising the conventions of financial accounting are open to us. First of all, there is a choice between the value and the cost approach, or perhaps rather a question how the two can best be combined. This combination is illustrated in the custom of carrying inventories at cost or market value, whichever is lower—one of the oldest of accounting practices.

There is a choice between different concepts of income and between different theories of allocation of income to periods. We have the concept according to which income arises gradually, and the concept which treats income as arising at a moment when realization is deemed to have occurred. Here again, both concepts are in practice adopted to some, but not to an unchanging, extent. Today, an interesting question is presented whether accounting is likely to move in the direction of a more complete adherence to the realization concept of income or towards wider application of the doctrine of gradual accrual.

There is also a choice between the enterprise and the legal entity that carries on the enterprise as the accounting unit. The system of consolidated accounts, freely employed in corporate reporting, is a departure from the strict separate entity theory. In recent years, the adoption by public service commissions of the concept of cost to the first person who devoted property to the public service, as the basis of property accounting of the present owners, has created a new interest in enterprise accounting, of which the concept is a crude and inadequate variant.

The range of possible choice of conventions might be extended if some postulates, commonly adopted, were discarded. It is, for instance, generally assumed that financial accounts must be in a continuous, related series, but it may be argued that there is no absolute compulsion that they should be. The problem of continuity presents difficulties when a substantial change of conventions occurs—as, for

instance, when public utility corporations are required for
financial accounting purposes (and not merely for rate purposes) to account for property on the basis of the cost to the
first purchaser who devoted the property to public service,
instead of on the traditional basis of cost to themselves; or
when straight-line depreciation accounting is substituted for
other methods of dealing with consumption of property that
have been employed and sanctioned for decades.

Again, the monetary unit is generally assumed to be substantially constant in value, but at times this assumption of
stability has to be abandoned, with the result that accounting
conventions have to be modified.

The choice of conventions in financial accounting as in
cost accounting is to some extent affected by the conflict
between considerations of speed, accuracy, and expense. The
accountant is called upon to produce general purpose accounts
within a few weeks of the completion of the fiscal period to
which they relate. Those accounts are expected to be final
and to serve a great diversity of purposes. Delay in preparation might permit of greater refinement but impair the usefulness of the statements; hence conventions must be such as
to be capable of prompt application.

*   *   *

In the chapters which follow, the elements of the process
of formulating or revising financial accounting conventions
will be considered in some detail. It, however, seems desirable
to indicate by brief consideration of one or more problems
the bearing of the observations already made.

In a pioneer economy, the great opportunity for making
profits is likely to lie in participation in the growth of the
country and in the increase of values which accompanies it.
At such a time capital will be relatively scarce, while labor—
particularly if there is free immigration—may be plentiful.
These causes will contribute to make capital investment rela-

tively small; and the proportion of assets that is readily salable, and may be expected to be realized in a short time, will be comparatively high.

In such circumstances, the value approach to accounting has a strong appeal. In reading American accounting literature, it is surprising to find how generally accounting was described at one time as a process of valuation, up to how recent a date this view was maintained, and how pronounced and rapid the change has been. In a more mature economy, when greater capital resources and perhaps, also, changes in labor conditions tend to produce constantly increasing capital investment, business units become larger and enterprises more complex. Then, the valuation approach becomes impracticable and resort to cost as the primary line of approach becomes almost inevitable.

The change from a value basis to a cost basis will be discussed at length in a later chapter. For the present, it is sufficient to note that it is a change of great importance in relation to such matters as the rate base and the "surplus assets" theory of limitation of dividends. It is undeniable, though not fully recognized outside the profession, that books of large enterprises are kept predominantly on a cost basis and do not, therefore, constitute evidence of the value of either the enterprise as a whole or the separate assets thereof, particularly the capital assets. This might be deemed to be a serious defect of accounting procedures but for two considerations: first, that the value of the enterprise is seldom a material fact; and, secondly, that when it is, it can only be measured by looking ahead. The sole relevance of accounts of the past is as throwing light on the prospects for the future. These considerations have additional force where the implicit assumption that the monetary unit remains stable is widely at variance with reality—as, for instance, in the case of property acquired before a decline in the purchasing power of the monetary unit such as occurred between 1913 and 1920.

Again, forty-five years ago the external influence on accounting that had the greatest effect was that of the credit grantor. In recent years there has been a marked shift of emphasis, and the use of accounts as a guide in the purchase or sale of securities has been more heavily stressed as a result of the efforts to impart liquidity to investments in long-term enterprises. In the early days, conservatism was the cardinal virtue of accounting; now, the virtue of conservatism is questioned, and the greater emphasis is on consistency. At that time, also, uniform classifications that were binding on particular forms of enterprises were practically unknown. Today, they are numerous and increasing in number and scope.

In this chapter the object has been to bring out the true nature of the accounting process and to prepare the way for a consideration of accounting conventions, not as something fixed and unalterable, but as something that, like the law, should have elements of stability and of flexibility. Times are changing and accounting conventions will change with them. Today, a study of the historical development of accounting conventions and of the causes which have brought about change may be more useful than a description of present practice. It has frequently been said that the changes revealed by successive balance sheets are more significant than the individual balance sheets themselves. The same may be true of the conventions upon which balance sheets are based.

APPENDIX TO CHAPTER I

Accounting Authorities

THE AMERICAN INSTITUTE OF ACCOUNTANTS is representative of the practicing accountants of the country but includes in its membership a considerable number of teachers of accounting. It maintains a research department under a Committee on Accounting Procedure (of which its Committee on Terminology is now in practice a subcommittee) and has issued a series of bulletins, now numbering seventeen. The American Accounting Association, whose membership is drawn to a greater extent from academic sources, has been engaged in studies in the same field. In 1936, it issued *A Tentative Statement of Accounting Principles Underlying Corporate Financial Statements* and in June, 1941, it put out a revised edition of that statement. In the interval, it sponsored a number of monographs including one entitled *An Introduction to Corporate Accounting Standards*, by W. A. Paton and A. C. Littleton.

The Securities Act of 1933 and the Securities Exchange Act of 1934, ·sometimes herein referred to as the Securities Acts, granted the Securities and Exchange Commission certain powers in relation to accounts. The accounting section of the Commission has kept in close touch with the Institute, and, in general, its object seems to have been to secure the recognition of desirable conventions through cooperative action. Through its accounting releases, and to a greater extent, perhaps, through its informal expressions of opinion and the positions it has taken on specific questions arising in relation to statements required to be filed with it, the Commission has exercised great influence on developments in this field in the last few years. The older regulatory bodies, such as the Interstate Commerce Commission and the various public utility commissions, have naturally been affected by the new interest and have advanced new accounting concepts.

The National Association of Railroad and Utilities Commissioners has an accounting section which has sought to strengthen the control of utility accounting. It has also been active in promoting the development and application of the doctrine according to which fixed property accounting is required to be based on cost to the person who first devoted it to the public service. This development has been strongly resisted.

The Institute Committee, in its first bulletin issued in September, 1939, indicated the standpoint from which it would approach the subject of financial accounting and made it clear that all its pronouncements should be read in the light of that indication. It said:

The Committee regards corporation accounting as one phase of the working of the corporate organization of business, which in turn it views as a machinery created by the people in the belief that, broadly speaking, it will serve a useful social purpose. The test of the corporate system and of the special phase of it represented by corporate accounting ultimately lies in the results which are produced. These results must be judged from the standpoint of society as a whole—not from that of any one group of interested parties.

The uses to which the corporate system is put and the controls to which it is subject change from time to time, and all parts of the machinery must be adapted to meet such changes as they occur. In the last forty years the outstanding change in the working of the corporate system has been an increasing use of it for the purpose of converting into liquid and readily transferable form the ownership of large, complex and more or less permanent business enterprises. . . .

As a result of this development in the field of accounting, problems have come to be considered more from the standpoint of the current buyer or seller in the market of an interest in the enterprise than from the standpoint of a continuing owner. The significance of this change is perhaps not yet fully appreciated. . . .

The American Accounting Association in its statement issued in June, 1941, expressed the view that

every corporate statement should be based on accounting principles which are sufficiently uniform, objective, and well understood to justify opinions as to the condition and progress of the business enterprise behind it.

Its "basic" assumption was that

the purpose of periodic financial statements of a corporation is to furnish information that is necessary for the formulation of dependable judgments.

The statement went on to assert that for this purpose "a knowledge of the origin and expiration of the economic resources of a company" was needed, and, finally, that "a unified and coordinated body of accounting theory" was required.

Neither of these pronouncements offers more than an indication of a general point of view. Usefulness, which the Institute adopted as its test, is an indefinite concept. In the Association's statement the word "sufficiently" denotes something short of completeness, and the text of the statement demonstrates the need for its inclusion in the passage above quoted. It may be questioned whether any degree of uniformity, objectivity, and comprehension will suffice to insure statements from which "dependable" judgments as to the condition and progress of an enterprise can be formed. It may be questioned, also, whether financial statements as customarily published are adequate for such a purpose or reveal the "origin" of economic resources of a company.

The Association seems to be in danger of overrating what

accounting can perform. In the statement of 1936, the Association spoke only of the possibility of forming "at least tentative business judgments," and this language may have been—more appropriate than the less guarded language of the revised statement. Here, as everywhere in accounting, it is important to recognize not only what useful results accounts and accounting can accomplish, but also the limitations on their possibilities.

The Association would scarcely claim that the principles and the specific applications thereof which it puts forward are so universally accepted as to constitute "laws or rules adopted or professed as a guide to action"; indeed, it is certain that some are not, and it is probable that some should not be so accepted. However, apart from a few minor proposals that would involve a complete change of practice, the subject matter of the differences between the Institute and the Association is relatively small, though important in the case of a minority of companies in normal times, and particularly in times like the present, when the degree of uncertainty in relation to profits and financial position is greatly increased.

Viewed philosophically, the contrast between the practicing and the academic accountants in their approach to problems may reflect their attitudes towards the risk of managerial misrepresentation. The dweller in the academic world, fearful, perhaps, of being deemed naïve, is apt to exaggerate the danger. The experienced practitioner not only rates it as less extensive but regards it as only a part of the risk entailed in the separation of management from beneficial ownership rather than as a major element of the accounting problem.

CHAPTER II

The Uses of Accounts and Their Influence on Accounting

Concepts of Income; the Accounting Unit

WHILE THIS VOLUME deals only with financial accounts, the materials upon which those accounts are based are the product of the recording function of accounting, and the form in which they are available is to a large extent affected by classifications adopted primarily for administrative purposes.

The balance sheet and the income account, which are the typical accounts under consideration, are products of the double-entry system of accounting. When concepts of income come to be considered, one will be presented which views income as an increase in net worth, and another, which regards it as the gain from the use of capital and labor. The first of these contemplates a process of enumeration and subtraction; the second involves an analytical process. A single-entry computation is sometimes thought to be sufficient for the application of the first of these concepts, but double-entry methods are far superior even for that purpose and are indispensable if the second concept is adopted.

In applying the first concept, income is measured from comparative balance sheets, and the income account merely supplements the determination by an analysis of its origin. Where the second concept is used, the income account discloses the amount of income, and the balance sheet shows what has become of it. In both cases the double-entry account-

14

ing supplies a check which is invaluable. Industrial experience has repeatedly demonstrated the dangers inherent in computations of costs or profits which are not so tied in with the financial accounts as to insure that all costs have been allocated in one way or another. Today, such integration is recognized as indispensable to the establishment of reliable factual bases for policies and actions.

The importance of this point and its wide applicability are apparent to anyone who has examined with care the purely statistical information in regard to the so-called national income and savings that has been officially disseminated, including that presented by distinguished economists in testimony before the Temporary National Economic Committee or in monographs published under the auspices of that body. If such material had always been the product of a rigorous system of double-entry accounting, many fallacies and unwarranted conclusions would have been avoided.

Professor Schumpeter, in discussing the practice which "turns the unit of money into a tool of rational cost-profit calculations," has spoken of double-entry bookkeeping as being its "towering monument." [1] It is to be feared that most economists and statisticians regard double-entry bookkeeping as just that—a monument to be admired from afar, rather than a technique to be acquired. They are less attracted by its humbler virtues than by the dangerous charms of extrapolation.

A few years ago I was drawn into a discussion of the question whether credit for work in accounting should be given to applicants for the doctor's degree in economics. The only legitimate doubt seemed to be whether such work should be the basis for a credit or whether an adequate understanding of the principles and a working knowledge of the methods of

---

[1] *Capitalism, Socialism and Democracy,* Joseph A. Schumpeter (New York: Harper & Brothers, 1943), p. 123.

double-entry accounting should be established as a preliminary requirement.

The separation of beneficial ownership from control and the recognition of a social interest in the corporations in which such a separation has occurred have created a management class which does not and should not consider itself as responsible solely to the securityholders, to whom in theory its members owe their positions, but recognizes a duty to the whole economy.

During this century, also, the immense value of accounting as an aid to administration has received full recognition. Hence the problem of providing appropriate financial statements is complicated not only by the variety of uses to which such accounts are put but also by demands for classification of transactions in the form that is most useful for administrative purposes.

It is manifestly economical where possible to use analyses for both administrative and financial accounting purposes, and within limits some sacrifice of maximum usefulness for either purpose may be justified to make a double serviceability possible. A practical limit is thus set on uniformity in financial accounting. This limit is particularly important in relation to allocations of costs between periods such as arise in accounting for inventories (see Chapter X).

There is always the danger that the administrative views about a corporation's accounting may be affected by the self-interest of the executive. Some look for a safeguard against this danger in an enforced uniformity. But events and transactions are many-sided, and it is not always easy to decide whether resemblances or points of difference should control the accounting treatment of them. The more effective protection lies in establishment of broad principles and in the acceptance of responsibility for their proper application by accounting officers and especially by the independent auditors whose primary duty is owed to actual and potential stock-holders.

The claims of administrative convenience cannot justify use in the preparation of financial accounts of classifications which do not conform to accepted principles. The treatment of selling expense or of interest as a part of cost will serve as an illustration of this point. Inclusion may be convenient for some administrative purposes but it is not sanctioned by accounting rules or principles. It is not permissible in the preparation of balance sheets or income statements or, therefore, in general accounting, though there is no objection to it in supplementary administrative calculations.

Emphasis on the fact that this volume does not deal with the recording and administrative uses of accounting is necessary to insure a proper perspective and to avoid the creation of an impression that the changes and conflicts of opinion regarding accounting methods that will be noted indicate a greater degree of uncertainty than has existed or exists. The ocean depths are unaffected by the winds and tides which disturb the surface waters. And the bookkeeper, immersed in the recording and administrative functions of accounting, may be unconscious of the changing tides with which the financial accountant must struggle. But as the tides may be harnessed or the surface waters may be diverted to serve great purposes, good or bad, so the direction given to financial accounting practices may have a profound influence on the economy. That the power to control financial accounting has often been abused in the past is undeniable; and the transfer of control from one policy-making group to another does not necessarily dispel the dangers of misuse.

An illustration of the dangers is afforded by the seemingly simple proposition that stock dividends may be treated as income to the extent of the value of the stock received. As will be shown later, acceptance of this rule was a vital part of a system which produced disastrous consequences in the financial orgy of the late 1920's. The New York Stock Exchange eventually set its face against it and the American Institute of Accountants has also expressed strong disapproval of the proposition. Yet qualified support, at least, was given to it in a recent dissenting opinion in the Supreme Court.[1]

In the simplest forms of cooperative activity accounting problems arise, and the way in which they are decided influences action. The administrators of even a non-profit institution—a club, for instance—are called upon to account to its members. Shall they limit the accounts to actual receipts and disbursements? Must they not at least exclude, or deal separately with, borrowings and repayments? If they ignore unpaid bills, may there not be a temptation to delay payments that ought to be made in order to present a more favorable showing? If bills owing by the club but unpaid are to be brought into account, should not amounts owing to the club also be taken into consideration? In technical language, should not the account be one of income and expenditure rather than one of receipts and disbursements? Taking a further step— in order to reduce the cost thereof, insurance has been written for three years; should the whole cost be charged against the one year and the next two years be relieved of any corresponding charge? Or, an automobile has been bought—should the cost be charged against the year or distributed over the probable useful life of the car? Speaking technically again, should not some accrual basis of accounting be employed?

From this example it is easy to see how considerations of policy may influence accounting, or how the form of accounting may influence the course of events. One form of accounting may show a balance for the year in favor of the club, with the result that the dues may be left unchanged or even reduced; another may show a balance against the club

---

[1] *Griffiths* v. *Helvering*, 308 U.S. 355. See also Chap. XI.

and lead to an increase of dues. Reluctance to put an increase in force may lead the administrators to choose the method which gives the seemingly more favorable result.

In a complex business organization, the problems are varied and difficult and the amount of profit shown for a period may differ greatly as one or another method of accounting is employed. The most appropriate method may vary with the purpose for which the account is required.

Financial statements are usually intended to be acted upon, and once issued they may be put to any one of many uses by those into whose hands they come. They are significant even more on account of the inferences that are likely to be drawn from them on account of their character as statements of fact or opinion.

Recognition of these truths, and of the responsibility that they impose on him, is a part of the fundamental professional obligations of the independent accountant. But to impose on a management or an accountant even a moral obligation to anticipate all the uses to which statements may be put, and to prepare them in such a way that no one may fairly claim to have been misled by them for whatever purpose he may have employed them, would be to set an impossible standard. A financial statement, like a word, must be interpreted in relation to all the circumstances attending its use. No one has a right to interpret a report of stewardship as though it were an invitation to invest.

In the first chapter, ten major uses of accounts were mentioned. An examination of that list will show that the first five might be regarded as the older, and the second five as the more modern, uses of accounting statements; and the distinction between the two is significant. Those in the first group are:

1. As a report of stewardship;
2. As a basis of fiscal policy;
3. To determine the legality of dividends;

4. As a guide to wise dividend action;
5. As a basis for the granting of credit.

American dividend laws vary so greatly that general purpose accounts are not likely to be adequate in every case for the determination of the legality of a proposed dividend. The remaining four uses in this group do not present any conflict so marked as to make difficult the formulation of general purpose accounting conventions that will serve them all reasonably well. In each case, there is an attempt to appraise the past, and to measure the cumulative achievement to date; there is no attempt to use the past as a measure of the future, nor any great stress on the allocations of past achievement to particular years. For each of these purposes, conservatism (a common term in accounting which may, perhaps, be defined as a disposition to resolve doubts in the measurement of assets or profit on the side of understatement) is a major virtue. If the doubts are more favorably resolved by the event, the benefit of the past conservatism will be reflected in the accounts at that time.

Accounting for these purposes recognized the provisional character of all measurements of income and the even greater uncertainty attaching to attempts to allocate income to particular short periods of time.

When a business was to be bought or sold, a reexamination of accounts used to be undertaken and new statements were prepared in the light of all the information then available and on a basis appropriate to the purpose. Reserves which had been made, and had later been shown to be excessive or inadequate, were revised. If, in the past, estimates had been made and later exact amounts had been ascertained, the differences between the estimates and the final charges or credits were brought into account in the period to which the latest information showed them to belong.

Into this, in retrospect idyllic, accounting scene, there

entered in rapid succession the disturbing influences of the regulator of rates; the assessor of income tax; and, most important of all, the dealer or speculator in securities intent on measuring the earnings per share to which his multiplier might be applied to arrive at a capital value.

It is difficult to overestimate the influences on corporate financial accounting of the second group of uses listed in Chapter I, which were thus created: viz.

  6. As information for prospective investors in an enterprise;
  7. As a guide to the value of investments already made;
  8. As an aid to Government supervision;
  9. As a basis for price or rate regulation;
10. As a basis for taxation.

Of these, three—Numbers 6, 9, and 10—were said to call for special purpose accounts.

The use of accounts as a guide to the value of investments already made was an outgrowth of the efforts to convert participations in permanent enterprises into liquid assets through distribution of corporate securities and the establishment of markets in which those securities could be freely bought and sold. This development has created the most crucial problems of financial accounting, and the present ferment in accounting thought is very largely due to conflicting objectives of those who would continue to regard financial statements as reports of progress or of stewardship, and those who would treat them as being in the nature of prospectuses.

Whether the experience of a company in the recent past is likely to be repeated in the near future is practically immaterial if financial statements are to be considered as reports of stewardship or as guides to the profits that may properly be distributed. It is of paramount importance if they are to be used as a guide in determining whether to buy, hold, or sell securities.

The prospective investor is not interested in past earnings

as such—they are significant to him only in so far as they are a guide to the future. It is not unreasonable, therefore, to require a management which invites subscriptions to a new issue of securities to choose between two alternatives if it has reason to believe that changes in conditions known to it but not to the potential investor make recurrence of past earnings unlikely. It should either refrain from making a representation as to past earnings; or, alternatively, should accompany any statement of earnings with a clear expression of the changed conditions, sufficient to indicate their probable effect on earning capacity. But it would be intolerable to place upon managements the burden of telling stockholders annually to what extent the recent past should be regarded as a fair indication of the probable future.

In England, the purely historical character of the annual report is not questioned. The managements of English companies do, of course, frequently discuss both the value of assets and the immediate outlook; but usually this is done cautiously, and the reference to the future is more likely to be found in the speech of the chairman at the annual meeting than in the formal annual report.

It seems desirable that the annual financial statements of American corporations should also be regarded as historical and in no sense prophetic, notwithstanding that the stock of the company may be listed and freely traded in. No doubt responsible managements will bear in mind that the statements, even though historical in character, will be used to some extent as a guide to the future; and at their discretion they may from time to time see fit to give expression to warnings or other comments based on recognition of this fact. How and when they should do so must, however, always remain a matter of discretion, and whether the discretion as to forecasting will be wisely exercised is but one of the hazards of management which the investor must run.

It has been said in Chapter I that special purpose accounts are called for in a prospectus. No doubt there are some who would not accept this view; but rejection of it would seem to be warranted only on the assumption that general purpose accounts should be so kept as to be appropriate for the quite exceptional case in which they are to be used in connection with a sale of securities. In a prospectus, accounts are normally presented covering a series of years. In respect to the earlier years the available information may be more extensive and accurate than it was when the accounts covering those years were first prepared. The intending investor should have the additional knowledge reflected in the statements of income submitted to him. It is not satisfactory that he should first be told what the results would have been if the earlier assumptions had been correct, and next, how far they have proved incorrect in the light of later knowledge, and be left to make his own computations.

An illustration of the point is afforded by an actual case in which the period for which income was reported in a prospectus under the present law included a year in which an important rate case had been decided. The income account for that year, as shown in the prospectus, reflected the adjustments made in respect of earlier years as a result of that decision. These adjustments affected not only revenues but depreciation charges, and as a result thereof there was a credit under the head of "depreciation" for that year instead of the customary charge. Of course, a full explanation was given in a footnote; but nothing could better emphasize the point that special purpose accounts are desirable in a registration statement or a prospectus, and that the practice of regarding an annual report as in the nature of a prospectus should be discouraged.

Similar evidence is afforded when railroad companies present in prospectuses accounts prepared in accordance with

Interstate Commerce Commission requirements, which are naturally designed for the primary purpose of meeting the needs of the Commission.

However, though annual reports are presented as historical documents and corporations sometimes take the precaution of attaching to them an intimation that they are not to be regarded as representations or invitations to purchase, the fact that annual statements are used as a guide to investment policy has materially influenced the development of accounting in recent decades. It is this fact that has caused the shift of emphasis from the balance sheet to the income account, that is, perhaps, the most significant change of recent years.

Conservatism in the statement of results of operations in the past may lead to overstatement of the profits of a later period. Therefore, while it may commend itself to the permanent investor, whose interest is in the cumulative total of profits, it may be regarded as misleading by one whose interest is to get as accurate an apportionment to particular years as is attainable. In the discussion of the parts that cost and value respectively should play in financial accounting (which will form the subject of later chapters), the influence of the new uses of accounts will become apparent.

Accounts as a report of stewardship by the management of a corporation are in many respects similar in purpose to reports of trustees to beneficiaries. It is natural that the management should account for the assets coming into its charge on the basis of cost to the corporation, and that only on rare occasions, if any, should any reflection of changes in value that have not been realized be considered.

The grantor of credit in the past was chiefly interested in what has been graphically called the "pounce" value. He was not greatly concerned with the basis on which the fixed assets were carried, since their value in case of default would have to be appraised in an entirely different way. He was, however, insistent that current assets, such as inventories, should be conservatively stated, and his support had much to do with the general adherence to the rule that inventories should be taken at cost or market, whichever is the lower. The influence of the grantor of credit has in recent years diminished, and his point of view has been affected by changes in the bankruptcy law designed to facilitate reorganization. These changes have restricted the right to "pounce" and shifted the emphasis from salvage value to earning capacity, where reorganization is possible.

The increase in intercorporate holdings of securities has enhanced the importance of accounting for interest, dividends, and other profits and losses arising out of holdings of such securities. Interest and dividends do not represent a creation of income but merely transfers of income. The distinction between the income which is created by a corporation or enterprise and that of which it is merely the transferee is important, but is inadequately recognized in most discussions of accounting principles and procedures. Realization is regarded as a crucial test in accounting; but a realization which represents the culmination of a process of creating income has an altogether different significance from that of a realization which is merely a transfer to a beneficiary of income already created by the transferor. A useful advance in corporate and financial practice would be effected if the distinction between "income from operations" and "transfer income" should become more universally emphasized.

Concepts of Income

Against the background that has been sketched the question may be considered of what concept of income is most appropriate in corporation accounting and what theory of allocation of income between years can most usefully be applied.

"Income" is a word of many meanings. In the terminology of manufacturing and trading it has displaced the older and more suggestive word, "profit." [1] (Both words have often been employed—sometimes with the prefix "gross"—to describe something that was not a clear gain to the corporation or enterprise in respect of which it was used.) The use of the terms "profit" and "profit and loss account" suggests the important truth that gain is usually a difference and must be measured by matching costs and expenses against revenue. This usage also provides a constant reminder of the fact that costs and expenses may exceed revenue and produce the loss that is the antithesis of profit.

The sacrifice of significance resulting from the substitution of the word "income" is not justified by the slight gain in brevity. However, in the accounting field there seems to be a constant disposition to sacrifice accuracy to terseness, and in this case the tendency is so encouraged by the existence of income taxation that it is perhaps necessary to accept the newer terminology.

The considerations recited, however, point to the desirability of adopting as the concept of income that which is suggested by the word "profit." The definition accepted by the Supreme Court in *Eisner* v. *Macomber* [2] reasonably fits this requirement, though the proviso which it contains may be reserved for future consideration. The main body of the definition, adopted from earlier cases, was: "Income may be defined as the gain derived from capital, from labor, or from both combined." To this the Court added the words: "provided it be understood to include profits gained through a sale or conversion of capital assets."

Another concept adopts the analogy of the tree and the fruit; but danger lurks in this as in many another analogy. It leads to the error, against which the Supreme Court definition guards, of treating the entire proceeds of sale as income

---

[1] The change may be noted in the 1921 edition of *Auditing Theory and Practice*, Robert H. Montgomery.

[2] *Eisner* v. *Macomber*, 252 U.S. 189.

without regard to the costs necessarily entailed. This error is common in economic analysis. The analogy does, however, suggest one view of income which is accepted to some extent in the United States and to a greater extent in England.

It is common to compute the income of a mine without regard to the exhaustion of the mineral areas; and the statutes of some states, such as Pennsylvania, expressly sanction this procedure. The same idea is carried to greater lengths in England both in corporate accounting and in the measurement of taxable income. There, it is clear that a company can be formed to acquire an inherently wasting asset and may determine income without regard to the wastage even if it is capable of being measured exactly, as in the case of a leasehold for a definite term. The larger enterprises, such as canals, railways, gas and other companies, which were incorporated by special acts or governed by what are called the Clauses Acts—which preceded the general law authorizing the creation of companies with limited liability—are regarded as permanent and, as explained elsewhere, follow the double account system of accounting.

The English income-tax law, first imposed in 1797 and repealed at the end of the Napoleonic Wars, was reenacted in 1842, twenty years before the passage of the famous Companies Act of 1862 which may be regarded as marking the beginning of the great period of company formation. Under the English income-tax law it has never been considered essential that provision should always be made for the maintenance of capital in measuring taxable income. This omission has often been criticized, but has been justified on two main grounds: first, that the income from professional and other services is taxed in full without regard to the fact that the source of income is not permanent; and, secondly, that when a man purchases an annuity he deliberately converts his capital into income, and that the State need not be more concerned to preserve his capital than he is.

This attitude is illustrated in the discussion of depreciation to be found in the report of the Royal Commission on the Income Tax of 1920. The Commission, while recommending the formal allowance of depreciation, suggested that the grant should be limited to property having a life of less than thirty-five years.

The specific proposal of the Commission has never been adopted, but the mode of thought indicated by it is reflected in various ways in the text and particularly in the administration of the income-tax law. The provisions of the general Company Law which allow the incorporators of companies wide latitude to decide how wastage of capital assets shall be dealt with are readily understandable in the light of the special company acts and the income-tax law.

American accounting in its earlier stages seems to have been based on a concept of income as an accretion to net worth. This concept goes further than that of the Supreme Court in recognizing capital gains as income, for it treats capital appreciation as income even when unrealized. But the two concepts may be considered together, and a single illustration will present the differences.

Suppose that at the commencement of a year a stock is earning and paying 10 per cent and selling on a "ten times earnings" basis at its par value of $100.00. During the year, changed conditions enable it to earn and pay 11 per cent, with a prospect of maintaining the increase. If stocks were selling on the same yield basis at the end of the year as at the beginning, this stock would presumably sell at 110 at the year's end. But assume that general conditions have brought down the yield of such stocks so that they are selling on an "eleven times earnings" basis—then the stock in question might be expected to sell at 121. If "income" is defined as the increase in net worth, the owner's income from a share of the stock would be $32.00, of which $11.00 would represent current earnings, $10.00 an increase in capital value due to increased earning capacity and $11.00 increased capital value due to a fall in the rate of yield obtainable on stocks.

The Supreme Court definition, through the proviso which was above reserved for later consideration, would produce the same result if the stock were sold on the last day of the year at 121; the income would then be made up of dividends of $11.00 and capital gain of $21.00. If the stock was not sold the income would be $11.00. The English definition would exclude the capital gain in any event and fix the income at $11.00. Without attempting to discuss the relative merits of the three different concepts it is clear that the significance of capital gains and of dividend income is very different where the problem under consideration is measuring capital value from earnings. Recognition of the truth is no doubt responsible for the provision in the Investment Company Act of 1940, which requires that no dividends shall be paid except out of net income, excluding profits or losses realized on the sale of securities or other properties, unless payment thereof is accompanied by a written statement which adequately discloses the source or sources of the payment.[1]

The combination of the concept of income as including capital gains and that of capital value as a multiple of income-producing capacity obviously may and, indeed, did in the financial boom of 1928 and 1929 produce fantastic results. The pyramiding of holding companies intensified the evil effects of the unsound combination of ideas; it also disguised them because what was capital gain to one company of a pyramid became dividend income as it passed on to the next. To a lesser extent the same effects were also manifested in the quotations for stocks of all corporations whose activities included investment.

An interesting illustration of the practical aspect of the question in the case of insurance companies may be found

---

[1] Investment Company Act of 1940, Sec. 19.

in the testimony in *Strong* v. *Rogers*.[1] The cross-examiner appeared really to doubt the honesty of a witness who did not accept the combination of concepts.

ALLOCATION OF INCOME TO PERIODS

The problem of allocation of income to particular short periods obviously offers great difficulty—indeed, it is the point at which conventional treatment becomes indispensable, and it must be recognized that some conventions are scarcely in harmony with the facts. Manifestly, when a laborious process of manufacture and sale culminates in the delivery of the product at a profit, that profit is not attributable, except conventionally, to the moment when the sale or delivery occurred. The accounting convention which makes such an attribution is justified only by its demonstrated practical utility.

It is instructive to consider how it happens that a rule which is violative of fact produces results that are practically useful and reliable. The explanation is, that in the normal business there are at any one moment transactions at every stage of the production of profit, from beginning to end. If the distribution were exactly uniform, an allocation of income according to the proportion of completion of each unit would produce the same result as the attribution of the entire profit to a single stage.

A number of conclusions immediately suggest themselves: first, that the convention is valid for the greatest variety of purposes where the flow of product is most uniform; second, that it is likely to be more generally valid for a longer than for a shorter period; and, third, that its applicability is seriously open to question for some purposes where the final consummation is irregular in time and in amount. Thus, the rule is almost completely valid in regard to a business which is turn-

---

[1] 14 AFTR, 1207. Quoted in *Twenty-five Years of Accounting Responsibility* (Vol. I, pp. 354-355).

ing out a standard product in relatively small units at a reasonably stable rate of production. It is less generally valid—or, to put it otherwise, the figure of profit reached is less generally significant—in the case of a company engaged in building large units, such as battleships, or carrying out construction contracts.

These considerations throw a useful light on the problem of the changing uses of accounts; they also explain a tendency which has been notable during the last fifty years in the accounting treatment of large contracts and similar enterprises. In earlier days, when the use of accounts as an indication of earning capacity was not considered, and when conservatism was clearly a virtue, the procedure of treating the gain on even a large contract as arising at the moment of its completion was unobjectionable—any other method might have resulted in taking credit for a profit that might never be earned. In recent years there has developed a much greater readiness to take credit for profits on uncompleted transactions, in order to secure a more useful guide to earning capacity. Another illustration of the problem presented, particularly as affecting the measurement of earnings for shorter periods, is provided in the moving-picture industry. These two illustrations will be discussed in more detail in a later chapter.[1]

The Accounting Unit

The Corporation—The Enterprise—The Ownership

In general practice, the corporation is regarded as the accounting unit. The costs, expenses, and revenues to be brought into account are determined from the standpoint of the corporation. There are, however, some accountants, especially in the academic field, who hold that the corporation should be

---

[1] See infra, Chapter X.

regarded more as a scheme of organization of an enterprise by its beneficial owners, than as a separate entity.

There are obviously practical limitations on the extent to which this concept can be applied. However, it is in fact accepted to an extent that is not, perhaps, generally recognized; there seems also to be reason to think that it may be more generally applied in the future. This seems probable in the fields of regulation and taxation, and while these uses are among those for which special purpose accounts are more appropriate than general purpose accounts, it is to be expected that practices initiated in one field will extend into others.

The oldest and most important departure from the principle of regarding the corporation as the accounting unit is the practice of preparing consolidated accounts for a parent company and its subsidiaries. In this procedure, even if the parent is treated as an accounting unit the activities of the subsidiary companies are regarded as if they were branches conducted by the parent directly. Alternatively, the group rather than the individual companies may be treated as the accounting unit. In either case, accounting looks through the corporation to the substance to a considerable extent.

Under the tax law, a further important extension of the principle of looking through corporate entities has been adopted in connection with corporate reorganizations. Under specified conditions, which from time to time have been changed, it has become possible to effect a reorganization without profit or loss accruing to the stockholders of the reorganized company and without affecting the basis for determination of profit or loss on the subsequent realization of assets in the course of corporate operations. In the depression years, reorganizations accompanied by readjustments of book values were frequent, so that today many corporations are reporting gains or losses on the realization of assets on the basis of the cost to them, while the taxes which they are called upon to pay are determined on the basis of the cost to their predecessors. The resulting net profit is thus measured in part in terms of profit or loss to the corporation and in part on the basis of profit or loss to the enterprise.

The device of consolidated accounts began to develop with the large combinations of corporations that took place in the period following the election of 1896. By the time we entered the first world war in 1917 the practice was so well established that the Treasury, without specific legislative authority, required consolidated tax returns under the Revenue Act of 1917. The Act of 1918 contained an express requirement for consolidation, and the regulations under the Act of 1917 were retrospectively confirmed in the Act of 1921. In an often quoted report, the Senate Finance Committee in 1918 justified this procedure as resulting in treating as a taxable unit what was, in fact, a single business unit. The principle of consolidation was perhaps carried to undue lengths in that law, and in the decade which followed it was certainly carried further in practice than the circumstances really warranted.

The state of incorporation of a subsidiary company necessarily possesses important powers in relation to the enterprise conducted by it; in times of stress the importance of these powers becomes manifest. Ownership of the entire capital stock of a subsidiary becomes relatively unimportant when the subsidiary is organized in an enemy country. And even in the domestic field the fact that a subsidiary such as a public utility is subject to the regulatory powers of the state in which it operates, negatives the idea that a group of such companies under a common ownership constitutes a single business or economic unit. There has therefore in recent years been some reaction from the undue extension of the practice of consolidation and a clearer understanding of the limitations on the significance of consolidated accounts.

In the Revenue Act of 1934 the Congress, rejecting the views of the Treasury, eliminated consolidated returns except in the case of railroads. But the validity of consolidation is shown by the fact that when taxation reached higher levels with the outbreak of war, restoration of consolidated returns was recognized as imperative if confiscation was to be avoided.

At times in the past there has been a disposition to regard what is a useful device as accomplishing more than can possibly be accomplished in the case of a complex business organization. Today, it is generally recognized that in many instances neither holding company statements nor consolidated statements alone are sufficient, and that both are necessary to a reasonable presentation of the financial picture. It must be recognized that the ownership of the entire common stock of a corporation is not substantially equivalent to ownership of its assets or enterprises if there are large amounts of prior securities outstanding and the enterprise is subject to a jurisdiction which limits the common stockholders' right or interest therein.

Looking through corporations to their ownership is a delicate problem, complicated by the fact that there may be either complete change of ownership without any change in the corporate structure, or a substantial change in the corporate structure without any change of ownership. In general, it seems unlikely that the courts will go further in looking through corporate entities than they have gone in the past, and in recent years the tendency in accounting has been to restrict rather than to extend this practice. The war, for instance, has made it no longer customary to include foreign companies in consolidated statements, and there has been a revival of interest in the accounts of parent companies as having a real significance, which is in addition to though not, perhaps, independent of the significance of the consolidated accounts.

Clearly, however, the ownership of an amount of stock sufficient to control a corporation is a fact to be taken into account in considering the proper accounting treatment, in the accounts of the controlling company, of dividends received or of the fact that no dividend has been paid. Where such a relationship exists, the declaration of a dividend has not the same value as objective evidence of the realization of income as the declaration of a dividend by a corporation over which the stockholder has no control.

In recent years, regulatory commissions have adopted the concept of "original cost" in utility classifications. This rule requires that units of property shall be recorded at their cost to the first person, legal or natural, who devoted them to public service. In the course of proceedings before the Supreme Court in the case of *American Telephone & Telegraph Co. v. U.S.* (299, U.S. 232), counsel for the Commission conceded that the difference between original cost and cost to the present owner should be recognized as such on the books and dealt with according to appropriate rules of corporate accounting. However, such differences are required to be assembled in a single account, and the Commissions have displayed a disposition to deal arbitrarily with them.

The adoption of this concept probably does not reflect an acceptance of the idea of enterprise accounting, but this would seem to be its only legitimate foundation. If cost to the corporation is still the controlling consideration in utility accounting, it cannot be right to make the cost to someone else the primary record and to give expression to cost to the corporation only through adjustment accounts which reflect in totals the difference between original cost and corporate cost of all classes of physical property in one figure. It seems clear that this new development calls for refinement and liberalization.

It is unfortunately true that corporate accounts are affected by the time when the corporation came into existence. This is particularly true in respect of such charges as depreciation and depletion. Corporations which are the result of refinancing in times of prosperity are likely to have larger depreciation and depletion charges than the predecessor companies would have had. Those that were created through reorganization in a period of depression have smaller charges. A substitution of enterprise accounting for corporate accounting might do something to mitigate this defect, but it is doubtful whether the advantage to be gained would be worth the price that would be entailed. As a practical matter, a large proportion of enterprises are at least partial failures, and reorganizations in which garments are cut according to the cloth are a practical necessity. The only course is to recognize such conditions as among those which make corporate financial accounts less significant than many would like or even believe them to be.

CHAPTER III

Accounting Principles and Postulates

THE TERM "ACCOUNTING PRINCIPLES" has assumed such a wide and varied importance as almost to demand a chapter for itself. It occurs, for instance, in every auditor's report under the Securities Exchange Act of 1934.

It used to be not uncommon for the accountant who had been unable to persuade his client to adopt the accounting treatment that he favored, to urge as a last resort that it was called for by "accounting principles." Often he would have had difficulty in defining the "principle" and saying how, why, and when it became one. But the method was effective, especially in dealing with those (of whom there were many) who regarded accounting as an esoteric but well established body of learning and chose to bow to its authority rather than display their ignorance of its rules. Obviously, the word "principle" was an essential part of the technique; "convention" would have been quite ineffective.

Today, we find utility commissions employing much the same device. In their efforts to avert judicial review of their decisions they constantly appeal to "accounting principles," and throw in the adjectival support of the word "fundamental" to enhance the impression of permanence and inevitability of the authority.

The American Institute of Accountants, which is representative mainly of the practicing accountants, has in recent years taken the position that the word "principle," if it is to be used at all, should be used only in the sense of "A general law or rule adopted or professed as a guide to action;

a settled ground or basis of conduct or practice" (*The Oxford English Dictionary*).[1] It therefore does not use the word "fundamental," but with more restraint speaks of "generally accepted accounting principles." A committee of the Institute has said that, initially, accounting rules are mere postulates, derived from experience and reason, and that only after they have proved useful and become generally accepted do they become principles of accounting. It has repeatedly recognized that accounting principles are founded on considerations of utility and are subject to modification as criteria of usefulness change.

The American Accounting Association, which is representative rather of the academic accountants, uses the word "principle" without indicating what precise sense it attaches to the word. In a statement, *Accounting Principles Underlying Corporate Financial Statements*, issued in June, 1941, which was a revision of a tentative statement issued in 1936, the Association speaks of "fundamental propositions concerning the functions of accounting in respect to cost, revenue realization, income, and capital." Under the heading of "Cost" it presents eight paragraphs, in commenting on which it speaks of "the cost principle stated above." Perhaps the most crucial of the eight paragraphs is No. 7, which reads as follows:

Values other than costs applicable to future periods should be treated in balance sheets as supplementary data, and then only when supported by substantial evidence. Such data should be adequately described and shown parenthetically, by footnote, or in separate schedules, to avoid obscuring the basic cost figures.

How costs applicable to future periods are to be determined is not made entirely clear, but under such a rule it would certainly not be permissible to carry fixed assets at more

---

[1] Accounting Research Bulletin No. 7, p. 60.

than cost or, probably, to carry inventories at market value because less than cost. But as will be made clear in Chapter V, the first part of this rule, although now fairly generally accepted in America, has only recently become established here and is not accepted in England, and the second part is far from being accepted in either country today—indeed, the rule that inventories should be stated at cost or market, whichever is lower, is not only one of the oldest but also one of the best established rules of accounting.

In a later chapter will be traced the history of the development which has made the precept that fixed assets shall not be carried at more than cost one of the best established rules of accounting. The fact there disclosed—that the rule of today is the result of a revulsion of feeling, and that it has passed through all the stages from being a postulate to a principle within a decade—illustrates in a most striking manner the nature of accounting principles and the character of accounting. The old rule, which permitted and in some cases encouraged the recording of unrealized appreciation on the books of corporations, fell into disrepute because of the abuses that were committed in its name, and because of a change in the general concept of the major objective of accounting from the determination of net worth to the measurement of income and earning capacity. Newly created regulatory commissions were quick to perceive that a change in the accounting rules might be helpful to them in their efforts to escape from the bondage into which their predecessors had been led by William Jennings Bryan and his associates in the famous case of *Smyth* v. *Ames*,[1] which established the predominance of value over cost in the field of public utility regulation. They have forbidden future, and excoriated past, "write-ups."

It is, perhaps, regrettable that the word "principle" should

---

[1] 169 U.S. 466.

be used to describe canons or procedures to which it can be applied only in a restricted sense. I must in fairness recognize that the word is used in the standard form of accounting reports, and that its use there grew out of the correspondence between the Institute and the New York Stock Exchange which began with a letter of September 22, 1932 (Appendix to Chap. IV), and which was conducted by a committee of which I was chairman. The form of report recommended by that committee was a radical change from the form which had been in use for many years; and since this volume is largely historical in character, it may be appropriate here to discuss its antecedents.

The standard form of audit report or certificate commonly in use prior to 1932 was of English origin. There, the auditor was required to say whether in his opinion the balance sheet to which it related was properly drawn up so as to exhibit a true and correct view of the state of the company's affairs as shown by its books of account. In England, the last seven words had a technical significance and were associated with the general rule that, within wide limits, the methods of accounting employed by a company might be determined by its directors acting within the authority of its memorandum of association. In our country they would have had no such specialized significance, and might have been construed as a reservation which impaired the value of the assurance given; they were therefore almost universally omitted. Moreover, a phrase such as "the financial position of the company" was substituted for "the state of the company's affairs."

When I became senior partner of a large accounting firm in 1911, a conviction that the public generally did not understand the nature of accounts or of audits as usually conducted caused me great concern. I felt that statements on the question by the profession itself would be regarded as self-serving and ineffective, and I was convinced of the desirability of associating responsible authorities with the profession in declarations which would help to define the auditor's responsibilities and enlighten the public.

An opportunity to deal to some extent with the nature of accounting occurred in 1917, when cooperation between the Federal Trade Commission, the Federal Reserve Board, and the American Institute of Accountants led to the publication of the pamphlet *Uniform Accounting*, though that pamphlet dealt mainly with audit procedures. A further opportunity occurred when accountants were called upon to play an important part in drafting the Revenue Act of 1918. They secured the introduction into Section 212 of the provision that returns should be made on the basis on which the taxpayer's books were kept unless that basis did not clearly reflect income, and the inclusion in Regulation 45 of an article (no. 24) which said: "the law contemplates that each taxpayer shall adopt such forms and systems of accounting as are in his judgment best suited to his purpose." While these provisions resulted in a somewhat better understanding, they did not make clear the real and limited significance of any statement that a balance sheet shows the "true position" of a company.

In 1932, the New York Stock Exchange was concerned over the variety in the methods of accounting employed by companies whose securities were listed. A cooperating Institute committee in its letter of September 22, 1932,[1] sought to do two things: first, to make unequivocally clear the existence of a variety of methods; and, secondly, to suggest a procedure by which the variety could be curtailed and the best methods gradually made practically universal. The latter objective, it proposed to achieve by a requirement that listed corporations must explain in adequate detail the basis on which their financial statements were made up, and under-

---

[1] Appendix to Chap. IV.

take not to change the basis without due notice to the Exchange and to stockholders. This procedure, it was thought, would insure consistency, or proper disclosure of any inconsistency, and gradually bring about the elimination of the less desirable practices by the pressure of public opinion.

The limitation on the significance of accounts and of auditors' reports thereon was to be emphasized by a change in the form of audit report so that it would become an expression of opinion on the question whether the financial statements were in conformity with the methods professed to be followed, and whether those methods were in harmony with good accounting standards. The question what word should be used to describe those standards was much discussed and finally decided in favor of the expression "accepted principles."

In the correspondence the Committee had used the words "rules," "methods," "conventions," and "principles" interchangeably. The word "methods" was being used in the suggested form of report in another sense; the word "rules" implied the existence of a ruling body which did not exist; the word "convention" was regarded as not appropriate for popular use and in the opinion of some would not convey an adequate impression of the authority of the precepts by which the accounts were judged.

Canons of accounting could not properly be described as "principles" in the more fundamental sense of that word but might be said to be principles in the narrower sense above quoted. It may well be that in agreeing on this word the Committee was resorting to the familiar expedient of securing unanimity by the adoption of a formula which was capable of sufficient variety in interpretation to cover the area of difference of opinion among its individual members. But the object to be sought was of major importance, and unanimity was highly desirable; its achievement was worth a minor ambiguity of this kind.

The response from all quarters to the Committee's proposal was surprisingly favorable and unanimous, and a movement was then initiated which has had lasting effects and might have been of even greater good but for the fact that the powers of the Stock Exchange were shorn by the Securities and Exchange Act of 1934.

Following the publication of the correspondence, the Institute appointed a Committee on Accounting Principles. Immediately the question was raised in what sense the word "principle" was used in the form of auditor's report which had been suggested. The new committee recommended adoption by the Institute of certain precepts listed in the appendix to the letter of September 22, 1932. In doing so it spoke of them as "rules or principles." Still later, a Committee on Accounting Procedure superseded the Committee on Accounting Principles and established a research department. In its first bulletin the new committee drew attention to the precepts which had been previously approved by the Institute membership, and in doing so spoke of them only as "rules." Still later, that committee approved a report of the Committee on Terminology in which the opinion mentioned earlier in this chapter was expressed, that the standard dictionary definition that came closest to defining the sense in which the word "principle" was used in accounting was: "A general law or rule adopted or professed as a guide to action; a settled ground or basis of conduct or practice." [1]

The pamphlet of 1917 (which later received the designation *Verification of Financial Statements*) and the correspondence published in 1933 under the title *Audits of Corporate Accounts* are important landmarks in the development of accounting. It is significant of a change in outlook that the

---

[1] Candor requires mention of the fact that the author was chairman of the several committees mentioned; but while this fact may impair the value of the reports as corroborative of the views here expressed, it lends authenticity to the narrative of the course of events.

earlier pamphlet was the result of cooperation with an institution concerned with the granting of credit, so that questions were viewed primarily from the standpoint of the credit grantor, whereas the latter pamphlet was the outcome of cooperation with a body concerned with the marketability of corporate securities and problems were considered from the standpoint of those who trade in such markets. It would be difficult to overestimate the importance of the change in emphasis thus illustrated upon the development of accounting.

Returning from this historical digression to a discussion of the question of accounting principles, it may be desirable to deal briefly with the suggestion that the word "principles" has a proper application to accounting as connoting certain fundamental qualities of good accounting, notably conservatism and consistency.

Many years ago, a manufacturer entered my office and said that he wished my firm to displace his former auditors. Upon my asking why, he said feelingly: "I'm through with optimistic accountants." He went on to say that he was himself of a sanguine temperament, and that what he needed in accounting advice was caution. He expressed the opinion that this was generally true of the relation between managements and accountants.

He was, of course, right; the great majority of ventures fail, and the fact that enterprise nevertheless continues is attributable to the incurable optimism (often dissociated from experience) as well as to the courage of mankind. In my experience, also, losses from unsound accounting have most commonly resulted from the hopes rather than the achievements of management being allowed to influence accounting dispositions. To me, conservatism is still the first virtue of accounting, and I am wholly unable to agree with those who would bar it from the books of account and statements prepared therefrom and would relegate it to footnotes.

Consistency is the second great virtue of accounting, and

the emphasis upon it in the form of auditors' reports that have been in use since 1932 is wholly desirable. However, accounting, like the common law, should have elements of flexibility and adaptability as well as of stability. Therefore, there can be no absolute rule of consistency, but only a general admonition that consistency should normally be maintained, and a rule that any significant departure therefrom and its effects should be adequately disclosed.

Some writers have suggested that the distinction between capital and income is a fundamental principle of accounting. However, the distinction in accounting today between so-called capital expenditures and income expenditures does not rest on any such essential difference in the nature of the property acquired as that between land and other property which is often stressed in the field of economics. The distinction rests rather upon the relation between the length of the useful life of the property acquired and the length of the accounting period for which income is being determined. A capital expenditure is one, the usefulness of which is expected to extend over several accounting periods. If the accounting period were increased from the customary year to a decade, most of what is now treated as capital expenditure would become chargeable to income, while if the period were reduced to a day, much of what is now treated as current maintenance would become capital expenditure.

Indeed, it is a practical test of the utility or significance of an accounting rule to consider the effect of its application if the accounting period were materially shortened or lengthened. For instance, an attempt to allocate the profits of a restaurant for a day to hours, some of which were hours of crowded activity and others hours of idleness, is easily undertaken in retrospect over the entire period and will suggest some of the limitations on the significance of allocations of the costs and profits of a complete business cycle to the individual years falling within that period.

Accounting practices must be considered in relation to the purposes and the principles or conventions which were deemed to be controlling when they were being followed. Moreover, when there is a change in controlling conventions, and some adjustments become necessary, these adjustments should be made upon the basis that a new viewpoint has been adopted—not that errors have been made in the past and are being corrected. Cases will, of course, arise in which revisions of past accounting are needed because methods were employed which were never justified by any accounting theory; but these cases are in a class apart.

The practice of speaking opprobriously of accounting treatments to which no ethical objection can be taken (such as honest revaluation or nonacceptance of straight-line depreciation), and which were in accord with legal and regulatory concepts of the time when they were adopted, is not calculated to inspire confidence in the impartial character of the discharge of quasi-judicial functions by those who indulge in it. Mr. Justice Holmes has pointed out that on occasion it is necessary to revise the judgment of posterity in the light of the judgment of the times. Never is this more necessary than when a change of judgment is the mere accompaniment of a change in interest.

The Postulate of Stability in the Monetary Unit

In formulating a statement of principles of accounting, as in a general discussion of principles of economics, it is customary to assume that the monetary unit is substantially stable in value; but as Taussig, for instance, points out in accepting this postulate for the purpose of his *Principles of Economics*,[1] it is not universally true, and in dealing with any case it is always necessary to consider to what extent the

---

[1] *Principles of Economics*, by F. W. Taussig, 4th ed., Vol. I, p. 105.

postulate is valid in the particular set of circumstances, or how its invalidity affects the conclusions to be reached.

Prior to the first world war, the postulate was regarded as accepted in respect of the principal commercial countries of the world. The events of the first world war, and even more, the postwar developments in Germany, France, and other countries, created conditions in which the postulate was clearly inapplicable, and which made the presentation of informative accounts in respect of enterprises in those countries a task of very great difficulty. Subsequent devaluations in Great Britain and in our own country, the concentration of gold in the United States, and the increasing acceptance of the notion of managed currencies have tended further to impair the validity of this postulate; and the prospect that the present war will lead to new developments of the same character makes reconsideration of accounting conventions, in so far as they rest upon it, inevitable.

Now that the main emphasis has shifted from the balance sheet to the income account, the effect of the change in the value of the monetary unit on the balance sheet is not the major question to be considered. The problem is rather to determine the form and content of the income account in such a way as to indicate as fully as possible its real significance. Here again the distinction between long- and short-term transactions is crucial.

In Chapter V it will be shown how during the decade following the last war there was a considerable movement to reflect the change in the value of the monetary unit in the balance sheet and, indirectly through depreciation charges, in the income account,[1] by restating capital assets on the basis of the then current prices which were, perhaps, roughly 50 per cent higher than immediately before the war and

---

[1] Cf. *Capital Consumption and Adjustment*, Solomon Fabricant (1938), pp. 213–222.

100 per cent above those at the beginning of the century. In the decade that followed, other forces brought about a situation in which it was apparent that capital assets generally had not appreciated in terms of the monetary unit even to the extent of a major fraction of the rise in price indices. As explained, also, in Chapter V, the regulatory commissions are making the most strenuous efforts to prevent any reflection of the decline in the purchasing power of the monetary unit in the rate base, by excluding value from consideration and measuring cost in terms of the monetary unit without regard to the fluctuations in its value.

In the light of this history it seems unlikely that there will be any general attempt to reflect a further fall in the purchasing power of the dollar in the capital-asset accounts of corporations generally, unless that fall assumes even larger proportions than it did in the first world war. In the other major phase of the problem—namely, in the valuation of inventories—there is a strong movement, to which the tax law has yielded, to exclude from the income account what may be regarded as nominal profits arising from changes in either the general price level or the price of particular products. It will be recalled that in and immediately after the first world war the index of wholesale prices rose from 100 in 1913 to over 250 in 1921. During this period, many efforts were made to bring about acceptance of the base stock method of inventory accounting, under which normal supplies of raw materials were carried at a fixed price instead of at the latest cost. The result of this method was, of course, broadly to put cost and sales in the measurement of income more nearly upon the basis of current price levels. This movement was successfully resisted by the Treasury, with the result that taxes were collected on large nominal profits due merely to increases in the price level.

In the last decade, a movement to secure the adoption of substantially the same principle was initiated. Its supporters discreetly avoided the terminology of the previous effort, and instead of pleading for the adoption of the base cost principle, asked for recognition of what was described as the last in, first out method of allocation in the determination of cost. This movement is more fully discussed in the chapter on inventories, but requires mention here in connection with the discussion of the historical development affecting the postulate of a uniform monetary standard.

THE POSTULATE OF CONTINUITY

It is an almost essential postulate of accounting that it shall be regarded as a continuous process. The emphasis on profits for particular short periods has sometimes led to attempts to isolate an accounting period from its past and future in some important respect. For special purposes, such a procedure may be necessary and practicable.

In the United Railways and Electric Company of Baltimore case,[1] the Supreme Court held that, in fixing service charges, depreciation as well as the rate base should be computed upon present values—not upon costs. Provision for depreciation for a series of years so computed would have no significance as an aggregate, and the method is quite inapplicable to the ordinary accounting processes. For current accounting purposes depreciation must be based on cost. The life of an enterprise, like that of a man, is continuous, and the gains and losses, the successes and failures, of one period are in a large measure the result of acts, omissions, and events of the past, and the results achieved cannot be appraised as successes or failures without regard to the future. The historical character of accounting cannot be too strongly emphasized; and attempts to divorce the present from the past in one respect, even where it may be practicable—as, for instance, by substituting a valuation for cost—are often objectionable because

---

[1] 280 U.S. 234.

they are at best partial adjustments and because they tend to obscure the true nature of accounting.

The point may be illustrated by assuming a purchase of high-grade securities financed by an issue of secured bonds at a time when interest rates are high. If interest rates fall, the value of the securities will tend to rise, and so will the market value of the bonds issued to finance the purchase. The bonds may then be refunded at a substantial cost in the form of unamortized discount and redemption premium. Current practice would permit the cost to be charged against earned surplus account, and if thereby a deficit were created, that deficit might be absorbed through what is called a quasi-reorganization. Thereafter the income available for the common stock would be determined by deducting from gross income only the reduced interest charge on the refunding bonds, though the gross income itself will be the result of opportunities to invest—which ceased with the advent of the conditions which made refunding of the debt advantageous.

It may be questioned whether this result is altogether sound. No doubt many cases arise where the inheritance from the past is so burdensome that a new start through reorganization or quasi-reorganization is, as a practical matter, desirable. But the concept of continuity should not lightly be discarded, and quasi-reorganizations which relieve a corporation's income account of burdensome inheritances from the past and ignore beneficial inheritances are of doubtful propriety. The whole problem of accounting in relation to reorganizations and quasi-reorganizations is an inviting field for study.[1] There will always remain here, as elsewhere, questions which can be rightly decided only by good judgment and regard for business morality.

---

[1] See Research Bulletin No. 3.

CHAPTER IV

Historical

IT HAS BEEN pointed out that accounting is utilitarian, and that the relative importance of different uses of accounts is subject to great and sometimes rapid change. It therefore seems worth while to trace briefly the history of the development of business and corporate accounts. For this purpose, the history may be divided into three periods according to the relative importance therein of three forms of business organization: (a) the individual venture or partnership; (b) the corporation with limited liability, owned and managed by a relatively small group of stockholders; and (c) the corporation owned by relatively large numbers of stockholders, the management of which is divorced from beneficial ownership and the securities of which are bought and sold freely on established security markets.

We are apt to forget how recently the change to these second and third forms of organization took place in our country. Judge Learned Hand, in his foreword to the fiftieth volume of the *Harvard Law Review* (1936–37) said: "It was during the last half century that the practice became common, by means of the private corporation, to conduct industry without personal liability." And the records show that in 1897 only thirty-seven industrial stocks were listed on the New York Stock Exchange.

In England, from which our accounting thought was in earlier days largely derived, general limited liability legislation was not enacted until after the middle of the nineteenth century. So long as the individual proprietorship and the partner-

51

ship were the typical, if not the only, forms in which business was conducted there the only restriction on the right of the owners to adopt such accounting methods as they thought fit was the obligation to do nothing that might be fraudulent as against creditors, and the fact that the owners of the business were personally liable for all its debts was a substantial assurance against this restriction being widely ignored.

The introduction of the principle of limited liability made the protection of creditors more important. The legal capital of companies was regarded as the main protection of creditors. Stringent rules were made to safeguard creditors against any reduction of the legal capital otherwise than in the manner contemplated by law—which involved notice to creditors and an opportunity for them to be heard before a reduction could be made effective.

Except for the important change in the matter of the protection necessary for creditors, the position of what is still called in England the private company presented, from the accounting standpoint, few differences from the earlier partnership; it was still permissible for stockholders to adopt such accounting methods for the determination of profits and of the amounts available for dividends as they might see fit, so long as these did not impair the just rights of creditors. For instance, Buckley explains a statement of Lord Justice Cotton that two apparently conflicting decisions were entirely consistent with each other, on the ground that in one case the memorandum of association of the company concerned expressly allowed capital to be sunk in a wasting property, and that whether depreciation should or should not be provided was therefore for the articles of association of that company, not the court, to determine. The rule in England is that no dividend may be paid otherwise than out of profits. And even this rule is not imposed by law, which provides only how capital may be reduced and leaves the rest to inference. Buckley, commenting on this provision, mentions the many cases that have been decided and the difficulty of reconciling the decisions; he then refers to the rule that dividends must not be paid out of capital, and goes on to say that, subject to this .provisio,

such questions as how the profit and loss account shall be made out, whether profits have been earned, and if so whether they shall be divided, are primarily business questions for the directors or shareholders to determine in accordance with the company's regulations, and provided they act honestly, and in accordance with such regulations in coming to such determination, they discharge all the obligations imposed upon them by the Act.

But the application of even such a plain abstract proposition as that dividends must not be paid out of capital may in practice raise questions of the utmost difficulty in their solution, and the question what are profits and what is capital may be a difficult and sometimes an almost impossible problem to solve. The House of Lords in *Dovey* v. *Cory* accordingly, whilst expressing the view that no great difficulty would arise in dealing with any particular case on its own facts and circumstances, declined to attempt to treat these questions in the abstract or to do that which Parliament has refrained from doing, namely to formulate precise rules for the guidance or embarrassment of business men in the conduct of business affairs.[1]

The introduction of the notion of free transferability, in theory and practice, of the shares of capital stock of corporations, lent new significance to these considerations. If corporations took steps such as listing securities on stock exchanges in the expectation that their securities would be freely held, bought, and sold by persons who were not in the councils of the enterprise, it was not unreasonable to insist that published accounts ought to be so framed as not to be misleading to those who were buying or selling these securities. Certainly,

---

[1] *The Law and Practice Under the Companies Acts,* 11th ed. (1930), p. 756, the edition which followed the passage of the Acts of 1928 and 1929, the last important revision of the English company law.

also, accounts should be made reasonably informative. The wholesale conversion of private enterprises into the new form that took place during the first three decades of the century, forced recognition of these aspects of corporation reports.

That the movement was a desirable one may be questioned; but it must be recognized that there were forces at work that made it almost inevitable. There existed a market, both foreign and domestic, for interests in successful American businesses, and there was a natural disposition on the part of some owners to take advantage of this market to realize at least a part of their investment. To these forces there was later added the pressure of heavy death taxes which made conversion into liquid form of a substantial part of ownership of private businesses necessary either before or immediately after death.

The first evidence of recognition on any considerable scale of an obligation to give to stockholders of American corporations a substantial amount of information in regard to their investment may be said to have come about in the first days of the present century. All authorities will probably agree that the first full report of the United States Steel Corporation, which was for the year ending December 31, 1902, was a landmark in the history of this development. The great importance of the corporation and the public discussion which its report evoked gave wide influence to its example. In the course of the next twenty years, while there were some conspicuous exceptions, corporations whose securities were listed on the public market tended to give more and more information to stockholders and the public. At the beginning of the Stock Exchange boom in the twenties the information that was currently being given by the great majority of listed companies was, I believe, reasonably satisfactory. Certainly it was so if judged on the basis of a comparison with the highest standards observed in other parts of the world.

The time came when pressure was clearly needed to compel those corporations whose standards were still unsatisfactory to improve their practice. In 1926, two events happened which tended to accelerate this movement: the New York Stock Exchange decided to take an active part in it and selected for that purpose an executive assistant to the Committee on Stock List, who carried on a persistent and effective campaign to bring about an improvement. At the same time, a recognition of other unhealthy developments in corporate practice had aroused concern, and critics of these practices found in the deficiencies of a minority of corporate reports a source of reinforcement of their attack on corporate abuses and a ground for demanding some form of regulation which would at least bring the practice of all up to the highest standard then being observed.[1] Their strictures may have indicated a lack of understanding of the problem and of its difficulties; their criticisms may have been in numerous instances gravely unjust; but at least public attention was drawn in a vivid way to a question of very real importance.

During the period in which the New York Stock Exchange was most actively concerned with corporate accounting problems I was closely associated with its work. The contribution in this field of J. M. B. Hoxsey, executive assistant to the Committee on Stock List, has been recognized by the Exchange, by Congressional committees and by writers on finance. Having worked with him during practically the whole of his term of office, I am able and bound to pay tribute to his courage, insight, and ability to reconcile theoretical and practical considerations. I would, however, emphasize as he would the fact that the picture of him which some have tried to present—as a lonely figure struggling against reactionary and sinister forces in the Exchange—is a false one. Credit for what was accomplished and was in course of being accomplished when the role of the Committee in effect passed to the Securities and Exchange Commission, should go only in part

---

[1] Cf. *Main Street and Wall Street*, William Z. Ripley (1927).

to him and largely to fair-minded and farseeing members of the Committee on Stock List and governing body of the Exchange.

In 1930, accounting cooperation in the work of the Exchange was increased by the appointment of a special committee of the Institute for that purpose. In the years that followed, consideration was given not only to specific problems but to the possibility of securing a greater degree of uniformity in practice and a public understanding of the nature of corporate financial statements. As a result, a far-reaching scheme was evolved which was set forth in a letter addressed by the Committee to the Exchange under date of September 22, 1932 (printed as an appendix to this chapter).

This scheme contemplated an adequate disclosure by listed corporations of the methods of accounting employed by them and an undertaking not to make any material change either in the methods themselves or in the way in which they were applied, without full disclosure to the Exchange and to stockholders. The independent auditors were to be charged with the responsibility of reporting whether accounts were in conformity with the representations made.

It seemed reasonable to expect that such a scheme, carried out under the active supervision of the Exchange, would result in gradually eliminating undesirable practices and a larger degree of uniformity, and thus in making corporate reports more valuable to stockholders. This was to be accomplished without the prescription of mandatory procedures or consequently any relaxation of the responsibilities of management, and with no compulsion except that of educated opinion.[1]

The scheme was warmly approved by the Exchange, by corporations, and by the Controllers Institute, and was made public in pamphlets issued by the Exchange and the Institute

---

[1] See note, *infra*, p. 61.

in January, 1934. Later, it was endorsed by the Investment Bankers Association and by the authors of a report prepared under the auspices of the Twentieth Century Fund.[1]

While these developments were occurring the depression came, in the course of which heavy losses on corporate securities were sustained by persons in all walks of life. It was inevitable that the same thing should then happen as had happened on numerous similar occasions in the past, and which is admirably described in a pamphlet (published under a pseudonym but attributed by some authorities to Lord Overstone) written in 1849:

Whenever the fingers are burned, a cure is always lustily called for by those who have been burned the most severely, and their object in this, as in the diversion that has hurt them is always the same—they call for the appointment of a government officer, who shall from time to time regulate how they shall hold their hands to the fire without being burned. Whether this special interference shall be crowned with success by keeping down the heat of the fire, or by increasing the distance at which the venturesome hand shall be allowed to approach it, is a perplexing difficulty which has not yet been solved. When duly considered, that difficulty must be held to be not a little perplexing; for evidently, if the heat of the fire should be kept so low, or the distance from it so great, as that no hands can be burned, why then there will be no fun in the thing, and the government officer will enjoy a sinecure.[2]

When with the passage of time it shall become possible to review dispassionately the history of the depression, it will, I think, be found that inadequate or misleading reports of established businesses played but a relatively unimportant part in causing the catastrophic losses that were sustained. The

---

[1] *Stock Market Control* (New York: D. Appleton-Century Co., 1934), p. 174.

[2] Cf. *The Development of the Business Corporation in England, 1800–1867,* B. C. Hunt, p. 115.

speculative fever which produced also the Florida land boom (in which corporate reports played no part whatever), the pyramiding of holding corporations, unsound treatment of stock dividends, and belief in a new economic order encouraged by persons high in the political and economic world, were far more potent influences.

However, the temper of the times demanded control of the dealings in corporate securities, and of corporate reports, and it was felt, with reason, that confidence would not be restored until a drastic measure designed to create this control had been enacted. It was apparent that Federal legislation was necessary. It took the form of the Securities Act of 1933 and the Securities Exchange Act of 1934.

When the question of enlightening investors is studied it becomes apparent that an improvement in the accounting information available, however substantial if measured by comparison with existing standards, can be of only minor value to the investor if this value is measured in relation to the risks necessarily run in speculation or investment in corporate stocks. I drew attention to this fact when the Securities Act of 1933 was under consideration, and again in 1934 in relation to the Securities Exchange Act of that year. It is a matter of profound regret to me that this truth has not been more emphasized by those in authority.[1]

The passage of the Securities Act of 1933 initiated a new era in the history of corporate finance and of accounting. The law was not the result of judicious inquiry and dispassionate legislative consideration; it was passed under the pressure of public indignation, enhanced by investigations which were lacking in judicial quality. The promoters of the law made claims for it, many of which were as open to question as the representations made in the prospectuses of which they

---

[1] Comments on this phase of the question will be found in *Twenty-five Years*, Vol. II, pp. 49-118.

complained. A law which ran counter to some of the most firmly established principles of English practice was portrayed as one the merits of which had been proved by English experience.

From the accounting standpoint, the irony of the law was that it gave legal recognition to the function of the *independent* public accountant, and at the same time, gave to a nonexpert body powers over the profession which went far to destroy its independence. From a pecuniary point of view, its effect on accountants was perhaps favorable, but this advantage was not worth the impairment of their professional status which the law effected, and which was neither necessary nor desirable for the purpose of holding them to a proper responsibility for the discharge of their auditing functions.

The prompt prosecution of Hatry and Kylsant in England had created a favorable impression of English company procedure. Few of those who cited these prosecutions in support of the penal provisions of the new law pointed out, or perhaps were aware, that neither of these convictions was secured under any company law. Hatry pleaded guilty to forgery and conspiracy to defraud, and Kylsant was convicted under the Larceny Act of 1861, which antedated even the Companies Act of 1862, which has been called the Magna Charta of limited liability enterprise.

The Securities Act of 1933 contained requirements as to disclosure of interests and of essential facts, and created liabilities (civil and criminal) for representations made, which were an adaptation or extension of similar rules which had long been in force in England; but it would seem that these provisions might almost have been spelt out of the common law. In other respects the Act was, in its antecedents, policy, and temper, the antithesis of the English law rather than its counterpart.

The Committee hearings, which were conducted as a prelude to the introduction of the bill, bore no resemblance to the typical inquiry through a Royal Commission or a Committee, which precedes legislation in England. The revision of the company law in England in 1928 was based on the report of a Committee, which in the course of its preliminary comments said: "Cases in which fraud or lesser forms of dishonesty or improper dealing occur are comparatively few and the public interest which such cases arouse tends to divert attention from the vast number of honestly conducted concerns and to create an exaggerated idea of the evils connected with limited companies and their activities."

That part of the law of 1933 which provided for prior scrutiny by a governmentally created body, accepted a policy rejected in England by successive committees and parliaments. The penalty provisions were harsh beyond anything known to English law and introduced new legal concepts of which England was certainly not the spiritual home. Nevertheless, the claim that the law followed English precedent was widely made by those who supported the bill or resisted any proposals to amend the Act after its passage. Even Professor (now Mr. Justice) Frankfurter in an article claimed that "what is asked of those engaged in its [i.e., corporate security] merchandising is well justified by British practice." [1]

A single quotation will indicate the character of the representations made to Congress and discussion of it will show their lack of foundation. An article which was read into the *Congressional Record* of January 12, 1934, contained the statement:

In substance, the Securities Act *is* the English Companies Act, modified to come within the constitutional power of the federal legislature to regulate interstate commerce, and to recognize the fact that in England, except for a very unusual Hatry or Kylsant, the distribution of securities is a decorous, traditional business, offering its wares only to institutions and wary family solicitors,

---

[1] *Fortune*, Aug., 1933, p. 55.

while in the United States it has been a high-pressure racket that jangled every housewife's doorbell.

As well might a historian claim that the French Revolution of 1789 followed the pattern of the English Revolution of 1688.

In point of fact, the Securities Act of 1933 did not even deal specifically with the evil of "jangling the housewife's doorbell"; but Section 356 of the English Companies Act of 1929 began with the words: "It shall not be lawful for any person to go from house to house offering shares for subscription or purchase."

In so far as the law of 1933 called for disclosure of a plethora of information of secondary importance, admittedly in the expectation that expert analysis would sift and digest that information so that it would be available and useful to the average investor, it relied on a machinery that did not exist in England. True, the investment analyst existed here; but he could not reasonably have been expected to function in the manner contemplated, and the hope that he would do so has been disappointed.

The creation of a governmental body which would scrutinize issues of securities before they were made was the heart of the Act of 1933. In England, Mr. Gladstone, whose prescience in other respects Professor Frankfurter lauded in the article above quoted, drew attention to the danger that such scrutiny would "increase the faith in the solvency and efficiency of the company," and that it would be "an almost impossible task to make such an inquiry as would tend to the real security of the public." [1] He therefore rejected such a solution of the problem, and the policy is still unaccepted in England.

The grant to such a body of power to prescribe accounting

---

[1] *Report of 1844,* Evidence, Q.795.

rules was equally at variance with English concepts. There, the view prevails which was expressed by the Greene Committee in 1926: "The matter of accounts is one in which we are satisfied upon the evidence before us that within reasonable limits companies should be left a free hand." [1] Whether the British views on regulation of corporations and of issues of securities are more or less sound than ours as reflected in the Acts of 1933 and 1934 may be debatable; it cannot be denied that they are vastly different.

Experience under the law during the last decade has served only to strengthen the conviction I then held, that the grant of powers to prescribe accounting procedure, was as unwise and unnecessary as it was inadequately considered. It struck a wanton and unjustified blow at the development of a profession which, despite lapses, had made remarkable progress in the forty years of its existence.

Whether the time was then ripe for making audits by independent accountants of statements filed under the Acts mandatory seemed to me to be doubtful. But if audits were to be required and a heavy liability placed on the profession for the proper discharge of the duty thus imposed upon it, there could be no reason for striking at its professional character by taking the responsibility for accounting rules and principles out of its hands and placing it in those of a policy-making body that was not expert, especially as there was not even any provision for a hearing or right of appeal to the courts against rules so made.

The provisions were manifestly written into the law by people who had no adequate understanding of the nature of accounting. One of the ablest of those associated with the origin of the law said in an address after the law was passed: "Accounting, as distinguished from law, has generally been

---

[1] Company Law Amendment Committee, 1925–1926, *Report* Cmd. 2657, p. 33.

portrayed as an exact science, and its representations have
been proffered to the unlearned as representations of fact and
not of opinion. If it insists upon such fact representations it
is, of course, fair that it should be burdened with the responsibility attendant upon such a portrayal of its results."

No doubt there have always been many who unthinkingly
have assumed that corporate financial statements were representations of fact, but no more than a moment's thought
is necessary to force the conclusion that they cannot be, and
that "the ascertainment of profit is in every case necessarily
matter of estimate and opinion," as Buckley (then Lord
Justice) wrote in 1909.[1] The reference to an "exact science"
may reflect a failure to distinguish between the inexorable
technique of double-entry bookkeeping and the broad interpretive function of financial accounting. So, far from its
being true that corporate financial statements had been generally portrayed as representations of fact, the words "in
our opinion" had been a part of the standard audit certificate
in England for generations and in America for decades. Dickinson, unquestionably the leading accounting authority on
the subject, in his *Accounting Practice and Procedure* published in 1913 had fully explained the need for and the significance of these words as used in the certificate.

The conclusion drawn from the erroneous premise in the
passage quoted is characteristic of the spirit of the legislation
in its emphasis on the retributive rather than the remedial
process. If corporate financial statements had, in fact, been
falsely portrayed to the unlearned as purely factual, the helpful course would seem to have been to enlighten the unlearned and to prohibit such portrayal for the future. Indeed
the desirability of bringing home to investors that financial
statements of corporations were not and could not be purely

---

[1] Buckley, *The Law and Practice Under the Companies Acts*, 9th ed.
(1909), p. 658.

factual had been urged upon the Congress before the Act was passed.

It may be said in extenuation of the statement criticized that, with notable exceptions, the legal mind has not been— at least until comparatively recent years—readily receptive to accounting ideas. Legal concepts of accounting ran in terms of cash accounts and similar statements which can and should be statements of fact. The increase in legal understanding of corporate financial statements is an outgrowth, first, as will be explained later, of income taxation, and secondly, of the laws here discussed and the regulations made thereunder.

The grant of jurisdiction over accounting rules and principles to a body on which there was no accounting representation struck at accounting in its most professional capacity. Auditing for the detection of fraud is an onerous and in many respects a disagreeable occupation which carries with it little prestige or professional satisfaction but substantial financial risks. The work of the financial accountant involves the assumption of responsibility to persons other than the immediate client in matters which require the exercise of judgment in the selection and application of appropriate rules or principles and the adherence thereto, if need be in the face of opposition from the client. It is clearly of a professional character. It gives the independent accountant that just ground for pride in his work which is essential to the establishment of a profession on a high ethical level. To make the accountant in this field responsible only for the application of rules laid down by a body which was not required to be expert or to be guided by expert opinion was to deprive his work of a large part of its professional chaiacter.

Looking to the future, I am convinced that the grant of power to the Federal Trade Commission, and later to the Securities and Exchange Commission, to control the accounting of general business corporations whose securities are listed, was not in the public interest. It seems to me to have been the more unnecessary since an alternative procedure, more in harmony with the American system of checks and balances and more likely to prove efficacious, was ready to hand.[1]

I am convinced that the transfer to a commission of the function assumed by the New York Stock Exchange under the plan formulated by the committee of the American Institute of Accountants, which has been mentioned, and which is printed as an appendix to this chapter, would have been preferable to the granting to the Commission of power over accounting, both from the standpoint of immediate results and from that of the long-term interests of the economy.

The requirement of adequate disclosure of accounting methods followed by corporations, coupled with the obligation imposed on accountants to assume or expressly disclaim responsibility for such principles, with the Commission judiciously stimulating the development of public opinion where uniformity or the elimination of particular procedures seemed desirable, would have achieved great results in a natural and orderly way. It would have been more effective in securing the adoption of sound accounting principles than the procedure actually followed has been; it would have enhanced the standing of the accounting profession and drawn into that body more men of high quality than it is likely, now, to attract. It would have avoided any acceptance of responsibility by a governmental agency for accounting methods and would have guarded against the danger of methods being prescribed on the basis of policy rather than principle. Unlike the provision enacted, such a course might justly have been presented as an American advance along the general line of English procedure.[2] That such an alternative, when recommended to the Congress, should have been dismissed without serious con-

---

[1] No doubt my regret that this alternative was not adopted is heightened by the fact that the alternative procedure was one to the formulation of which I had given many years of study.

[2] Since this chapter was written a friend has brought to my notice a sentence from Bagehot: "In England we can often effect by the indirect

sideration was perhaps due to the temper of the times; but now, as then, I am convinced that the action taken was unwise.

If further argument in support of this alternative be necessary, it can be found in the fact that the law created a body authorized to lay down accounting rules whose point of view might be expected to differ from that of two other types of governmental agencies performing similar functions—the Bureau of Internal Revenue and the utility commissions, such as the Interstate Commerce Commission and the Federal Power Commission. It is well known that efforts to effect agreements between the Securities and Exchange Commission and the Bureau of Internal Revenue on accounting questions have proved unsuccessful. This is only natural, since the objectives of the two bodies are directly opposed. The Commission should be concerned to see that accounting is conservative, whereas the Bureau must be constantly on its guard against the recognition of income being improperly deferred.[1] The regulatory commissions are concerned primarily with the protection of consumers, whereas the Securities and Exchange Commission's primary concern is with investors.

Fortunately the Securities and Exchange Commission has up to now exercised the power to prescribe accounting rules under the Acts of 1933 and 1934 with restraint, and judiciously. Its decisions on general accounting questions have usually been reached after consultation with the Institute. Its influence on accounting practice in the field of general business has undoubtedly been beneficial. However, this bene-

---

compulsion of opinion what other countries must effect by the direct compulsion of Government."

[1] In the course of a discussion of this phase of the question a member of the Securities and Exchange Commissions told me of a case which strikingly illustrated the conflict. A corporation, desiring to avoid the undistributed profits tax in 1936, contemplated an issue of securities. It was informed by the Commission that a stop order would be issued if in its registration statement it claimed profits as great as those on which its liability to the undistributed profits tax was, according to the Treasury, properly computed. He did not tell me the outcome of the matter.

fit has arisen from the enforcement of rules which were laid down prior to its creation, and from strengthening the position of the accountant in relation to the corporation, rather than from the formulation of new rules—indeed, it is not too much to say that its power to prescribe rules has not been an important element in its usefulness. The latent dangers in the system of vesting power to formulate accounting rules in non-expert bodies, especially those vested with policy-making functions, has been clearly indicated by the action of other Commissions which have laid down so-called accounting principles with which independent accounting opinion does not agree and have asserted the power to relax the application of such principles as a matter of expediency or out of concern for particular classes of stockholders.

Admittedly, accounting is utilitarian, and its "principles" are not immutable. But while they are in force they should be of general application. If different rules are to apply in similar but not identical situations, or if alternative procedures are to be permissible (which they may well be in some cases), the distinctions and alternatives should be provided for in advance in the formulation of the rules. This subject will be further discussed in the final chapter.

Income taxation has affected financial accounting to an appreciable extent, and a brief historical review of developments in England and the United States in this field will reveal points of major interest in relation to both the art and the profession of accounting.

In England, the present series of income-tax laws began in 1842, and thus antedated by many years the passage of the first general limited liability company law of 1855. Subject to specific principles embodied in the law, which affect particularly the treatment of rent, interest, and amortization, the determination of income has been regarded there as a matter of good business practice.

The first modern tax levied by the Federal Government on

corporate income was the Excise Tax imposed in 1909. It was a hasty political maneuver and made its appearance in the Senate as an amendment to the tariff bill. Framed by distinguished lawyers, it contemplated the measurement of income through the use of accounts of a form to which the legal mind was accustomed—a statement of receipts and disbursements—though an allowance for "depreciation" and losses was incompatibly included in the scheme. The introduction of this proposal was the occasion for one of the first organized presentations of the accounting point of view. A group of leading firms protested against the naïveté and unworkability of the proposal. The Attorney General, however, brushed aside the protest with an ironical expression of his faith in the ability of the accountants to overcome any difficulty which the law might present, and the measure was enacted substantially as originally proposed.

The Treasury, called upon to administer the law, soon realized the justice of the criticisms that had been offered. It found it impossible to solve the problem without, in effect, adopting the substance of the proposals that the accountants had made. After conferring with advisers, such as W. J. Filbert, comptroller of the United States Steel Corporation, and A. Lowes Dickinson, a leading practicing accountant, it adopted a regulation which provided that the term "actually paid" used in the law did not necessarily contemplate that there should have been an actual disbursement of cash or even of its equivalent, but that under the law an item would be deemed to be paid as soon as the taxpayer recognized that it had to be paid by recording it as a liability. This artificial rule, made practically necessary by the unfortunate wording of the law, had a permanent effect on the development of our taxing system.

The authority and prestige of accountants in the tax field were greatly enhanced when the first world war made high taxation necessary. Once more the law as passed proved quite

unworkable. The second Revenue Act of 1917 had to be supplemented by regulations which were practically legislation.
In the formulation of these regulations and of the Revenue
Act of 1918 and the regulations thereunder, accounting influence rose to a high point. The provisions that income should
be determined in accordance with the method of accounting
employed by the taxpayer; the provisions relating to consolidated returns, and the regulations relating to inventories
(amongst others) were expressions of accounting concepts that
marked a departure from the previous practice of the Bureau.
The creation in 1924 of a Board of Tax Appeals, which as
originally planned was expected to operate more like the
English commissioners of taxation than as a court, was a
further acceptance of the accounting, or business, rather than
the legal approach to tax problems. However, the civil servant
has never taken the place in Federal taxation that he occupies
in England.

Since 1924, the tax law has tended more and more to deal
specifically and in highly technical ways with questions which
in England would be decided by the surveyors of taxes or
commissioners in accordance with broad provisions of law
and established business usage. As a result, tax practice has
passed to an increasing extent into legal hands. Moreover,
persistent efforts have been made by bar associations to restrict the activities of accountants in the field. Today, it may
often be necessary to call in the accountant to deal with tax
problems; but in all but the simplest cases it is necessary to call
in, also, a lawyer. Indeed our federal income-tax law might
be called a towering monument of legalism and is an outstanding illustration of the need of a different mode of thought to
counteract that influence in the formulation of laws in the
business field.

No feature of American business life impresses the visitor
from abroad more strikingly than the extent of the activities
of the legal profession in this as in other fields of our life.

The fact that in England the number of practicing members of the Bar is less than four thousand goes far to explain the difference between American and British company practice.

No doubt the difference has its roots in the history of the two countries. The English bar developed in an economy dominated by landholders, in which society was definitely stratified; it is not and it has never been a business profession. As the needs of business grew, there was ample scope and opportunity for the accountants to form such a profession, and in doing so they met with little or no resistance from the bar. Today, the accountants of England assume the duties of trustees and receivers, and they conduct the greater part of the discussions in relation to taxation, up to the point where litigation becomes necessary. As the commission sent by the Treasury to England in 1934 noted with surprise, such litigation is infrequent—over a period of five years, the number of tax cases carried to the courts averaged only fifty-two.[1] In addition, accountants act as business advisers, and of course conduct the audits of the accounts of companies, private and public, that are required by law. The profession thus has a broad basis and is strong enough to take a leading part in all developments affecting business.

The development of such a profession has a social value. Its existence, together with the high prestige and authority of the upper branches of the English Civil Service, has made the approach to business questions much less legalistic in England than in America.

Here, the legal profession early assumed a dominant position in the business life of the community, and the position thus created has tended to perpetuate itself. The fact that admission to the bar opens the road in so many directions naturally draws into the profession a large proportion of the

---

[1] *A Summary of the British Tax System* (Washington: Government Printing Office, 1934), p. 9.

best brains of the country and makes more difficult the development of an independent profession which might usefully take over a part of its functions. Only in comparatively recent years have any considerable number of college graduates of more than average qualifications entered the accounting profession. The work of trustees and receiverships, for which accounting experience forms an admirable qualification, has long been, in the main, the function of the legal profession. Developments in the field of income taxation have already been described. Intimate contact with outstanding members of both professions here and in England convinces me that the habit of mind that accounting experience develops, with its emphasis on essentials and willingness to disregard form, is a valuable corrective to the legal mode of thought.

If 1918 saw the authority of the accounting body in America at a peak, the years 1933 and 1934 saw it at a low point. It may well be that its rise was too rapid to be altogether healthy, and that it can now reestablish itself on a sounder basis. It cannot, however, do so unless it can regain the professional ground of which the Securities Act of 1933 deprived it. How this can be accomplished is a question discussion of which may be left until the problems of accounting have been reviewed and some issues now facing the accountants have been outlined. One such issue is suggested by the warning given in 1938 by a student of finance who was neither an accountant nor a rugged individualist, that "every administrative body has a specific job to do. . . . Its views on accounting accordingly are conditioned by its desire to reach that result, rather than by any interest in the healthy growth of accounting as a whole," and that the accounting profession might "all too easily, find itself merely the ciphering agency for virtually unreviewable bureaucrats." [1]

---

[1] A. A. Berle, Jr., "Accounting and the Law," *Accounting Review*, Vol. XIII, pp. 11, 15.

APPENDIX TO CHAPTER IV

Report of the Special Committee on Cooperation with Stock Exchanges of the American Institute of Accountants to the Committee on Stock List of the New York Stock Exchange, dated September 22, 1932.

Note: The members of the Institute Committee were:
Archibald Bowman
Arthur H. Carter
Charles B. Couchman
Samuel D. Leidesdorf
William M. Lybrand
George O. May (*Chairman*)

The Committee on Stock List,
New York Stock Exchange,
New York, N. Y.

Dear Sirs:

In accordance with suggestions made by your Executive Assistant, this Committee has given careful consideration to the subject of the general line of development of the activities of the Exchange in relation to annual reports of corporations.

It believes that there are two major tasks to be accomplished —one is to educate the public in regard to the significance of accounts, their value and their unavoidable limitations, and the other is to make the accounts published by corporations more informative and authoritative.

The nature of a balance-sheet or an income account is quite generally misunderstood, even by writers on financial and accounting subjects. Professor William Z. Ripley has spoken of a balance-sheet as an instantaneous photograph of the condition of a company on a given date. Such language is apt to prove doubly misleading to the average investor—first, because of the implication that the balance-sheet is wholly photographic in nature, whereas it is largely historical; and, secondly, because of the suggestion that it is possible to achieve something approaching photographic accuracy in a balance-sheet which, in fact, is necessarily the reflection of opinions subject to a (possibly wide) margin of error.

Writers of text-books on accounting speak of the purpose of the balance-sheet as being to reflect the values of the assets and the liabilities on a particular date. They explain the fact that in many balance-sheets certain assets are stated at figures which are obviously far above or far below true values by saying that the amounts at which such assets are stated represent "conventional" valuations. Such statements seem to involve a misconception of the nature of a balance-sheet.

In an earlier age, when capital assets were inconsiderable and business units in general smaller and less complex than they are today, it was possible to value assets with comparative ease and accuracy and to measure the progress made from year to year by annual valuations. With the growing mechanization of industry, and with corporate organizations becoming constantly larger, more completely integrated and more complex, this has become increasingly impracticable. From an accounting standpoint, the distinguishing characteristic of business today is the extent to which expenditures are made in one period with the definite purpose and expectation that they shall be the means of producing profits in the future; and how such expenditures shall be dealt with in accounts is the central problem of financial accounting. How much of a given expenditure of the current or a past year shall be carried forward as an asset cannot possibly be determined by an exercise of judgment in the nature of a valuation. The task of appraisal would be too vast, and the variations in appraisal from year to year due to changes in price levels or changes in the mental attitude of the appraisers would in many cases be so great as to reduce all other elements in the computations of the results of operations to relative insignificance.

Carrying the thought one stage further, it is apparent that the real value of the assets of any large business is dependent mainly on the earning capacity of the enterprise. This fact is fairly generally recognized by intelligent investors as regards capital assets such as plant and machinery, but it is not equally generally recognized that it is true, though to a lesser extent, in respect of such assets as inventories and trade accounts receivable. Those, however, who have had experience in liquidations and reorganizations realize that in many industries it becomes impossible to realize inventories or accounts receivable at more than a fraction of their going-concern value, once the business has ceased to be a going concern. To attempt to arrive at the value of the assets of a business annually by an estimation of the earning capacity of the enterprise would be an impossible and unprofitable task. Any consideration of the accounts of a large business enterprise of today must start from the premise that an annual valuation of the assets is neither practical nor desirable.

Some method, however, has to be found by which the proportion of a given expenditure to be charged against the operations in a year, and the proportion to be carried forward, may be determined; otherwise, it would be wholly impossible to present an annual income account. Out of this necessity has grown up a body of conventions, based partly on theoretical and partly on practical considerations, which form the basis for the determination of income and the preparation of balance-sheets today. And while there is a fairly general agreement on certain broad principles to be followed in the formulation of conventional methods of accounting, there remains room for differences in the application of those principles which affect the results reached in a very important degree.

This may be made clearer by one or two illustrations. It is

a generally accepted principle that plant value should be charged against gross profits over the useful life of the plant. But there is no agreement on the method of distribution. The straight-line method of providing for depreciation which is most commonly employed by industrial companies, the retirement-reserve method used by utilities, the sinking-fund method, the combined maintenance-and-depreciation method, and others, are supported by respectable argument and by usage, and the charges against a particular year may vary a hundred per cent or more according as one or the other permissible method is employed.

Again, the most commonly accepted method of stating inventories is at cost or market, whichever is lower; but within this rule widely different results may be derived, according to the detailed methods of its application. For instance, at times like the present, cost of finished goods may be deemed to be the actual cost, as increased by subnormal operation, or a normal cost computed on the basis of a normal scale of operations. It may or may not include interest during the period of production or various kinds of overhead expenses. Market value may be either gross or net after deducting direct selling expenses. The choice between cost or market may be made in respect of each separate item or of classes of items or of the inventory as a whole. Frequently, whether a profit or a loss for the year is shown depends on the precise way in which the rule is applied. And since the conventions which are to be observed must, to possess value, be based on a combination of theoretical and practical considerations, there are few, if any, which can fairly be claimed to be so inherently superior in merit to possible alternatives that they alone should be regarded as acceptable.

Most investors realize today that balance-sheets and income accounts are largely the reflection of individual judgments, and that their value is therefore to a large extent dependent on the competence and honesty of the persons exercising the necessary judgment. The importance of method, and particularly of consistency of method from year to year, is by no means equally understood.

In considering ways of improving the existing situation two alternatives suggest themselves. The first is the selection by competent authority out of the body of acceptable methods in vogue today of detailed sets of rules which would become binding on all corporations of a given class. This procedure has been applied broadly to the railroads and other regulated utilities, though even such classifications as, for instance, that prescribed by the Interstate Commerce Commission allow some choice of method to corporations governed thereby. The arguments against any attempt to apply this alternative to industrial corporations generally are, however, overwhelming.

The more practicable alternative would be to leave every corporation free to choose its own methods of accounting within the very broad limits to which reference has been made, but require disclosure of the methods employed and consistency in their application from year to year. It is significant that Congress in the federal income-tax law has definitely adopted this alternative, every act since that of 1918 having contained a provision that the net income shall be computed "in accordance with the method of accounting regularly employed in keeping the books of such taxpayer" unless such method does not clearly reflect income. In its regulations the Internal Revenue Bureau has said, "the law contemplates that each taxpayer shall adopt such forms and systems of accounting as are in his judgment best suited to his purpose." (Reg. 45, Art. 24.) The greatest value of classifications such as those imposed on regulated utilities lies in the disclosure of method and consistency of method which they tend to produce.

Within quite wide limits, it is relatively unimportant to the investor what precise rules or conventions are adopted by a corporation in reporting its earnings if he knows what method is being followed and is assured that it is followed consistently from year to year. Reverting to the illustrations already used, the investor would not need to be greatly concerned whether the straight-line or the sinking-fund method of providing for depreciation were being employed by a given corporation, provided he knew which method was being used and knew that it was being applied in the same way every year. But if depreciation is charged in one year on the straight-line basis applied to cost and in another is charged on a sinking-fund basis applied to a valuation less than cost, the investor may be grossly deceived unless the change is brought to his notice. For this reason, the requirement of the Exchange that the depreciation policy of a company applying for listing shall be stated in the application is valuable, and it might well be amplified to include an undertaking to report to the Exchange and to stockholders any change of policy or any material change in the manner of its application.

Again, it is not a matter of great importance to investors whether the cost-or-market rule for stating inventories is applied to individual items or to the inventory as a whole, but it is very important to the investor that he should be advised if the test is applied to individual items at the beginning of the year and to the inventory as a whole at the close thereof.

It is probably fairly well recognized by intelligent investors today that the earning capacity is the fact of crucial importance in the valuation of an industrial enterprise, and that therefore the income account is usually far more important than the balance-sheet. In point of fact, the changes in the balance-sheets from year to year are usually more significant than the balance-sheets themselves.

The development of accounting conventions has, consciously or unconsciously, been in the main based on an acceptance of this proposition. As a rule, the first objective has been to secure a proper charge or credit to the income account for the year, and in general the presumption has been that once this is achieved the residual amount of the expenditure or the receipt could properly find its place in the balance-sheet at the close of the period, the principal exception being the rule calling for reduction of inventories to market value if that is below cost. But if the income account is to be really valuable to the investor, it must be presented in such a way as to constitute to the fullest possible extent an indication of the earning capacity of the business during the period to which it relates. This Committee feels that the direction of the principal efforts of the Exchange to improve the accounting reports furnished by corporations to their stockholders should be towards making the income account more and more valuable as an indication of earning capacity.

The purpose of furnishing accounts to shareholders must be not only to afford them information in regard to the results being achieved by those to whom they have entrusted the management of the business, but to aid them in taking appropriate action to give effect to the conclusions which they reach regarding such accomplishments. In an earlier day, stockholders who were dissatisfied with the results secured by the management could perhaps move effectively to bring about a change of policy or, failing that, a change of management. With the growth in magnitude of corporations and the present wide diffusion of stock holdings, any such attempt is ordinarily impracticable because of the effort and expenditure that it would entail. The only practical way in which an investor can today give expression to his conclusions in regard to the management of a corporation in which he is interested is by retaining, increasing or disposing of his investment, and accounts are mainly valuable to him in so far as they afford guidance in determining which of these courses he shall pursue.

There is no need to revolutionize or even to change materially corporate accounting, but there is room for great improvement in the presentation of the conclusions to which accounts lead. The aim should be to satisfy (so far as is possible and prudent) the investor's need for knowledge, rather than the accountant's sense of form and respect for tradition, and to make very clear the basis on which accounts are prepared. But even when all has been done that can be done, the limitations on the significance of even the best of accounts must be recognized, and the shorter the period covered by them the more pronounced usually are these limitations. Accounts are essentially continuous historical record; and, as is true of history in general, correct interpretations and sound forecasts for the future cannot be reached upon a hurried survey of temporary conditions, but only by longer retrospect and a careful distinction between permanent tendencies and transitory influences. If the investor is unable or unwilling to make or secure an adequate survey, it will be best for him not to rely on the results of a superficial one.

To summarize, the principal objects which this Committee thinks the Exchange should keep constantly in mind and do its best gradually to achieve are:

1. To bring about a better recognition by the investing public of the fact that the balance-sheet of a large modern corporation does not and should not be expected to represent an attempt to show present values of the assets and liabilities of the corporation.

2. To emphasize the fact that balance-sheets are necessarily to a large extent historical and conventional in character, and to encourage the adoption of revised forms of balance-sheets which will disclose more clearly than at present on what basis assets of various kinds are stated (e.g., cost, reproduction cost less depreciation, estimated going-concern value, cost or market whichever is lower, liquidating value, et cetera).

3. To emphasize the cardinal importance of the income account, such importance being explained by the fact that the value of a business is dependent mainly on its earning capacity; and to take the position that an annual income account is unsatisfactory unless it is so framed as to constitute the best reflection reasonably

obtainable of the earning capacity of the business under the conditions existing during the year to which it relates.

4. To make universal the acceptance by listed corporations of certain broad principles of accounting which have won fairly general acceptance (see Exhibit I attached), and within the limits of such broad principles to make no attempt to restrict the right of corporations to select detailed methods of accounting deemed by them to be best adapted to the requirements of their business; but—

(a) To ask each listed corporation to cause a statement of the methods of accounting and reporting employed by it to be formulated in sufficient detail to be a guide to its accounting department (see Exhibit II attached); to have such statement adopted by its board so as to be binding on its accounting officers; and to furnish such statement to the Exchange and make it available to any stockholder on request and upon payment, if desired, of a reasonable fee.

(b) To secure assurances that the methods so formulated will be followed consistently from year to year and that if any change is made in the principles or any material change in the manner of application, the stockholders and the Exchange shall be advised when the first accounts are presented in which effect is given to such change.

(c) To endeavor to bring about a change in the form of audit certificate so that the auditors would specifically report to the shareholders whether the accounts as presented were properly prepared in accordance with the methods of accounting regularly employed by the company, defined as already indicated.

This Committee would be glad to discuss these suggestions with you at any time, and to co-operate with the Exchange in any action it may see fit to take along the lines indicated.

Yours very truly,

GEORGE O. MAY, *Chairman.*

EXHIBIT I

It is suggested that in the first instance the broad principles to be laid down as contemplated in paragraph 4 of the suggestions should be few in number. It might be desirable to formulate a statement thereof only after consultation with a small group of qualified persons, including corporate officials, lawyers and accountants. Presumably the list would include some if not all of the following:

1. Unrealized profit should not be credited to income account of the corporation either directly or indirectly, through the medium of charging against such unrealized profits amounts which would ordinarily fall to be charged against income account. Profit is deemed to be realized when a sale in the ordinary course of business is effected, unless the circumstances are such that the collection of the sale price is not reasonably assured. An exception to the general rule may be made in respect of inventories in industries (such as the packing-house industry) in which owing to the impossibility of determining costs it is a trade custom to take inventories at net selling prices, which may exceed cost.

2. Capital surplus, however created, should not be used to relieve the income account of the current or future years of charges which would otherwise fall to be made thereagainst. This rule might be subject to the exception that where, upon reorganization, a reorganized company would be relieved of charges which would require to be made against income if the existing corporation were continued, it might be regarded as permissible to accomplish the same result without reorganization provided the facts were as fully revealed to and the action as formally approved by the shareholders as in reorganization.

3. Earned surplus of a subsidiary company created prior to acquisition does not form a part of the consolidated earned surplus of the parent company and subsidiaries; nor can any dividend declared out of such surplus properly be credited to the income account of the parent company.

4. While it is perhaps in some circumstances permissible to show stock of a corporation held in its own treasury as an asset,

if adequately disclosed, the dividends on stock so held should not be treated as a credit to the income account of the company.

5. Notes or accounts receivable due from officers, employees, or affiliated companies must be shown separately and not included under a general heading such as Notes Receivable or Accounts Receivable.

The exchange would probably desire to add a rule regarding stock dividends.

EXHIBIT II

The statement of the methods of accounting contemplated in paragraph 4a of the suggestion would not be in the nature of the ordinary detailed classification of accounts, nor would it deal with the machinery of bookkeeping. It should constitute a clear statement of the principles governing the classification of charges and credits as between (a) balance-sheet accounts, (b) income account and (c) surplus account, together with sufficient details of the manner in which these principles are to be applied to enable an investor to judge of the degree of conformity to standard usage and of conservatism of the reporting corporation. Its content would vary according to the circumstances of individual companies, but some of the more important points which would be disclosed thereby would be as follows:

THE GENERAL BASIS OF THE ACCOUNTS:

Whether the accounts are consolidated, and if so, what rule governs the determination of the companies to be included in consolidation; also, a statement as to how profits and losses of subsidiary and controlled companies not consolidated are dealt with in the accounts of the parent company.

THE BALANCE-SHEET:

(a) In respect of capital assets, the statement should show:
(1) What classes of items are charged to property account

(whether only new property or also replacements and improvements);

(2) Whether any charges in addition to direct cost, either for overhead expense, interest or otherwise, are made to property accounts;

(3) Upon what classes of property, on what basis, and at what rates provision is made for, or in lieu of, depreciation;

(4) What classes of expenditures, if any, are charged against reserves for depreciation so created;

(5) How the difference between depreciated value and realized or realizable value is dealt with on the sale or abandonment of units of property;

(6) On what basis property purchased from subsidiary companies is charged to property account (whether at cost to subsidiary or otherwise).

(b) In respect of inventories: The statement should show in fairly considerable detail the basis of valuation of the inventory. The statement under this head would be substantially a summary in general terms of the instructions issued by the company to those charged with the duty of preparing the actual inventories. It would not be sufficient to say that the inventory was taken on the basis of cost or market, whichever is lower. The precise significance attached to these terms should be disclosed, for the reasons set forth on page 3 of the letter.*

The statement should include a specific description of the way in which any intercompany profit on goods included in the inventory is dealt with. It should show under this head, or in relation to income or surplus account, exactly how reductions from cost to market value are treated in the accounts and how the inventories so reduced are treated in the succeeding period. It is, for instance, a matter of first importance to investors if inventories have been reduced to cost or market at the end of the year by a charge to surplus account, and the income for the succeeding year has been determined on the basis of the reduced valuation of

---

* Page 75.

the inventory thus arrived at. Obviously, under such a procedure the aggregate income shown for a series of years is not the true income for the period.

(c) In respect of securities: The statement should set forth what rules govern the classification of securities as marketable securities under the head of "current assets" and securities classified under some other head in the balance-sheet. It should set forth in detail how any of its own securities held by the reporting corporation, or in the case of a consolidated statement any securities of any company in the group held by that or any other member of the group are dealt with in the balance-sheet. (Stock of subsidiaries held by the parent will of course be eliminated in consolidation.) The disclosure of the basis of valuation of securities is covered in paragraph 2, page 6 of the recommendations contained in the letter.*

(d) Cash and receivables present few questions, though where sales are made on the instalment plan, or on any other deferred basis, their treatment should be fully set forth, including a statement of the way in which provision is made for future collection or other expenses relating to sales already made but not liquidated and to what extent deferred accounts are included in current assets.

(e) Deferred charges: The statement should set forth what classes of expenditures are in the company's practice deferred and what procedure is followed in regard to the gradual amortization thereof. (This question is of considerable importance as substantial overstatements of income may occur through deferment in unprosperous periods of expenses ordinarily chargeable against current operations, possibly followed by writing off such charges in a later year against surplus account.)

(f) Liability accounts: There is normally less latitude in regard to the treatment of liability accounts than in respect of assets. The statement should clearly show how unliquidated liabilities, such as damage claims, unadjusted taxes, etc., are dealt with. The statement should disclose whether it is the practice

---

* Page 79 hereof.

of the company to make a provision for onerous commitments or to deal with such commitments in any way in the balance-sheet.

(g) Reserves: A statement of the rules governing credits and charges to any reserve account (including both those shown on the liability side and those deducted from assets) should be given in detail. It is particularly important to know whether losses, shrinkages or expenses which would otherwise be chargeable against income accounts are in any circumstances charges against contingent or other reserves, and whether such reserves are built up partly or wholly otherwise than by charges to income account.

THE INCOME ACCOUNT:

An adequate statement in regard to the treatment of balance-sheet items discloses by inference what charges and credits are made to income account or surplus. The additional points required to be disclosed are the principles followed in allocating charges and credits to income account and surplus account respectively and the form of presentation of the income account. The form should be such as to show separately (a) operating income; (b) depreciation and/or depletion if not deducted in arriving at (a), in which case the amount of the deduction should be shown; (c) income from companies controlled but not consolidated (indicating the nature thereof); (d) other recurring income; (e) any extraordinary credits; (f) charges for interest; (g) income taxes and (h) any extraordinary charges.

The company's proportionate share of the undistributed earnings or losses for the year of companies controlled but not consolidated should be disclosed in a note or otherwise on the face of the income account. Stock dividends if credited to income should be shown separately with a statement of the basis upon which the credit is computed.

CHAPTER V

Cost and Value

THE QUESTION HOW far cost and value respectively shall be reflected in books of account and financial statements, may be regarded as perhaps the central question of accounting. It presents so many phases and gives rise to so many questions, terminological, theoretical, and practical, that much confusion has arisen in discussion of it. Considerations which may be determinative with respect to the treatment of fixed property are not necessarily applicable to the treatment of inventories. The case where value exceeds cost may call for different treatment from that in which it is less than cost. Acceptance of the postulate of continuity naturally leads to emphasis on cost, while recognition of the limited truth of the postulate that the monetary unit is stable may lead to wider recognition being given to value. In this chapter, the question will be considered in its broad aspects and in relation to fixed property; the case of inventories will be considered later.

The first major difficulty is that the word "value" has a great variety of meanings; indeed, Professor Bonbright in his well-known work on the subject says that it is impossible to reconcile even the uses of the word in American judicial decisions except by defining it so broadly as to include any monetary statement about property.[1] The English Companies Act provides that every balance sheet shall disclose how the fixed assets are valued, and the leading commentators agree

---

[1] *The Valuation of Property*, J. C. Bonbright (1937), Vol. I, p. 38.

that they may be said to be "valued" at cost even though they are admittedly worth only a far smaller sum. It has been said that in another English statute the word "value" is used in twenty-seven different senses.

In this discussion the word "value" will connote an attempt to determine worth except where it is italicized, in which cases it will be used in the broadest sense of a monetary statement about property.

When property is new, cost and value are normally the same, and for a considerable time thereafter cost may be the best guide to value. Even when this condition has ceased to exist, cost may be used as a conventional measure of *valuation*. It is important to distinguish between the cases in which property is stated at cost as such, and those in which cost is merely a conventional measure of *value*.

When an election between cost and value has to be made, the choice may differ according as cost or value is the greater. There are many cases in which value will be preferred to cost if it is the lower of the two, but not if it is the higher. The alternative basis of cost or market value, whichever is the lower, for *valuing* inventories, is an outstanding illustration. This rule may be accepted on a pragmatic basis because of its demonstrated merits; alternatively, it may be defended on the ground that only useful costs should be carried forward, and that the fact of value being less than cost is evidence of a loss or cessation of utility. When value is in excess of cost, any attempt to recognize it in accounting must have regard to the definition of income as realized gain, to which there are no recognized exceptions in the accounting for manufacturing and trading operations (though there are in the accounting for transfer income, such as interest). There is not the same insistence on realization as a condition precedent to accounting recognition in the case of losses as in the case of gains.

The question whether cost or value should govern in

specific cases is clearly one that might be answered differently according to the purpose for which accounting statements are designed. In particular, a conflict may be recognized between the requirements necessary to meet the older uses of accounting statements and those that will serve the newer use as a guide to earning capacity (see page 21).

Changes in the value of property may be due to a variety of causes. An appreciation of property in terms of a stable monetary unit has a different significance from one that reflects only a decline in the value of the unit. Perhaps the most difficult of all problems in this field is presented where a decline in value as the result of use or obsolescence is either accelerated or offset by a change in money value due to fluctuations in the price level. The disentanglement of the elements in such cases is essential to sound accounting treatment.

With this formidable catalogue of difficulties in mind, the specific case may be considered of fixed assets having a value that is greater than cost. Fixed assets by definition consist of property which is intended to be used and perhaps ultimately consumed in connection with the business, and is not ordinarily offered for sale.

The question at once arises—how can value be measured in such a case? Clearly there is no exchange value for such property in the sense in which the economists use that term, since no market for the property exists. If the fact that value is higher than cost is due to a decline in the value of the monetary unit, the solution may be to adhere to the cost basis but to accept the view that cost must be expressed in a unit that is uniform, and adjust the dollar cost accordingly.

Apart from this case, the efforts to find a measure of value for fixed property not intended for sale have proved unsatisfactory, and the justification of the cost basis rests, perhaps, more on the inherent defects of any suggested method of valuation than upon the abstract merits of the cost approach, itself. However, there are cases in which value is clearly in excess of cost when both are measured in terms of the same monetary unit, and the question whether recognition should be given to the higher value in such cases should not be decided solely on the grounds of the practical difficulties of measuring value. This is particularly true in an economy like ours, in which capital gains are regarded as income and capital values are important for a variety of purposes, such as taxation and determination of the validity of dividends.

Upon this question the history of British practice may be particularly illuminating, since in England capital gains are not regarded as income and the emphasis is on the annual yield rather than on capital values.

The Companies Act of 1862 included an appendix, known as Table A, in which model articles of association were set forth. This model was not compulsory, but was deemed to have been accepted unless expressly excluded by the articles actually adopted by a company. Under Table A, provision was made for the submission annually to shareholders, by the company, of a balance sheet, and the accompanying instructions were that property should be stated at cost "with Deductions for deterioration in Value as charged to the Reserve Fund or Profit and Loss." [1] The only statutory limitation on the payment of dividends was afforded by provisions which set forth how capital might be reduced. Table A contained a model article on the question which originally provided that dividends should be paid only out of "profits arising from the business of the company." Because of uncertainties as to their interpretation, the last seven words were omitted in the revision of the statute in 1908.

As has been indicated, the English law permits a wide latitude to corporations in determining how profits shall be

---

[1] Buckley, *The Law and Practice Under the Companies Acts*, 6th ed., p. 523.

measured, and it is clear that an English company may, if its memorandum of association so provides, distribute profits without making any allowance for wastage of capital assets, however readily determinable that wastage may be. Not only may the profits of a mine be determined without allowance for depletion, but the profits from a lease or an annuity for a fixed term may be determined without amortization of the price paid therefor.

It is equally clear that a realized appreciation in the value of capital assets may be distributed, and Palmer states [1] that upon the basis of the authorities a clearly realizable appreciation is apparently an adequate basis for a distribution even if it has not, in fact, been realized. However, as he goes on to point out, the directors in such cases assume the heavy burden of proving the realizability; and for this reason distributions based on unrealized appreciation are rare. A stock dividend could not conceivably involve a return of capital, so that there is no bar to a stock dividend based on unrealized appreciation, assuming that the articles of association permit such an issue.

It may be said, therefore, that in English practice the emphasis is strongly on cost, but that nevertheless there has been and is no prohibition against the recording of appreciated values on books of account, though such adjustments are infrequent.

In America, the emphasis on valuation was in earlier days far greater than in England, and it is only in very recent years that the propriety of recording appreciation on books of account has been questioned. Many citations from American writers could be given in support of the foregoing statement. It will suffice to offer a single quotation from an author of unquestioned standing, whose English background made him thoroughly familiar with the case for carrying assets at not more than cost. A. Lowes Dickinson in 1913 said:

---

[1] F. B. Palmer, *Company Law*, 15th ed. (1933), p. 224.

It is necessary to recognize that there are causes at work, particularly in young and growing communities, which may render a statement prepared on the basis of cost of capital assets misleading and even prejudicial to the proper interests of present owners.[1]

This quotation is interesting not only because of its author's eminence and English origin but because of its date, which just preceded the first world war. From the depression that began in 1893 there had been a steady rise in prices, which from 1896 to 1913 averaged about 2 per cent per annum cumulatively for wholesale prices. As Professor F. C. Mills has said, this rise "provided one of the most fundamental of the conditions under which business men of that era worked." [2]

The war brought a further rise, so that in 1922 the wholesale price index was roughly 50 per cent greater than in 1913. It is not surprising, therefore, that the view expressed by Dickinson in 1913 is to be found in Paton and Stevenson, 1918, and Montgomery (4th edition), 1927.[3]

In discussion of tax problems such as those of invested capital, replacement reserves, and capital gains, the late Dr. T. S. Adams during the first world war stressed the point that cost figures gradually lost their significance, and he expressed the view that capital assets should be revalued at intervals—say once in a generation.

When the Special Committee on Cooperation with Stock Exchanges of the American Institute of Accountants addressed its letter of September 22, 1932, to the New York Stock Exchange (see Appendix to Chapter IV) it undertook to list certain generally accepted accounting principles. It is sig-

---

[1] Dickinson, *Accounting Practice and Procedure* (1913), p. 80.

[2] *Recent Economic Changes in the United States* (1929), Vol. II, p. 609.

[3] Some arguments against reappraisal were discussed in an article entitled "The Problem of Depreciation," which appeared in the *Journal of Accountancy*, Jan. 1915, and is reproduced in *Twenty-five Years*, Vol. I, p. 149.

nificant that no prohibition against recording unrealized appreciation was included in this list.

During the last decade there has been a change of viewpoint which may be regarded as the result of an unusual combination of financial, political, and social forces. Today, it is a fairly generally accepted rule of accounting that unrealized appreciation should not be recorded on books of account. Write-ups of fixed assets are in many quarters strongly disapproved. Not only is this so, but past write-ups are condemned, as if they had been originally violations of a fundamental principle instead of being merely something that is outmoded today.

Even those who regard capital gains as income concede that an apparent gain due to a fall in the value of the monetary unit is not true income. Economists have pointed out that currencies are really suitable as a medium only for transactions which do not require any great length of time for their completion. They have endeavored to formulate plans for a standard of value that would be better suited to the adjustment of long-term transactions. In doing so, Marshall (in 1887) pointed out that the need was a modern one; that in earlier ages contracts to make definite payments at distant times were rare, though now they had become common.

The assumption of stability in the monetary unit was clearly not valid in respect of the measurement of income derived from the conversion after 1920 of assets acquired in the years of the century prior to the first world war.

Following the war and immediate postwar rise and a precipitate fall, the price level became stabilized in 1922; and in the years that followed, as Bauer and Gold [1] point out in their discussion of utility valuation, the new price level came to be regarded as virtually permanent. At the same time, the effort to impart liquidity to securities representing enterprises of

---

[1] *Public Utility Valuation for Purposes of Rate Control* (1934), p. 105.

a permanent character, to which reference has more than once been made, became intensified, with a corresponding increase in emphasis on the income account as a measure of earning capacity and thus a guide to value.

In measuring earning capacity it is advantageous to express revenues and charges against revenue in terms of a monetary unit of the same value. The recent movement in favor of the last in, first out method of valuation of inventories reflects this desire.[1] Many of the write-ups of fixed properties between 1920 and 1930 were efforts to reflect the change in the value of the monetary unit in the subsequent depreciation charges against income. So long as these write-ups were based on reliable evidence and the resulting credits were excluded from income and from earned surplus (so that the rule against including unrealized gains in income was not infringed) there was ample theoretical and practical support for them. If the verdict upon them is made to depend on whether they were reasonable in the light of the circumstances when the entries were made, such write-ups must be held to have been fully justified. It is only in the light of later developments and on the basis of new modes of thought that they can be indiscriminately condemned.

Unfortunately, in some cases write-ups were not based on satisfactory evidence and had no justification whatever, and criticism, warranted in these cases, has too often taken the unjustified form of condemnation of the procedure itself.

However, even during the 1920's the emphasis on income and earning capacity had produced other effects than a disposition to express depreciation charges in terms of current purchasing power. The strange anomaly came to be recognized that lower book *values* meant lower depreciation charges, which in turn would result in larger reported earnings per share and so in higher *values* per share as measured by the

---

[1] *Vide infra*, p. 177.

process of capitalizing earnings. At the same time, the shift of emphasis made the lowering of the book *value* per share of minor significance. Recognition of these facts afforded a strong check to the movement to record appreciated values on books of account.

Reference to prospectuses of the period will show that in many cases the book *values* were left unchanged and the higher appraised values were recorded only as notes on the balance sheet or in the text of the prospectus itself. By adopting this procedure it was possible to bring the higher values. to the notice of the investor without the necessity of increasing depreciation charges. It was even possible to get a third benefit in the form of credit for conservatism and for conformity to academic thought, which then, as now, favored recording values other than cost only in footnotes or supplementary statements.

The depression that began in 1929 created new conditions favoring a close adherence to cost as the basis of fixed asset accounting. Overcapacity and a resulting lack of earning power tended to offset the earlier rise in the price index as a factor affecting the dollar value of fixed assets. We had passed out of the pioneer stage into the first stages of a controlled economy. Regulation and other political forces, as well as taxation, were limiting the opportunity to secure profits based on increments in real value, to say nothing of mere increments in dollar reproduction costs. The tendency to write up properties was not only checked but reversed, and write-downs became frequent. At the same time, particularly in the public utility field, past write-ups—some of which were warranted and others unjustifiable—were being scathingly criticized in the course of a movement to strengthen governmental controls. In a conference with members of the Federal Trade Commission, following the passage of the Securities Act of 1933, the use to be made of the power granted the Commission to prescribe accounting methods was under discussion. A commissioner dilated on the necessity for stringent rules against the vice of write-ups. I suggested that the necessity had already passed, and that, in private industries at least, the danger was, rather, that assets would be unduly written down for the purpose of reducing depreciation charges against income. I had made a similar comment in an article published in 1932.[1]

The forces which were tending to bring about a change in the rule which permitted and in some cases even encouraged recognition of value in excess of cost in the accounting of unregulated industries, met strong support from some commissions charged with the regulation of the rates and practices of public utilities. These bodies in general found in this movement support for the prudent investment theory of the rate base, to which under the leadership of Mr. Justice Brandeis they had resorted in an effort to free themselves from the shackles of Supreme Court decisions which insisted on value as the measure of the rate base.

The record of the Supreme Court on the question of value is suggestive of the attitude of the Court in A. P. Herbert's discussion of *Fardell* v. *Potts* in his *Misleading Cases*. There, Lord Justice Morrow is made to say that there is no problem which an English court cannot resolve by putting the question, "Was this or was it not the conduct of a reasonable man?"— and leaving the jury to answer the question.

In a series of cases beginning with *Smyth* v. *Ames*, the Court found itself barred by the nature of the issue from requiring value to be computed with reference to earning capacity, which it recognized as being the principal determining factor. It therefore undertook to prescribe a method of computing value by combining a variety of minor elements in undisclosed proportions. The confusion and uncertainty

---

[1] "The Influence of the Depression on the Practice of Accountancy," *Journal of Accountancy*, Vol. LIV, p. 336.

which was produced by the rule then laid down led eventually to a situation in which, as Bauer and Gold put it, the Court came to recognize reproduction cost less allowance for depreciation (which must not be computed by a mere formula) as virtually determining value, whereas commissions, according to Mr. Justice Brandeis, "while admitting the evidence in obedience to *Smyth* v. *Ames*, failed in ever-increasing numbers to pay heed to it in fixing the rate base." [1]

The decisions of the Court unquestionably influenced to a great extent the prices at which public utility enterprises were actually bought and sold in the 1920's and also gave strong support to the practice of recording on books of account values computed in accordance with the Court's views. A minority of the Court and many commissioners persisted in advocacy of cost as the measure of the rate base—sometimes on the ground that cost was the best measure of value, and at other times on the ground that cost was the appropriate measure without regard to value. The abuses of the holding company device and other vices into which the financial world lapsed in the late 1920's, and the unexampled intensity of the depression which followed, brought the Commissions both new arguments and new powers.

Commissions not only pressed more vigorously for the adoption of the prudent investment theory, but undertook to apply it in an extreme form by the adoption of the concept of cost to the first person who devoted property to the public service. This may be regarded as a crude and illiberal variation of the old concept of enterprise accounting, which treats as the accounting unit the enterprise rather than the corporation which is carrying on the enterprise.

To what extent a modification of the position of the Supreme Court has been effected is a debatable question. In the Natural Gas Pipeline case, decided in 1942,[2] three judges in

---

[1] Southwestern Bell Telephone Co. case, 262 U.S. 276.

[2] *Federal Power Commission, et al.* v. *Natural Gas Pipeline Company, et al.* (315 U.S. 575).

a concurring opinion interpreted the decision of the Court
as an abandonment of the rule laid down in *Smyth* v. *Ames*
more than forty years earlier. There are, however, some who
regard this view of the Court's position as at least premature
if not erroneous.

In a recent case, a commission had said: "With the decline in favor of 'fair value' as the only mode of public utility
rate regulation, its keystone, reproduction cost, crumbles.
Bona fide investment figures now become all important
in the regulation of rates." The Circuit Court of Appeals,
however, rejected this view, the majority opinion saying:
"What has declined in favor is not, as the Commission thought,
the 'doctrine' of fair value, but the cumbersome and misleading reproduction cost theory as a means of determining it." [1]

It is undoubtedly a grave objection to the reproduction-
cost theory that there are many properties which no one
would reconstruct as and where they exist. In a famous merger
case both parties agreed that a particular plant had no value,
or even had a negative value. It would have paid to demolish
the plant and build another in a better location, but this could
not be done because of probable repercussions on the local
attitude towards a more important plant near by.

In the last few years the Supreme Court has felt itself
compelled to consider the question of value in connection
with reorganizations of railroads and other companies. For
such purposes, earning capacity—which it felt bound to exclude from the elements entering into the determination of
value for rate purposes—has been recognized as practically
determinative. Indeed, the Court has insisted that those on
whom the burden of finding value falls must peer into the
future and determine value on the basis of prospective earning
capacity estimated with regard not only to past experience
but also to probabilities in the future.

---

[1] *Hope Natural Gas Company* v. *Federal Power Commission,* United States
Circuit Court of Appeals, Fourth Circuit, decided Feb. 16, 1943 (pp. 6 and 12).

The practical consequences of such rulings are themselves extremely difficult to foresee. Today, it is apparent that in many lines of activity the future course of regulation and legal decisions—which apparently may have a retroactive as well as a prospective effect—and the course of governmental policy in relation to such matters as prices, taxation, and interest rates, are the crucial uncertainties affecting future expectations and their discounted value. Commissions have asserted and ruthlessly exercised the right to change accounting principles with unlimited retroactive effect. Assuming that such procedures are legally permissible, what real validity can a process of discounting a so-called expectation for the future possess, or what measure of value can there be of enterprises subject to these risks except the pragmatic test of the occasional purchase and sale? (A more technical discussion of the problem of valuation is given in an appendix to this chapter.)

Writing many years ago, I spoke of the pursuit of the will-o'-the-wisp of value which the Court had initiated in *Smyth v. Ames*. In *Palmer* v. *Connecticut Railway & Lighting Company*,[1] the Court seems to me to have required the attainment of an even more illusory objective. It may well be that eventually it will be compelled to recognize the impracticability of the concept of value set forth in that decision, and accept the alternative suggested by Mr. Justice Frankfurter of a "tough business basis," which would presumably be determined by the testimony of "tough businessmen." Accountants are constantly being reminded in their professional experience that ideas, which in the abstract seem perfectly adapted to a purpose, are subject to a high mortality rate when they undergo the test of the "tough business world."

While, in the past, to record appreciated values on books of account has been regarded as permissible, this has never been considered as compulsory, however large and well as-

---

[1] 311 U.S. 544. *Infra*, p. 103.

sured the appreciation may have been. The question arises whether managements should be permitted to recognize or refuse to recognize such appreciation at their option, and if so, what terms should be attached to the exercise of such an option. Clearly the formation of a new corporation would create a right and, indeed, an obligation to record the values of the assets acquired at the date of acquisition, and it may well be that the recognition of new value on books of account of a continuing company should be regarded as a quasi-reorganization.

In the case of downward adjustments, this concept of quasi-reorganization has been developed, and it would seem desirable that it should be applied, also, to recognition of increases in value. This would mean that the readjustments in either direction would require to be disclosed to and approved by stockholders with substantially the same formality as would be required to effect an actual reorganization. Subject to this requirement it would seem to be wise to recognize the propriety of upward readjustments to values which are adequately demonstrated and are clearly not of a purely ephemeral character.

A special case is presented where an excess of current value over depreciated book *values* is clearly due to overestimation of depreciation in the past. This question, however, forms a part of the general subject of corrections of past estimates rather than a part of the problem of deciding to what extent cost and value respectively should be recognized in accounting.

The case in which value is less than the balance of cost which has not been amortized is of more practical importance and presents more problems than the case in which value is the higher figure. The fact that earnings are large may result in an increase in the value of an enterprise, but in the case of manufacturing and trading corporations that increase in value does not ordinarily attach to the physical properties employed in carrying on the enterprise. The question how far a decline in earnings calls for adjustment of property values is one of great difficulty. Depreciation schemes today normally aim to provide for obsolescence as well as for physical deterioration, and a decline in earning power may be evidence of obsolescence—not only in particular units of property but in complete plants or even enterprises.

No important accounting problem has, perhaps, received less adequate discussion than the question whether a decline in earnings for any considerable period should be regarded as calling for a downward adjustment of the book *values* of the property, and if so, how that charge should be treated in the accounts.

In England, it is clear that such an adjustment is not called for. In general, American practice would seem to be in accord with that of England, though no doubt passages could be found in accounting literature to support the view that such adjustments ought to be made.

Manifestly it is not easy to determine whether declines in earning capacity are temporary or relatively permanent, nor is it easy to decide to what extent they are inherent and how far they may be due to poor management. Moreover, the accounting considerations bearing on the question may differ according as the decline in earning capacity appears to be due to competitive inferiority or to a decline in the earning capacity of an entire industry. As has been suggested (see page 29), an attempt to reflect changes in the capital value of prospective income in measuring current income or surplus raises difficult technical problems and important questions as to the significance of the resulting figures.

Where the decline in value is not due to a fall in earning capacity caused by competitive inferiority it would seem undesirable to lay down any rule which would require a write-down. Managements should, perhaps, be encouraged to give recognition to such declines through reorganization or quasi-reorganization. There is something incongruous in basing accounting on property *values*, which, if real, would imply a value for the stock of the corporation of $100 per share when the stock persistently sells at from $10 to $15 per share. But as an English judge, in discussing a somewhat similar question, said: "It may be a precept of prudence and yet be far removed from the sphere of the categorical imperative."[1] Just how such an adjustment should be made will form part of the question of the treatment of capital gains and losses in general, which is reserved for discussion in a later chapter.

The obligation, or right, of a management to write down property cannot be determined without consideration of the equitable rights of the owners of different classes of securities that may be outstanding. If a corporation has issued preferred stocks or bonds on the basis of a balance sheet, this may be regarded as implying an obligation to provide out of revenues for any decline in the useful value of such assets before making any distribution on junior securities. In such circumstances a corporation should not be permitted to reduce the book *value* of the assets to current value and thereafter compute depreciation on the basis of the reduced value, if that action would prejudice the position of the senior security which the corporation has a legal or a moral obligation not deliberately to impair. Subject to appropriate recognition of these equities, accountants should encourage corporations to deal through quasi reorganizations with inheritances from the past which have lost their old significance. Such readjustments are likely to promote efficiency as well as to remove possible causes of misconception on the part of stockholders. However, they should, if undertaken, be comprehensive, and not limited to readjustments which will improve future earnings made without regard to offsetting favorable inheritances.

The conclusion to which this discussion leads is that pri-

---

[1] *Ammonia Soda Co. v. Chamberlain* (1918), I Ch. 275.

marily the accounting for fixed assets should be based on cost, but that perhaps the strongest argument in favor of this procedure is the difficulty and uncertainty that are encountered in determining value. Therefore, where despite these difficulties it is clear that the existing value is markedly at variance with a book *value* determined on the basis of cost, it should be regarded as permissible and in some cases desirable to recognize current values in the books of account and in financial statements prepared therefrom. However, such readjustments should not be lightly undertaken and should in all cases be subject to the approval of stockholders, given with a formality comparable to that required for the purpose of actual reorganization. Care should be exercised to distinguish between readjustments which represent corrections of past estimates of depreciation and those due to causes to which recognition is not ordinarily given in current accounting practice. In all cases, the fullest consideration should be given to the equitable rights of different classes of stockholders in determining whether a readjustment shall be effected and what changes in the method of determining income may properly result therefrom.

When it is said that accounting should be based on cost, the implication is merely that cost should form the starting point for the determination of the sum at which the property shall be carried. There remain certain questions as to the determination of cost and also the question what deduction from the initial cost should be made from time to time in respect of the fact that the life of property units is not perpetual, or, to use the common language of accounting, for depreciation. These subjects will be considered in the chapters that follow.

APPENDIX TO CHAPTER V

THE PROBLEM OF MEASURING the capital value of enterprises has assumed so much importance in connection with reorganizations that it may be worth while to discuss it in a note more fully and technically than would be appropriate in the text.

The position is rightly stated by Mr. Justice Holmes in the decision in *Galveston, Harrisburg & San Antonio Ry. Co. v. Texas:* [1] "the commercial value of property consists in the expectation of income from it," i.e., in the expectation that it will produce some income. But from this starting point to a valuation of a particular enterprise is a long and uncertain road.

A reference by Mr. Justice Douglas in *Palmer v. Connecticut Railway & Lighting Company* to the need for "an estimate" of what will occur in the future might give rise to a misunderstanding if too literally interpreted. For obviously there are many possible estimates of future earnings to which varying degrees of probability attach. The valuation of an enterprise according to this general theory depends upon:

(a) The range of reasonable expectations of income for each future year for a period of years. The period ends at the point where the present value of a sum receivable thereafter becomes immaterial.

(b) The degree of probability attaching to the expectations within various parts of the range.

(c) The rates of discount deemed appropriate to convert a sum assumed to be receivable in the future to a present value.

---

[1] 210 U.S. 217–226.

True, calculations are often made by a process in which averages are applied (a) to earnings as between years; (b) to expectations, and (c) to rates of discount. But those who employ such methods know, or should know, that they involve a simplification of the problem scientifically unwarranted, though perhaps necessary or convenient in reducing it to manageable proportions.

It should be noted, also, that a calculation of the value of an enterprise made in such a way cannot be used to determine the value of interests therein which are not upon an equality. If the most probable average expectation were treated as the actual expectation, and if that were less than the amount of fixed charges ahead of junior securities, those junior securities would have no value. Observation shows that securities to which no earning capacity attaches, on the basis of the seemingly most probable estimates of future income, nevertheless are bought for appreciable sums by persons who have no interest in the property otherwise than as investors or speculators. The reason lies, of course, in the possibilities of more favorable expectations being realized, and the value varies with the chances of these more favorable possibilities happening.

In the Palmer case, Mr. Justice Douglas said:

The value of a going enterprise is dependent on earnings. A forecast of earnings must take into consideration the numerous and variable factors which affect income-producing capacity. Those factors vary from business to business. Here we are dealing with passenger transportation by bus. Certainly any forecast of earnings should embrace an expert study of problems peculiar to this field—the territory served, population trends, competitive conditions, the record of companies in comparable territory, and the like.

However, political and economic changes, such as a trend towards higher taxation or inflation, and the prospect of changes in the policy of control, are likely to affect the course of future earnings as much as or more than changes in operating conditions, and the appropriate rates of discount will depend on interest rates which may be governmentally controlled. The evidence required must, therefore, include not only that of managers, engineers, and accountants, but also that of political and economic experts.

There is an incongruity in applying highly refined mathematical processes to assumptions that are of a highly speculative and doubtful character, and obviously such inquiry as is theoretically called for is not ordinarily undertaken even in crude form by those who buy or sell properties. As Keynes points out,[1] the outstanding fact in relation to the application of this theory of value is the extreme precariousness of our knowledge of the future. It is common, therefore, to assume that it will be similar to the present and the recent past except in so far as we have definite reason to foresee change. This assumption is adopted even though all experience goes to show that it is itself contrary to probability.

The question then arises whether, if by value we mean the price that a willing purchaser will be likely to pay to a willing seller, we should resort to theory or should seek to ascertain what procedures are commonly followed by those who buy or sell. If we adopt the former course, there is a danger that we shall arrive at a figure which indicates what ought to be the value rather than one that represents the actual value. If we adopt the latter course, we encounter the difficulty that there are as a rule no individuals or groups of individuals, or corporations, willing and able to buy the entire enterprise—except with the assurance that they can resell interests in it. This, in turn, raises the question of the relations between the value of an enterprise and the prices or

---

[1] John Maynard Keynes, *The General Theory of Employment, Interest and Money* (1936), Chap. XII.

values of securities that represent an interest in the enterprise. Mr. Justice Brandeis in the Ray Consolidated Copper Company case pointed out:

The capital stock of a corporation, its net assets, and its shares of stock are entirely different things. The value of one bears no fixed or necessary relation to the value of the other.[1]

A question often overlooked is the quality of management to be assumed. An extremely well managed enterprise will earn far more than one badly managed. It would be wrong to attach to an enterprise the exceptional efficiency of its management, especially if their services are available only because of their ownership interest in the enterprise. To do so would be scientifically incorrect as well as unduly exalting the material and depreciating the human contribution.

The next point to be noted is that capital value is a multiple of annual yield, and that this multiple is often much larger than the number of years for which we can pretend to foresee the probable course of earnings. This increases our doubts as to the realism of the methods by which the general proposition laid down by Mr. Justice Holmes is to be applied to reach conclusions in specific cases. This doubt is further strengthened by a reading of history.

It may be worth while to consider a case which happened many years ago, so that what was then the future can now be viewed in retrospect.

The Atchison, Topeka & Santa Fe Railway was reorganized in 1895. The reorganized company had a capital structure consisting of fixed interest-bearing debt, conditional interest-bearing debt, preferred stock, and common stock. For the four years preceding reorganization, the income of the railway (before interest charges) averaged roughly six and three-quarters million dollars. In the year preceding reorganization and also in the first year thereafter, the income was about six

---

[1] 268 U.S. 373.

million dollars. In the best year of the five, the earnings would have yielded one per cent on the new preferred stock. Income of six million dollars would suffice to pay the full fixed interest and about one-half of the conditional interest. At the end of the first year after reorganization, the conditional-interest bonds were selling at about 40, preferred stock at about 20, and the common stock at about 13. Obviously, these prices reflected varying possible expectations and varying degrees of probability attaching to those expectations. This point is emphasized by the fact that five years later the railway was earning its full interest and preferred-dividend charges and a substantial margin per share on the common stock. The quoted prices of the securities at that date were: conditional-interest bonds, 90; preferred stock, 105; common stock, 90.

The experience in this case reinforces the conclusions suggested by analysis of the problem. Clearly the prices for Atchison junior securities, if based on expectations of income, reflected the possibility that income would exceed any sums then foreseeable and an estimate of the odds against such an event happening. They may, of course, have represented instead, as Keynes suggests market prices often do, an estimate of what other people might be willing to pay for the securities in the future.

The more the question is studied, the more convinced accountants must be of the wisdom of avoiding valuation of enterprises or capital assets as far as possible. They will recall with approval the dictum of Dr. T. S. Adams, our greatest modern authority on taxation: "I think that no one thing so conduces to delay and complexities of tax laws as the necessity for valuations. . . . It would follow from that, then, that valuations should be omitted and eliminated wherever possible." [1] Valuations are unavoidable in so many cases that their number should not be multiplied unnecessarily.

---

[1] *Hearings*, Select Committee on Investigation of the Bureau of Internal Revenue, United States Senate, Sixty-eighth Congress, 1924, p. 269.

CHAPTER VI

Cost

IN THE PRECEDING CHAPTER it has been suggested that one of the strongest arguments for adopting cost as the basis of general purpose accounting for fixed property is the impracticability of determining value. It must be recognized, however, that the measurement of cost itself presents difficulties, though these are not comparable in magnitude with those encountered in an attempt to appraise the value of the fixed properties of a large and complex modern business.

When property is acquired for cash the amount paid normally measures its value, subject to reservations in respect of wasteful or injudicious expenditure or forced sale. When property is acquired for a consideration not substantially equivalent to cash, the measurement of cost involves some process of valuation.

The simplest case arises when property of one kind is exchanged for other property, itself homogeneous, as when capital stock all of one kind is issued for a piece of land. More complex cases are frequent, in which neither that which is received nor that which is given in exchange consists of homogeneous units of property: as when all the assets of a going business are acquired through the issue of stocks—perhaps of more than one class—and bonds, and the assumption of existing liabilities, some payable immediately and others at a distant date. In every instance the problem of valuation arises, though in some cases nothing more than a conventional valuation may in practice be undertaken.

108

Where the consideration received is not homogeneous, a further problem arises of allocating the aggregate value to separate units of property. Since it is normally assumed that the considerations exchanged are equal in value, the problem may usually be approached by valuing whichever of the two seems more susceptible of accurate appraisal. In some cases exchange of securities of a newly formed corporation for property is in the first instance a mere change in the form in which ownership exists; the real change of ownership occurs when the securities are distributed by sale. In theory, corporate accounting requires valuation at the moment when the property is acquired by the corporation and is not directly concerned with the subsequent dealings in the securities which the corporation issues and the recipient later disposes of. But the sums so realized have a probative value which may be almost conclusive.

At one time it was common by a combination of a legal fiction and an accounting convention to record property acquired through an original issue of securities by a corporation at the par of the securities issued, provided that the directors had made a formal, even though perfunctory, finding that the property acquired was worth that aggregate. How unreal many such proceedings were has been abundantly illustrated by the subsequent history of companies which adopted it. For instance, the United States Steel Corporation has written off a total sum of over $700,000,000 in respect of the values originally recorded on its books in excess of the value of the tangible assets represented by the stocks of other companies which were received by it in respect of its original issue of securities. While no doubt the Corporation acquired intangible assets of substantial value through the original issues, it is clear that a considerable part of the excess of book cost over tangible values which was ultimately written off represented *values* in only a conventional sense.

It may, however, be said that in many cases valuations

which were largely in excess of those suggested by the record of earnings during the depression years of the 1890's, and which were made in the latter part of that decade, have been shown to have reflected expectations which were reasonable and have been justified by the event. At the low point of a depression, the future outlook is brighter than people generally assume it to be, just as the reverse is true at the height of a boom. Looking backward may in either case result in a misleading view of the future.

With the coming of stocks of no par value and other changes in corporate law and practice, purely arbitrary assumptions as to the value of the consideration paid for property in the form of capital stock have become discredited. It is, however, still common to assume that bonds issued or assumed as a part of a purchase price should be taken at par, though this assumption may not be entirely realistic.

The procedure so far outlined met only the requirement of placing a *value* on the assets acquired as an aggregate, and left the problem of allocation to individual assets to be undertaken. The determination of the *value* to be allotted to current assets which would be realized within a short time in the ordinary course of business offered no problems differing from those encountered in closing the books of a company at the end of an accounting period. Frequently, the remainder of the consideration was carried to a single account, representing the fixed assets and the intangible *values* in total.

Even if this course was followed for balance-sheet purposes, a subdivision of the fixed property accounts became essential in order to ascertain the values that were subject to depreciation, depletion, or other forms of amortization of cost. Gradually, therefore, it became recognized as the best practice to subdivide the fixed property on the books into categories that were appropriate for the purpose of computing such charges. The distinction between tangible and intangible fixed assets is by no means clear, and further discussion of the problem of drawing the line between them will be necessary later in this chapter.

Where subdivided fixed-asset accounts had been carried on the books of a predecessor company and had been maintained on acceptable lines, it was a common practice to carry over such figures to the books of the acquiring corporation. Strictly speaking, the cost to the predecessor company was not an appropriate basis for recording on the books of the new owner; but if price levels had not changed the method was, perhaps, as nearly correct as any available alternative. In some cases, recognition of the fact that the new owner had paid for particular assets a price greatly in excess of the sum at which those assets were carried on the books of the previous owner, was indispensable to proper accounting for income in the subsequent period. (A striking illustration of this point can be found in the case of the United States Steel Corporation in relation to the interests in iron-ore properties which it acquired upon its formation.)

Even if an attempt is made in good faith by competent persons to express in terms of a monetary unit the value of fixed properties which have never been sold and are not intended to be exchanged for cash, the proceeding is in some respects artificial. Inevitably there is a range, which may be wide, within which a valuation that can never be put to the test of realization would be justifiable. Plants might perhaps with reason be valued at any figure from, say, twenty to thirty million dollars where manifestly they would be undervalued at ten million dollars and over valued at fifty million dollars. For, as has been stated, value is based largely on future expectations, and expectations are subjective and cannot be formed with any certainty.

What choice should, in theory, be made between the valuations falling within the reasonable range as the basis for an accounting? The accountant will normally seek a conservative course; but the question arises whether it is more conservative to take the higher or the lower figure. If the sole purpose were to present a balance sheet at the date of the valuation, the answer would clearly be in favor of the smaller valuation. But the more important significance of the determination is likely to be its bearing on the ascertainment of profit in subsequent periods, and from this standpoint the choice of the higher figure may be the more genuinely conservative. In considering this question, not only the total value but the way in which it is allocated is material when what is called a "mixed bag" is acquired.

It has been pointed out in the preceding chapter that placing a low *value* on depreciable assets results in lower depreciation charges and so in higher reported earnings. This being so, great importance attaches to the allocation of the total price between (a) current assets, which will be liquidated in the near future and the value of which can therefore be determined with reasonable accuracy; (b) depreciable fixed property; and (c) land and intangibles which normally are not regarded as subject to amortization. Clearly, fixed properties cannot be regarded as worth more than the cost of replacing them (except to the extent that their earning capacity during the period required for replacement may be a material element of value). Normally, it would be neither mandatory nor justifiable to record assets at more than cost of reproduction less a reasonable deduction for depreciation. It is not, however, uncommon for interested parties to propose to record such amortizable capital assets at far less than depreciated reproduction cost; and at times difficulty is encountered in resisting such proposals, which have a superficial appearance of conservatism.

In some cases the proportion of the purchase price that remains after deducting current assets may be less than the depreciated reproduction cost of fixed properties. In such a case, the whole amount will naturally be attributed to the tangible assets. A question of theoretical interest and often great practical importance is presented in regard to the subsequent determination of profits. Consideration of this question will throw further light both on the problem of value and on the significance of income statements.

A distinction may properly be made between cases in which the fixed property will be exhausted in the course of operations and not replaced, and the case in which the enterprise is regarded as a continuous one so that property retired will have to be replaced, not necessarily with identical property but with property that cannot be acquired at a bargain price.

If provisions in respect of depreciation and retirements of property are based on a capital sum which, because of lack of earning capacity of the enterprise is substantially less than normal depreciated cost, the profits so computed are not overstated; but it is clear that they are in part in the nature of liquidating profits rather than operating profits and will continue only so long as the liquidation of low-priced property goes on. If the enterprise is regarded as permanent, then— assuming for the sake of simplicity stable price levels and earnings—there will be a steady increase in fixed property accounts as units are retired and require to be replaced through purchases in the ordinary markets. And when a cycle of replacement has been completed there will have been added to the capital account an amount roughly equal to the amount by which the original valuation of the fixed property fell short of depreciated reproduction cost. Profits shown while this process is going on have a limited significance.

These considerations were recognized by the Interstate Commerce Commission as being of national importance in connection with the accounting of railroad corporations created or to be created through reorganizations made necessary during recent years by lack of earning capacity. The Commission, reversing one of its divisions, met the situation thus presented by the application of the enterprise concept to the accounting of these reorganized companies. In a notable decision,[1] the Commission said:

It must be borne in mind that property which is carried in the accounts at a depreciated value continues in usual course to function in the operation of the railroad, and when retirement becomes necessary, it must ordinarily be replaced with new property whose cost has suffered no reduction. Gradually, therefore, as property is retired and replaced, the property investment accounts will tend to become reestablished on the basis of full original cost, and there will also be a corresponding increase in capitalization, unless the excess cost is met by appropriations of income which would otherwise be available for the payment of contingent interest or dividends.

In the paragraph which followed, the Commission indicated its clear understanding of the problem by distinguishing between the case of property which is replaceable and that which is retired and not replaced. It, however, decided that as a practical matter it was not possible to foresee which units of property would be abandoned, and that errors in judgment on this point might have serious financial consequences in the future. It therefore left this phase of the subject for further consideration and disposition.

The practical importance of the accounting questions presented became strikingly manifest when war brought the prospect of new war taxes. It became apparent that unless the principles laid down by the Commission were implemented in the tax law, reorganizations contemplated would have to be abandoned, and that where reorganization had been consummated the tax burden on the new companies would be ruinous. The anomaly already pointed out, that lowering the book value of depreciable assets results apparently in higher earnings, would have taken an almost tragic form. A railroad

---

[1] The Chicago Great Western Railway Company accounting case (Ex Parte No. 138) decided June 16, 1941.

which through lack of earning capacity had been forced to reorganize would have been liable to an excess profits tax from which another company which had been and still was more successful would (not having been reorganized) be free.

This development is of intense accounting interest for the reasons that have been indicated in the foregoing discussion, and also for the light that it throws on the whole question of the distinction between corporate accounting and enterprise accounting. It strikingly illustrates the point often overlooked, that a seeming conservatism in the present may easily lead to overstatement of income in the future. This fact and its importance have been gaining steadily-growing recognition as the shift of interest to earning capacity has proceeded, and as the basic approach to income measurement has become more and more one of offsetting costs against revenues, and less one of measuring increases in net worth. It is also relevant to the discussion of depreciation and other methods of providing for the cost of property exhaustion which forms the subject of the next chapter.

So far, only properties acquired at the initiation of a corporate enterprise have been considered. Accounting for additions subsequently made by the corporation itself presents problems, particularly where the construction of the additions is carried out by the corporation itself and constitutes a substantial part of its activities, as frequently happens in the case of public utilities. In such cases the problem arises of allocating costs between products, which is admittedly one of the most intractable of all accounting problems.

In accounting for fixed properties, if a company carries out its own construction, two theories of allocation of costs, such as engineering, supervision, and general administration, are recognized. In industrial practice, where construction of fixed property constitutes a relatively small proportion of the corporation's activities, the incremental method is commonly applied. Only those expenses are charged to construction which would not have been incurred had the construction not been in progress. The proportion of other costs which might theoretically, at least, be allocated to construction, is ignored. This procedure is in conformity with the practice followed in many other cases in which costs incurred primarily for one purpose have a minor value for another—thus advertising expenses may create a residual goodwill but are commonly written off as incurred.

In the case of public utilities the extent of the construction carried out by the corporation's own staff and facilities frequently is an important element, and today a process of allocation of overhead costs is commonly required or at least permitted. In the treatment of such costs, as in the treatment of property consumption, great changes in practice have taken place in the public utility industry and in the history of individual companies during the last quarter of a century. In the reclassifications that have been made necessary by the exercise of the powers of federal and state commissions in recent years, these changes of practice have given rise to difficult questions and acute controversies.

The line between fixed property accounts and maintenance and other expense accounts is not precisely drawn. Primarily, the distinction rests, as already stated, on the relation between the length of life of a unit of property acquired and the length of the accounting period, which is normally a year. A fixed property expense is one the benefit of which is expected to extend over a number of accounting periods; what number, is a question to which no uniform answer can be given. As the emphasis on earning capacity has increased, the tendency has been to reduce this number and to treat more and more expenditures on the basis of allocation to accounting periods instead of as direct charges to the expense account of the current period.

An illustration of a difference of practice, involving large sums, is afforded by the treatment in the accounts of General

Motors Corporation and Chrysler respectively of tooling costs. In one case, these expenditures are passed through fixed property accounts and reach the income account in the form of depreciation charges; in the other case, they are not. Obviously, this difference is of great significance in comparing the depreciation charges of the two companies.

In the case of any corporation that has been long in existence the recorded costs of its fixed properties are likely to lack homogeneity in regard to the methods of computing cost, the classes of expenditures capitalized, and the treatment of replacements. Because this is so, and because, also, the costs lack homogeneity in respect of the purchasing power of the dollar—the expenditure of which they reflect—the significance of all such figures is limited. Usually an attempt to readjust them to a uniform basis would entail an expense that would not be warranted by any increase in accuracy and homogeneity, in view of the inescapable limitation, upon the significance of even the best of accounting statements. A partial review is likely to involve a sacrifice of continuity without the attainment of uniformity. This is a frequent and seemingly just ground for criticism of recent reclassifications under the jurisdiction of commissions for the purpose of determining original cost. Either property accounting must be accepted on a historical basis or, if revision is to be made, it should be complete and bilateral.

CHAPTER VII

Depreciation

DEVELOPMENTS TO 1918

THE ESTABLISHMENT of the modern theory of depreciation in the field of private industry is a purely accounting development. In the railroad and utility fields, however, it is a political history with a legal—not an accounting—background. In private industry the theory became generally accepted at a relatively early stage of development, when its usefulness was at a maximum. In the railroad and utility fields, adoption of the theory has, broadly speaking, been delayed until a state of maturity has been reached, at which its usefulness is seriously limited if not, indeed, questionable.

Before undertaking to review this record it is desirable, first, to draw attention to changes that have occurred in the meaning of the word "depreciation" as applied to fixed property of corporations, and then to discuss briefly the early history of the subject in England and America.

Depreciation, as applied to fixed property, is now a word of art, used to describe broadly the cost or expense due to all the factors which cause the ultimate retirement of property in so far as that cost is not included in current maintenance.[1] Annual depreciation charges are an amortization of cost over useful life; they are not an attempt to measure a change in value; they have nothing to do with replacement.

---

[1] For a fuller discussion see Accounting Research Bulletin No. 16 of the American Institute of Accountants, Oct., 1942. See also footnote to this chapter.

The word "useful" is a necessary but troublesome part of the definition. In depreciation accounting, usefulness is neither an absolute nor a wholly objective conception. Useful life does not continue until a property is absolutely useless, nor does it end when the unit ceases to be the most useful available. Where between these two extremes useful life ends is a question of judgment and to some extent of policy, upon which no general rule can be laid down.

The word and its implications go far to vitiate the alluring but misleading analogy sometimes suggested between plant mortality and human mortality. Jones and Bigham, in their *Principles of Public Utilities*, citing E. B. Kurtz,[1] go so far as to say: "The case is like life insurance. No one can tell how long a particular person will live; but reasonably accurate determinations can be made of the 'expectancy of life,' and an enormous and profitable business has been built up on the basis of such estimates. So it is with public utility property."

But no actuary would undertake to prepare life tables to be used both by a community which provided old age insurance and by one which dispatched its members as soon as they ceased to make what was deemed an adequate contribution to the tribal life. Nor would tables derived from the combined experience of the two communities be useful to either. What makes life insurance possible on a reasonably exact basis is that the conditions which cause the great majority of deaths are inherent, foreseeable, and subject only to gradual change, so that the past forms a reliable guide to the future. Only a minor fraction of plant mortality is due to causes of which the same can be said, and the major fraction is attributable to such causes as obsolescence, of an external character, unpredictable and irregular in the time of their incidence. Moreover a plant does not have the right and the will to live which are postulated in the system of life insurance.

---

[1] *Life Expectancy of Physical Property* (1930), E. B. Kurtz.

Facile talk about determining depreciation, including obsolescence, from experience tables ignores the vital importance of timing in relation to expenditures on fixed property. When radically new methods are coming into use an immediate change to the new technique creates an immediate advantage. But the new methods are apt to be improved, with the result that in a short time the first installations may be relatively obsolete in comparison with the still newer units. Business success, particularly in fields that involve a large capital investment, depends to a considerable extent on choosing the right time to make changes. The failure of a great steamship company was in large measure occasioned by the building of ships with engines of a new type before the type had been adequately developed. Vessels of competitors built only a little later were manifestly superior, so that the ships of the line were comparatively obsolete soon after their launching. Numerous similar illustrations can be found in the history of the steel industry in recent years. Clearly the impact of obsolescence is not the same on "the first by whom the new are tried" and "the last to lay the old aside."

In an earlier day, when value played a larger part in accounting, depreciation was considered as a change of value; depreciation due to wear and tear might be offset by appreciation due to fortuitous circumstances, such as a change in the price level, and in that event required no recognition. Moreover obsolescence, which is now recognized as a major factor in depreciation, has not always been so regarded. Where property was replaced with new units, which resulted in a marked economy of operation, it was at one time common to capitalize the whole cost of the new installation without making provision for the obsolescence of the unit displaced.

It will be convenient to consider the history of the depreciation movement in relation to three different types of corporations: railroads, public utilities, and industrials.

Most of what has been said on the merits of depreciation

accounting for railroads in the last twenty years was said, and
to some extent acted upon, nearly a hundred years ago both
in America and in England. In England, a select committee of
the House of Lords took accounting and other testimony
upon the subject in 1849 and in its report favored the creation
of depreciation reserves. It did not use the expression as the
equivalent of amortization of cost in the way in which it is
now employed. It contemplated, rather, an adequate provision
"for the maintenance of railways in a due state of efficiency,
as relating to the way, the buildings, the rolling stock and other
property." Speaking of the reserve or depreciation fund contemplated by the Companies Clauses Act of 1845, the Committee said: "it seems now to be generally admitted as necessary, and in some instances, the Committe rejoice to observe,
it is practically adopted."

The Regulation of Railways Act of 1868 accepted the
theory that the investment in a railroad was permanent. It
required only certificates that the property had been adequately maintained, though provisions for depreciation were
made permissive. This policy was implemented in the double
account system of railroad accounting to which reference
has already been made.

Some early American railroad reports showed provisions
for depreciation, but in the railroad cases of 1878 the Supreme
Court disallowed a "depreciation reserve" as an element in
determining net earnings, but allowed a deduction for improvements which had actually been financed from earnings.
The decision in *Union Pacific Railroad Company* v. *United
States* (99 U.S. 420) is historically interesting to the accountant
today because in discussing interest the Court recognized
the distinction between the enterprise and the corporation,
saying that interest was a distribution of earnings from the
standpoint of the enterprise although an expense from the
standpoint of the corporation. This case, in so far as it dealt
with the charge of improvements to operating expenses, was

distinguished in the decision in the Illinois Central Railroad Company [1] case in 1906, to which reference will be made later. But through the great era of railroad development its authority was unquestioned and it was common practice for carriers to charge improvements to operating expenses or income but not to provide specifically for depreciation.

In the industrial field depreciation provisions were not, in the earlier days, customary either in England or in America. From 1842, when the present series of income tax laws began, to 1878, nothing in the nature of depreciation allowances in respect of even plant or machinery was granted under the English income tax system. However, the absence of such an allowance became recognized as a grievance, and some commissioners began to grant unauthorized allowances, while others adhered to the legal position. In 1878, annual allowances in respect of the diminished value of plant and machinery by reason of wear and tear during the year of assessment were authorized by law. It may be noted that in 1907, an express provision was enacted providing that where the allowance for depreciation was greater than the assessment for the year, the unexhausted balance might be carried forward and availed of in later years.[2] Our law has not accepted this principle.

In America, the dictum that "The public, when referring to the profits of the business of a merchant, rarely ever take into account the depreciation of the buildings in which the business is carried on, notwithstanding they may have been erected out of the capital invested," doubtless expressed the general practice in 1876, though the case in which it was uttered (*Eyster v. Centennial Board of Finance*, 94 U.S.) was not a typical one.

---

[1] *Illinois Central Railroad Company v. Interstate Commerce Commission* (206 U.S. 441).

[2] See Report of the Royal Commission on Income Tax, 1920, Paragraphs 208–9.

My own earliest experience was mainly in two fields—the accounting of recently reorganized railroads, and mergers of industrial companies. In the railroad field, as already noted, depreciation provisions were not commonly made. In the process of industrial consolidation, however, it became necessary to place the accounts of the various companies proposed to be merged upon a uniform basis. This almost inevitably entailed the elimination of charges to expense of capital items (made in a manner that was irregular and varied with fluctuations in prosperity) and the substitution of charges for exhaustion of property on a systematic and consistent basis. Proposals to make such adjustments gave rise to many controversies, particularly where appreciation of assets, such as real estate, were claimed to be a legitimate offset to depreciation, or where economies due to the installation of new units were claimed to make provisions for obsolescence of the old units unnecessary. But the overriding necessity of securing comparability was manifest and eventually prevailed.

The depreciation accounting which had been adopted in order to place accounts of companies on a uniform basis as a part of the plan of merger was carried over naturally into the accounting of the resulting new corporation. Since consolidations were frequent between 1897 and 1903, a great impetus was thus given to depreciation accounting in the industrial field.

Between the railroads and the industrial companies were the public utilities. The sad history of street railway accounting, in which the costs of adaptation to new sources of power were capitalized cumulatively without any absorption in operating expenses of the costs of property abandoned, emphasized the superiority of depreciation accounting for such companies over methods adapted from those of the railroads.

In the case of the electric utilities, clearly much of the equipment was of an experimental character and destined to have a relatively short life, so that the income or profits of such enterprises could not properly be ascertained without provision for what has come to be called depreciation. Insistence on this view became the settled policy of some leading accountants, though unfortunately the result was all too often a restriction of their activities in the field rather than any conversion of operators of public utilities to the policy.

In 1906, the Interstate Commerce Commission was called upon to formulate classifications for carriers by rail, and the introduction of depreciation into railroad accounting was extensively discussed. Clearly the question was even at that stage of far less importance in this field than in the case of industrial and public utility enterprises, which were at an earlier stage of development.

Depreciation accounting is one of those habits which is not really beneficial unless acquired in early youth. The time element is vitally important in regard to every aspect of the depreciation question. A scheme which would be manifestly desirable if adopted in the early stage of an enterprise, is of doubtful value when the enterprise has reached maturity, so that in terms of property units, replacements substantially equal exhaustion; and the doubt is greater if in the interval there has been a decline in the value of the monetary unit.

In 1906, the straight-line amortization concept of depreciation was in fairly general use in the industrial field. In that year, the Supreme Court decided the case of *Illinois Central Railroad Company et al.* v. *The Interstate Commerce Commission* (206 U.S. 441). The Court, after distinguishing the *Union Pacific Railway Co.* case of 1878, reached a decision which, as stated in the report of the Interstate Commerce Commission for 1907, was that

improvements which added to the permanent value of the property, which had presumably increased the earning power of the property, which were not to be used for a single year, but for many years, should, as between the public and the railway, in estimating a reasonable transportation charge, be made out of net income and not out of earnings.

The Commission welcomed the decision, and its first classification prohibited the charge of additions and betterments to operating expenses. At the same time, depreciation accounting, for equipment only, was introduced.

This procedure might be regarded as an acceptance of the newer idea without departing from the basic conception of railroads as permanent. Way and structures must be reasonably maintained so long as operations continue. But equipment units may become obsolete and for all practical purposes go out of service, though still kept alive, while an improved service is conducted with new units that are classified as additional equipment. It was no doubt in connection with equipment that railroad accounting was most open to abuse, and the Commission was wise to select it as the first subject of depreciation accounting.

The Commission, in discussing the new requirement, said that perhaps its most important result would be "to protect investments and to prevent the management from paying dividends by depleting the property." This was extravagant language. The scheme was defective in that it contemplated amortization of the cost of equipment over the potential life as extended by rebuilding, and the rate of depreciation was left to the reporting carriers. The introduction of depreciation accounting and the prohibition of charges to operating expenses for betterments together did little if anything to preserve railroad investment or to make railroad accounting sounder. The accounts of the less provident railroads were made somewhat more conservative and those of the most conservative, less so. Our railroad system was at that time approaching maturity, though the Commission in the same report spoke of the inadequacy of transportation facilities as being little less than alarming. In 1914, the regulations in respect of depreciation of equipment were made more stringent and provisions for other classes of property were made optional.

In 1907, the Supreme Court for the first time expressed itself fully on the subject of depreciation in relation to the rate base. Its decision in the *Knoxville Water Company* case [1] was adequate, judged by the standards of the time, but it did not recognize nor draw a clear line between two concepts of depreciation—one, as a provision for future replacement; the other, as an amortization of past cost. "The Company," it said, "is not bound to see its property gradually waste without making provision out of earnings for its replacement." In the *Minnesota Rate Cases*,[2] decided in 1913, the Court said: "And when particular physical items are estimated as worth so much new, if in fact they are depreciated, this amount should be found and allowed for. If this is not done the physical valuation is manifestly incomplete." Here it clearly accepted the valuation concept of depreciation which has come to be known as "observable depreciation" as distinguished from the "amortization of cost" concept which now prevails.

New interest in the question of depreciation was aroused by the enactment of the first corporation excise tax in 1909 and the subsequent adoption of the income tax amendment to the Constitution and the passage of the first income tax law thereunder in 1913. In the Act of 1909, an allowance for depreciation was incongruously made a factor in the determination of taxable income, which in the main was to be measured on a strictly cash basis. The deduction was preserved in the Act of 1913. In the Revenue Act of 1916 the word "depreciation," which had appeared in the earlier Act,

---

[1] *Knoxville* v. *Knoxville Water Company* (212 U.S. 1).
[2] 230 U.S. 352.

was discarded, and there was substituted a phrase which, with an addition in 1918 to provide explicitly for the inclusion of obsolescence, became and has since remained "a reasonable allowance for the exhaustion, wear and tear of property used in the trade or business, including a reasonable allowance for obsolescence." The deduction is still referred to in Treasury regulations, "for convenience," as being for "depreciation."

In the earlier Treasury Regulations allowance of depreciation deductions was made conditional on their being reflected in the corporation's own accounting (Reg. 33, Art. 130). Later this limitation was held to be unenforceable, but in the meantime it had served its purpose in the industrial though not in the utility field.

The first world war brought wider recognition of the importance of depreciation accounting in the determination of income. In the war taxation the logic of it was fully accepted, since it was recognized that under a system of very high taxation, preservation of the capital employed was essential to the continued effectiveness of the industrial machine. By the end of the war, depreciation accounting in the unregulated industries was fully established and the history of the development may be regarded as having then come to an end though a footnote was written in connection with the tax legislation of 1934.

At that time, the House tax bill proposed to secure a part of a needed increase in tax yield by arbitrary reductions in depreciation allowances. Such a proposal could, of course, only be justified on the assumption that the deductions were ex gratia allowances and not necessary deductions in arriving at a balance that might properly be described as income. The Treasury opposed the suggestion but undertook to accomplish substantially the same purpose by a rigid scrutiny of the actual allowances made. This pledge was implemented in a regulation. In the ensuing years, depreciation deductions were curtailed and the reduction was frequently if not generally reflected in the corporation's own accounting.

This development, it may be noted, was in marked contrast to the English policy under the same conditions. In 1932, when the British Government found it necessary to raise the rate of taxation, it contemporaneously made provisions for increases in depreciation allowances. This action was based upon the broad ground that as the rate of tax became higher the importance of guarding against taxation of capital under the guise of income increased.

Apart from this development little has happened since 1919 to change the position in regard to depreciation in private industry.

Among public utilities there developed a system which became known as "retirement reserve accounting," the general purpose of which was to provide for the cost of property about to be retired over a few years in advance of its actual retirement.[1] In so far as retirement within a few years was not definitely foreseeable the certainty that it would some day occur was ignored. The result of the application of this concept was to create reserves which bore a closer relation to the observable depreciation of the engineers than to the accrued amortization contemplated by the income-tax law and commonly set aside in private industrial accounting.

Retirement reserve accounting never seemed to me to possess much theoretical merit. The amortization theory regards fixed property as a store of usefulness that is constantly being depleted. It is not concerned with the questions how, whether, and at what cost property may be replaced. A replacement theory regards fixed property as an investment that is an indivisible whole and is practically permanent. Its sole concern is with the actual or probable cost of replacing parts

---

[1] See classification promulgated by National Electric Light Association. 1914.

if and when replacement becomes imminent. The retirement reserve theory combines elements of the amortization and replacement theories in a manner that seems to me illogical and incongruous.

However from the practical standpoint retirement reserve accounting had much to recommend it to those charged with regulation of rates in communities in which the encouragement of further utility-development was desired. It placed a lower burden than the cost amortization method upon the earlier years of operation and it resulted in reserves which were not greatly out of line with the observed depreciation which the courts had found to be deductible in fixing the rate base. The sharp upturn in prices during the war following on the steady rise that had occurred between 1896 and 1914 had raised rate bases to high levels. Insistence on the amortization of cost concepts would have both created a demand for higher rates and discouraged new enterprise. In such conditions retirement reserve accounting met with little opposition though there were those who regarded it as in the longer view unwise.

Thus in the three fields of activity here considered there were at the end of the first world war three or more distinct ways of dealing with exhaustion of life of fixed property.

In the private industrial field, cost amortization was practically universal and the straight-line method was that most generally employed.

In the railroad field, cost amortization was being applied to equipment, and replacement or retirement accounting to other property.

In the public utility field a hybrid "retirement reserve accounting" was being employed the requirements under which were determined largely by the fears or the hopes of management.

CHAPTER VIII

Depreciation and Regulation Since 1918

THE GENERAL ESTABLISHMENT of depreciation accounting (using that term in the modern sense as meaning amortization of cost or other initial base value) had been in private industry a natural development closely related to essential accounting concepts. It recognized the major importance of the income account and the historical cost concept that underlies modern accounting. It also accepted the postulates of continuity in accounting and of reasonable stability in the monetary unit. According to this mode of thought, it was the charge against income that was important; the other side of the entry was of minor significance. For the property accounts were records of unamortized cost which did not pretend to reflect value or to have more than historical significance.

In the regulated industries the dual character of depreciation charges is of crucial importance. There, accounting concepts came into conflict with legal notions which were in part supported by engineers but which have been more recently opposed on pragmatic grounds by regulatory commissions, whose power has steadily grown.

The legal treatment of depreciation as a function not of cost but of value, both in the determination of the rate base and in measuring the consumption element of the cost of service (as set forth in the cases from *Smyth* v. *Ames* to *United Railways & Electric Co. of Baltimore* v. *West*) was no doubt internally consistent, but its consistency with the whole theory of regulation was less clear, and it ignored the problem of continuity which is nowhere more essential than in accounting for property exhaustion. It was discontinuous and a treatment that could not be fitted into the general theory of double entry accounting.

The objectives of the Commissions which attacked this treatment therefore came to be, first, to substitute cost for value in rate regulation and, secondly, to relate the charge for property exhaustion in operating expenses to the deduction for exhaustion in computing the rate base. The first objective has been discussed in Chapter V. The second calls for historical consideration here.

In 1920, the Interstate Commerce Commission, which was then engaged on the valuation of the railroads, was authorized and required by Congress to determine "the classes of property for which depreciation charges may properly be included under operating expenses and the percentages of depreciation which shall be charged with respect to each of such classes of property." [Section 20, Paragraph 5.] [1]

The use of the term "percentage of depreciation" is significant in view of the attitude of the Supreme Court on the question, which will be discussed later.

The National Association of Railroad and Utilities Commissioners in its first standard classification, promulgated in 1922, did not adopt depreciation accounting; instead, it gave the seal of its approval to retirement reserve accounting. In presenting its classification it said:

An account is provided in which to include charges made in order that corporations may, through the creation of adequate reserves, equalize from year to year, as nearly as is practicable, the losses incident to important retirements of buildings, dam, etc., or of large sections of continuous structures like electric lines, or of definitely identifiable units of plant or equipment.

---

[1] This grant and its relation to the problem of valuation on which the Commission was then engaged are discussed in *Twenty-five Years*, Vol. I, p. 168.

"Losses" used above means in each case the excess of the original cost to the accounting company of the property retired plus the cost of dismantling or removing, over its salvage value at the time of its retirement.

The contrast between the attitude of the Interstate Commerce Commission, as indicated in the legislation secured by it in 1920, and decisions made under that authority, and the attitude of the National Association of Railroad and Utilities Commissioners, is striking and significant. The Supreme Court, in its decisions in rate cases, had approved decisions of lower courts which had rejected deductions from new value in respect of depreciation determined by any system of percentages, and had insisted on the importance of observation. To fix the rate base on the theory of observed depreciation, and at the same time to allow depreciation on an amortization basis as a part of operating expenses might, as the Commissioners insisted, impose a double burden on the public.

The Interstate Commerce Commission sought to meet this situation by prescribing percentage depreciation charges as a part of its control over accounting, in the expectation that this procedure would ultimately result in a deduction of depreciation in a similar manner in the computation of the rate base. Its first report, pursuant to the provisions of the Act of 1920 above noted, was made in 1926. The Commission said:

In our consideration, therefore, of the relative burdens imposed by the depreciation and retirement methods of accounting, we must start with the premise that the former presupposes full deduction of accrued depreciation in ascertaining the rate base value . . . [Case 15–100, pp. 310–11.]

The National Association of Railroad and Utilities Commissioners, in its classification of 1922, accepted the other alternative of providing through retirement accounting for the creation of reserves more nearly corresponding to the observed depreciation, which was then currently being recognized by the Supreme Court as the only permissible deduction from new value in the determination of the rate base.

To the detached accounting observer the position of the commissions in the postwar period was a difficult one. No generally acceptable solution of the problem created by the decisions of the Supreme Court was, perhaps, possible—certainly none could be found which would result in accounts being equally appropriate for purposes of rate determination and for general financial purposes.

The issue of the NARUC classification of 1922 had a decisive effect on those accountants who had theretofore declined to recognize the retirement reserve method as affording adequate provision for the exhaustion of property. With the Supreme Court accepting the idea of observed depreciation and the NARUC expressly approving retirement reserve accounting, it became impossible for them to maintain the position that accounts which conformed to that requirement were unacceptable because they failed to meet accepted accounting standards. The utmost that they could do thereafter was to say, in substance, in their certificates that the accounts were in accordance with accounting principles as set forth in the classification.

No history of depreciation accounting can ignore the significance and far-reaching effect of this action of the NARUC. The dilemma which the commissions faced has been recognized and may to some extent explain the action taken. The rule laid down was no doubt favored by a great majority of utility corporations; it was perhaps more likely than a cost amortization rule to encourage new utility development. But in any retrospective judgment upon retirement reserve accounting, the influence of this endorsement of it, given after long study at a time when the significance of cost amortization procedures had been fully recognized in tax laws and in general accounting practice, cannot be over-estimated. The NARUC must accept a large share of criticism that may be directed against the method of accounting and the results which it produced. It was not until 1936 that it advocated depreciation accounting. In a report made by its committee on depreciation in 1937 the partial responsibility of the NARUC for what the committee then regarded as inadequate depreciation provisions was definitely recognized.

The issue of double burdens resulting from deduction of only observed depreciation in the computation of the rate base and of straight-line depreciation in calculating operating cost of service, was presented most acutely in cases involving telephone rates. The Bell Telephone System has from its early days followed a system of straight-line depreciation accounting· which, because of the experimental and developing character of its business, must be regarded as, from the accounting standpoint, highly appropriate and conservative. In the *Southwestern Bell Telephone Company* [1] case, decided in 1923, the Supreme Court, rejecting a comprehensive and vigorous protest of Mr. Justice Brandeis, handed down a decision which was regarded as establishing reproduction cost, less observed depreciation, as almost determinative of the rate base. And in later cases, notably the *United Railway Company of Baltimore* case,[2] it held that the charge against earnings for depreciation should be based on current values rather than original cost, and that existing depreciation for the purpose of measuring the rate base could not be established from depreciation tables.

A proceeding in the *Illinois Bell Telephone Company* [3] case,

---

[1] *Southwestern Bell Telephone Company* v. *Public Service Commission of Missouri* (262 U.S. 276).

[2] *United Railways & Electric Co. of Baltimore* v. *West* (280 U.S. 234).

[3] *Lindheimer* v. *Illinois Bell Telephone Company, et al.* (292 U.S. 154).

begun in 1923, slowly found its way through the courts, and was finally decided in 1934. In that case, the contrast between observed depreciation as a factor in measurement of the rate base and straight-line depreciation as a measure of the operating charge was strikingly presented. The Court decided against the Company on the grounds that it had failed to prove "the necessity for the annual charges for depreciation as claimed by the Company in order to avoid confiscation through the rates in suit." It stressed "the disparity between the actual extent of depreciation as ascertained according to the comprehensive standards used by the Company witnesses and the amount of the depreciation reserve."

The interest of this case is enhanced by the fact that the opinions set forth more adequately than earlier decisions the judicial views of depreciation. The Court, speaking through Mr. Chief Justice Hughes, adopted a definition of depreciation which marked a great advance from the decision in the *Knoxville Water Company* case, saying:

Broadly speaking, depreciation is the loss, not restored by current maintenance, which is due to all the factors causing the ultimate retirement of the property. These factors embrace wear and tear, decay, inadequacy and obsolescence. Annual depreciation is the loss which takes place in a year.

The first two sentences may be regarded as the final acceptance by the Court of the general concept of depreciation which accountants had held and fought for in the industrial field for more than a generation. The statement that annual depreciation is the loss that takes place in a year may seem a truism. But actually the words "takes place" are far from unambiguous and present a crucial question which must, however, be reserved for later discussion.

Mr. Justice Butler, in a concurring opinion, set forth in clear terms what has been called the double account or replacement concept:

From the foregoing it justly may be inferred that charges made according to the principle followed by the company create reserves much in excess of what is needed for maintenance. The balances carried by the company include large amounts that never can be used for the purposes for which the reserve was created. In the long run the amounts thus unnecessarily taken from revenue will reach about one-half the total cost of all depreciable parts of the plant. The only legitimate purpose of the reserve is to equalize expenditures for maintenance so as to take from the revenue earned in each year its fair share of the burden. To the extent that the annual charges include amounts that will not be required for that purpose, the account misrepresents the cost of the service.

The company's properties constitute a complex and highly developed instrumentality containing many classes of items that require renewal from time to time. But, taken as a whole, the plant must be deemed to be permanent. It never was intended to be new in all its parts. It would be impossible to make it so. Amounts sufficient to create a reserve balance that is the same percentage of total cost of depreciable items as their age is to their total service life cannot be accepted as legitimate additions to operating expenses. [Pp. 181–82.]

While the *Illinois Bell Telephone Company* case was gradually progressing through the courts, the Interstate Commerce Commission was also making somewhat hesitant advances towards conclusions on the question of depreciation under the law of 1920.

In 1926, the Commission handed down a decision which excited much opposition, and which it decided to reconsider. In 1931, it issued a modified decision and ordered depreciation accounting on a straight-line basis to be applied to other property as well as to equipment after January 1, 1932. However, while the case had been under consideration, the economic situation had been changing rapidly. In 1932, the time was obviously not opportune for imposing on the railroads either the initial expense of adjusting their accounting to the new regulations or the added burden on operating expenses which those new provisions would themselves have imposed. Not only was the Commission constrained by circumstances to suspend the enforcement of its new rules, but despite the inadequacy of existing depreciation charges it felt compelled to alleviate the difficulties of some of the railroads in the depression period. In Statistics of Railways for 1934 it explained the situation in the following statement:

When permitted by the Interstate Commerce Commission, a carrier may charge retirements and repairs to profit and loss which are ordinarily chargeable to operating expenses. Such items appear in the profit and loss statement as "Delayed income debits," or to some extent as "Miscellaneous debits" and "Loss on retired road and equipment." Charges to account "Delayed income debits" have varied in recent years as follows:

Dec. 31, 1928	$ 6,049,545
Dec. 31, 1929	7,369,919
Dec. 31, 1930	37,616,254
Dec. 31, 1931	65,629,895
Dec. 31, 1932	28,439,318
Dec. 31, 1933	42,779,220
Dec. 31, 1934	60,906,646

Charges to this account result in smaller charges to operating expenses than if the ordinary accounting procedure were followed, but it cannot be said that they result in understating the true operating expenses of the accounting period because these charges usually relate in large measure to operations of preceding years.

It was not until January 1, 1943, eleven years after the date originally fixed and when the war traffic was swelling the revenue of the railroads that the Commission found it possible to put its depreciation order, modified in important respects, into effect. The long deferment throws a shadow on many of the arguments advanced in the original decision.

In the meantime, the National Association of Railroad and Utilities Commissioners had issued in 1936 a revised classification. The decision in the *Illinois Bell Telephone Company* case had not reversed the Court's views on percentage tables, but it had seemed to justify the confidence expressed by the Interstate Commerce Commission in its report of 1930—

that the courts, when the issues and facts are made entirely clear to them, will recognize the connection and interrelation between depreciation in accounting and in valuation which have been pointed out hereinbefore [p. 413].

The Association's classification adopted the principle of depreciation accounting wholeheartedly. In a report by a NARUC Committee on Depreciation issued in 1938 it was admitted (as already noted) that part of the responsibility for the small depreciation reserves (they were not, of course, depreciation, but retirement reserves) among utilities was attributable to systems of accounting recommended by the NARUC prior to 1936.[1] In large part the responsibility rests, also, on the Supreme Court. Yet in decisions of the Federal Power Commission, the "failure" to provide what the Commission now considers adequate depreciation is often imputed solely to utility managements.

A change from the double account principle, or from retirement accounting to depreciation accounting, creates the major problem of dealing with depreciation which under the new classification is deemed to have accrued in the past in so far as that sum exceeds, as it naturally will, reserves that were adequate under the previously existing classification. Neither the Interstate Commerce Commission nor the National Association of Railroads and Utilities Commissioners has faced this problem fairly and squarely, or presented adequate proposals for its solution in an equitable manner, though

---

[1] Report, p. 31.

some commissions have dealt with it more or less satisfactorily in specific cases.

Viewed in retrospect, the adoption of depreciation accounting in railroad and utility regulation cannot be regarded as an accounting reform but only as a change of policy inspired by purely practical rate-making considerations. To effect such a change with retroactive effect at the expense of the railroads and public utilities would be a grave injustice. To impose on shippers and consumers of the future the burden of creating a reserve which it is now thought should have been accumulated in the past, might also be unjust. It has not even been made clear that a useful purpose would be served by setting up such reserves at this late date. Even if straight-line depreciation is to be adopted for the future, justice and practical wisdom would dictate that no effort should be made to require from either investors or customers the sacrifice necessary to bridge the gap between the retirement reserve and the theoretical depreciation reserve at the date of the change.

What has occurred is in the nature of a change of rules in the middle of the performance of a quasi-contract. It has become the fashion of some commissions to justify such changes on the ground of pragmatism (which Professor Josiah Royce is said to have defined as the philosophy according to which you can change your mind as often as you like and are always right). Whether retroactive pragmatism is to be approved or condemned is not an accounting question—it is, therefore, outside the scope of this work.[1] It may, however, not be inappropriate to consider the questions whether, if commissions as zealous to protect customers as those of today had been in office when the railroads and utility enterprises were begun, they would have been likely to recommend the accounting treatment that commissions now advocate, and

---

[1] See the decision of the Circuit Court of Appeals in *Hope Natural Gas Co. v. Federal Power Commission*, 1943.

whether upon similar assumptions managements would then have accepted their views and have gone ahead with the undertakings. In an article which appeared in the *Quarterly Journal of Economics* in 1929 I said, in discussing the first of these points:

Let us assume that it is agreed between the promoters of the railroad and the community that the former shall be entitled to a reasonable opportunity to earn a fair return on their investment in the line, and that the community shall have the right to restrict closely to that fair return the profits of the railroad. Would competent economic advisers of the community advocate a system of depreciation charges, and, if so, of what type? The result of a depreciation plan is obviously to throw an added charge for use and exhaustion of property upon the earliest years of operation, years in which the traffic development would be in progress and in which consequently the charge would be more burdensome than in later years. Such a condition would seem to be exactly the reverse of that which would be economically desirable from the standpoint of the community. Its interests would be served by keeping the charges in the early years down to the minimum consistent with maintaining the efficiency of the property, thus enlarging the volume of the commodities that could profitably be transported, and building up both the traffic and the community more rapidly than would otherwise be possible. The best interests of the community in such a situation would be served, it would seem, by a mutual agreement to ignore the depreciation on the property in so far as it could never be made good while the property was being operated, the owners of the railroad agreeing that this depreciation should not be treated as a part of cost of operation, and the community agreeing on the other hand that in computing return no deduction should be made from the original investment therefor.

Such a solution, which is practically that favored by Mr. Justice Butler (*supra*) and adopted in the English Regulation of Railways Act of 1868 and might have been acceptable in England, had the idea of regulating rates of charges by a sys-

tem based on the rate of return on investment ever been seriously considered there. Here, in the early days, regulation
was not contemplated—the sole anxiety of the community,
as of the promoters, was to get railroads built.[1] Acceptance of
the arrangement above outlined would increase the investors'
hazard in respect of the possibility of the enterprise failing
or becoming obsolete in its entirety, but the present value as
at the date of investment of such a hazard would be negligible
in proportion to the other elements of risk.

In concurring in the depreciation order of the Interstate
Commerce Commission in 1926, Commissioner Woodlock
expressed the view that straight-line depreciation was desirable in the interests of the owners of carrier property assuming that the present value concept of the rate base was to be
preserved (though quite logically he regarded any depreciation as unnecessary upon the original cost theory of the rate
base). It may be conceded that depreciation accounting *from
the beginning of operations* would have benefited the owners
of railroads and other enterprises as it had benefited the telephone investors.

It is not uncommon to assume that such a benefit would
take the form of an accumulation of cash assets equal to
the amount of depreciation reserve, but such an impression
is wholly unfounded. If depreciation is conceived as amortization of a cost already incurred, it is no necessary part of the
scheme that the reserve should be set aside in cash and the
charge has no relation to the problem of replacement. Practically, in an expanding enterprise, depreciation accounting
tends to result in the assured retention in the business of funds
which might have been distributed as profits. The practical
benefit to investors is that these retentions will reduce the
amount of capital required to be raised and exposed to the
risk of being lost ultimately as a result of the enterprise becom-

---

[1] A. T. Hadley, *Railroad Transportation*, 1885, p. 125.

ing obsolete, as happened in the case of the street railways.

Depreciation schemes do not, of course, eliminate such losses, though advocates of them often speak as if they did. If, when the decline of an enterprise begins, it has a depreciation reserve of 30 to 35 per cent, investors are likely to be better off than if only a retirement reserve of 10 or 15 per cent, or no reserve at all, had been created out of revenue. The advantage may lie in the fact that their investment is smaller, or that the assets other than fixed property are greater. But investors will still face a large loss of capital which they will be unable to recover through earnings in the declining days of the enterprise.

Let it be assumed for illustrative purposes that salvage will average 15 per cent of investment and that a depreciation reserve would be 35 per cent and a retirement reserve 15 per cent of investment at the beginning of a final decline. It is not to be expected that any provision for loss on ultimate abandonment will be capable of being made thereafter except at the expense of the investors, so that the loss to investors becomes measurable at this point (which has no doubt been reached and passed by some railroads). On the retirement basis the inevitable loss is 70 per cent; on the depreciation basis, 50 per cent. The difference of 20 per cent between the two reserves is no doubt substantial but the loss in either case is more so. If the increase of 20 per cent is to be effected by a mere transfer from surplus or taken out of the investor's fair return, it is difficult to see how he is benefited by the change.

The statement that depreciation accounting is better for the investor is true only if depreciation accounting is assumed to be in force from the beginning of the enterprise. Since, broadly speaking, this has not been the case in respect of either railroads or utilities, the statement is as to them only a part of the truth and apt to mislead. If not only is the depreciation adjustment to be taken out of surplus but the rate base is to be reduced to the extent thereof, then the introduction of depreciation accounting today is bound to be detrimental to investors collectively and to most separate classes of investors.

New interest in the broad questions here discussed results from the rise in the price level that has taken place in the last two years, and the prospect of a further rise. In the case of permanent enterprises that have matured, annual replacements measured in terms of property will roughly equal the annual exhaustion of property. This being so, there is much to be said in favor of charging replacements against operations, with a reasonable system of reserves to provide for equalization and for cases in which replacements that are due to be made are deferred. The great advantage of such a procedure would be that the money expression of the consumption of property would be reflected in terms of the current purchasing power of money. As the Interstate Commerce Commission recognized in the *Chicago Great Western Ry. Co.* case (*supra*) it is undesirable that if property is retired and replaced exactly in kind there should be a charge to capital simply because the cost of the new unit in terms of a depreciated currency is greater than that of the old. Closely related to this question is the question whether the prudent investment theory of determination of the rate base applied without any provision for adjustment in respect of changes in the purchasing power of the monetary unit, is equitable.

Once the amortization concept of depreciation is accepted a further problem is to find an appropriate method for allocating depreciation over the life of property. A technical discussion of the merits of different systems of allocation would be beyond the scope of this volume, but it seems desirable at least to discuss alternative methods sufficiently to indicate the nature of the annual depreciation charge and the relation of different systems to the broader problems of the part that cost and value respectively should play in accounting and regulation. This is the more desirable since commissions have at times sought to minimize the importance of the differences between methods. The Interstate Commerce Commission, for instance, in its decision of 1926 above mentioned said of the straight-line and sinking-fund methods: "Nor are the practical results of the two methods very different." But, as will appear, this statement is far from correct.

CHAPTER IX

Depreciation Methods—Depletion—Intangibles

CHARGES FOR DEPRECIATION (amortization) may be allocated to years on the basis of time or use, or a combination of the two. They may or may not take account of interest. The fundamental concept of depreciation today is that property may be regarded as a store of future usefulness that is constantly being diminished. If for the sake of simplicity it be assumed that the store will be exhausted by equal instalments over a fixed period of years, then the value of the unexhausted store declines in the same way as that of an annuity for a fixed term. Hence if the object is to insure that the store of future usefulness shall always be carried at the sum which a purchaser could afford to pay therefor (still upon the same hypotheses) the depreciation charge can properly be computed from annuity tables at an appropriate rate of interest. The residual value so shown will always be greater than the balance that would remain if the original sum were amortized by equal annual instalments, but the difference will vary as the life of units varies.

If salvage be ignored, the proportion of cost of a unit un-amortized at mid-life on a straight-line basis will in every case be 50 per cent. The percentage of cost which a purchaser could afford to pay at mid-life would vary considerably. If total life is assumed to be twenty years, this price would be, on a 6 per cent basis, 64 per cent of new value; if the life is fifty years, it would be no less than 81 per cent.

Three points must therefore be recognized: First, the results of a straight-line method are very different from those of a

145

sinking fund (or annuity) method. Second, two computations which give such widely different allocations to years cannot measure the loss that "takes place" in a year, to quote the Supreme Court's definition. The depreciation charge in the first year of property with a life of fifty years, computed on a sinking-fund basis with interest at 6 per cent, is about one-sixth of the charge on the straight-line basis. Manifestly it cannot be said even that each is a reasonable estimate of the loss that takes place within the year. Third, only the sinking-fund method even approximates the course of value, as measured by the price a purchaser could afford to pay on the assumed basis of useful life and supposing the price level to remain unchanged. These three points have an important bearing on the relationship between depreciation, conceived as a process of amortization, and the determination of value.

The straight-line method has the great merit of simplicity. It is almost universally employed in industrial practice (where, however, there is no pretense of an effort to reflect realizable value in property accounts); and in view of the hazards which cannot be foreseen, its conservatism gives it a strong appeal for the average accountant. In private industry the greater part of fixed property has a life of from fifteen to twenty-five years. It is within that range that straight-line depreciation has the strongest support in theory.[1] Where property has a probable useful life considerably exceeding twenty-five years, it is less defensible, and where the unexpired life is fifty years or more, a provision for depreciation on a straight-line basis—or perhaps on any basis—is theoretical and unrealistic. As noted earlier, in Chapter II, the Royal Commission on the Income Tax of 1920 in England recommended that depreciation on property whose unexpired life was more than a generation should be ignored.

---

[1] See *Journal of Accountancy*, Vol. LX, p. 182.

In Paragraph 186, the Commission laid down the principle thus:

. . . as all material assets waste,· and as no income emerges from a source which is so permanent as not to be subject to the possibility of wastage in capital value, there shall be a time limit to the recognition of wastage. In fixing this time limit regard should be paid, we think, only to that wastage which is important when considered in relation to human life and human expectation. If a man has an income which will apparently last for 60 years it is to him practically a permanent income. Contingencies happening after the lapse of a period of time exceeding 35 years appeal very little to the mind of the average individual; for example, it is only when the period of deferment is something less than 35 years that reversionary interests begin to have any appreciable value. Moreover, the longer the life of the asset the greater the difficulty of estimating it with any reasonable approach to accuracy. These considerations, amongst others, have led us to recommend that NO ALLOWANCE SHOULD BE MADE WHEN THE LIFE OF THE WASTING ASSET IS ESTIMATED TO BE 35 YEARS OR LONGER. This is no doubt an arbitrary time limit without any special or intrinsic merit, but if some period of time beyond which wastage will not be recognized is not fixed the number of minute adjustments in every class of income will become so great that it will almost disintegrate the administration of the tax. We think that a period of time which approximately covers a generation is a fair time limit to impose.

If the accounting of railroads and public utilities is conducted on the implicit assumption of their permanence and of the existence of a quasi-contract between the utility and its customers, the considerations which make straight-line depreciation preferable for private industrial purposes have little weight in the utility field.

A depreciation scheme necessarily assumes continuity. For this reason, a system of computing depreciation for rate purposes on the basis of the fair value of the property at the time when the service is being rendered, which necessarily implies discontinuity, is quite unsuitable for adaptation to ordinary accounting purposes. Such a method was insisted upon for rate purposes in the *United Railways Company* case. Depreciation must be based on estimates, and therefore a machinery for the correction of estimates must be provided. Recognition of these facts and of the notion of quasi-contracts would seem to afford an admirable way of dealing in public utility accounting with the difficult problem of obsolescence.

Depreciation schemes contemplate that obsolescence will frequently lead to the retirement of property before its physical life is exhausted, but the extent to which this obsolescence will affect the length of life is apt to be a matter of mere conjecture. In practice, allowances are made with the realization that circumstances may make them either excessive or quite inadequate. The problem of making adjustments when the reserve proves to be excessive offers no great difficulty; but sometimes retirements occur much earlier than was contemplated and present difficult problems. For ordinary accounting purposes it is difficult to justify carrying forward a balance in respect of an asset which has ceased to have usefulness but under the doctrine of quasi-contract such a procedure might be in the interest of both the utility and the consumer. It would be justifiable on the theory that the asset in respect of which the balance is carried forward is not the property unit itself but a right to recover the unamortized cost thereof out of subsequent operations. Regulatory commissions have frequently adopted the substance of this proposal, but have justified it on the doubtful ground of regulatory expediency rather than as a reasonable application of the concept of quasi-contract between the utility and its customers, which seems a logical part of the general theory of regulation on which commissions are now generally operating.

Such a proposal seems clearly valid if the doctrine of prudent investment, or a variant thereof, is accepted as the basis for rate regulation. Manifestly it has not the same validity where value is the sole test of the reasonableness of rates, for in such cases no value can fairly be asserted in respect of property that has ceased to exist or of rights growing out of its former existence.

A phase of depreciation accounting, the importance of which is not widely recognized except by accountants who have had to deal with the problem in practice, is the treatment of charges against depreciation provisions. In many cases in the past, corporations adopted a system of creating depreciation reserves without making any change in the distribution of expenditures in connection with fixed property. As a result, they charged to maintenance accounts expenditures which the depreciation provision was designed to meet and thus made a double charge to operating expenses. This aspect of the question received steadily increasing attention from the Bureau of Internal Revenue in connection with the determination of taxable income, so that inconsistencies of this kind are less extensive than they formerly were. However, it should never be forgotten that what is charged against a depreciation reserve is almost as important as what is credited thereto.

Again, depreciation provisions may be made in respect of specific units of property or of groups of units. Since rates of depreciation are based on averages, the group method is theoretically preferable where the alternative exists. At the same time, accounting on this basis is more technical and requires even greater watchfulness than is called for when the unit method is employed. Frequently, also, single units are large, or groups of units are so interrelated that the retirement of one involves the retirement of all, and it is in these special cases that depreciation accounting is most useful—in fact, railroads that have opposed a general depreciation scheme have recognized its appropriateness and applied it in the case of some large units, such as important bridges.

Depletion

Depletion, by which is meant the exhaustion of natural resources through extractive processes, is quantitatively much less important in accounting than depreciation but it presents more points of interest and in some cases presents them more clearly. Depletion differs from depreciation in that it relates to property which has not been created by an expenditure of capital. This point is interestingly illustrated in the treatment of it under English tax law. A deduction is allowed in respect of foreign mineral areas acquired (which from the English standpoint may be regarded as having been created by expenditures of capital) though none is allowed in respect of properties in England. That this should be so is natural in view of the general philosophy of the law as outlined earlier, in Chapter II.

In the same way, no deduction for depletion is mandatory or customary in England in determining the profits of companies available for distribution as dividends. Indeed, a mine affords as good an illustration as can be found of the reasons which are deemed to justify omission for such purposes of any provision for wastage of assets which do not require to be replaced. In America, corporate laws vary, but there are many states in which depletion may be ignored in determining divisible profits.

The treatment of the extractive industries under our federal income tax laws is in striking contrast to that accorded to them in England. With us, they are the beneficiaries of special grants. The allowed deductions are not limited to those necessary to amortize actual outlays but extend to values which have neither been created nor paid for by those to whom they are allowed. The contrast in the attitude of legislators towards those who are developing through extractive operations our natural resources, and those who are conserving them, by putting water power to valuable uses, is an interesting subject for analysis that would, however, go beyond the scope of this work.

A limitation of depletion allowances to 5 per cent of the value of the product at the mine was enacted in 1913, but this limitation was soon removed—first the right to recover the full value of the natural resources at March 1, 1913, and then the masterly concept of "discovery depletion" were written into the law. Still later came percentage depletion as a supplement to depletion of the tax base.

The right to recover the value of the mineral resources as at the date when the income tax amendment to the Constitution became effective involved a stupendous task of valuation. The performance of that task forms an interesting chapter in the history of the valuation problem. In general, the method adopted was a strange compound of highly speculative assumptions and meticulous mathematical computations. There was a curious lack of perspective and proportion in the procedure by which valuation engineers in or as of 1913 reached their conclusions. First they made assumptions as to future prices and production over long periods of years (fortunately in ignorance of the events that would mark those years). Next, they expressed these estimates (by an averaging process that was scientifically unwarranted) in the form of a uniform net annual yield. Finally they applied to this assumed yield discount tables extended to many places of decimals. The crowning touch of incongruity was afforded by the introduction into the discount process of a questionable actuarial refinement which has raised Hoskold's formula to an amazing prestige and immortalized its author in the tax world. But as courts have pointed out the main responsibility for the unrealities rests upon the legislature—if laws call for valuations, valuations must be made as best they can, even though that best is manifestly and inevitably very imperfect.

Whether inclusion of a charge for depletion makes accounts more useful than those in which no such provision is made, but the omission is clearly noted, is a question to which no universal answer can be given. Mines differ in their essential characteristics, and the depletion problem varies correspondingly. Where, as in the case of many coal and iron mines, the mineral bodies are measurable with what for all practical purposes is substantial accuracy, a depletion charge is desirable. This is particularly true if the mineral deposits form the basis of an industrial operation as in the steel industry, and may therefore be regarded as analogous to inventories. In cases where the mineral content is highly uncertain the balance of advantage may well lie in making no estimate of depletion (disclosing the fact clearly) rather than in making one that is wholly conjectural. Once more it becomes evident that attempts to secure uniformity based on points of similarity, without regard to points of difference, may lead to unsatisfactory results.

If depletion is to be provided for, much the same questions arise concerning the way in which the provision should be made, as have been already discussed in relation to depreciation. It can fairly be argued that for the purposes of amortization, a mine may be regarded as analogous to a terminable annuity. This would mean that the amount to be written off in the first year of n years of assumed life would be the difference between the value of an annuity of n years and the value of one for $n - 1$ years. However, the perhaps less logical but more conservative alternative of amortizing the investment on the basis of a uniform rate per unit is almost universally employed in practice. In the case of a mine having an extremely long probable life, the conservatism of a fixed charge per unit may be excessive—in fact, the considerations set forth in the discussion of depreciation (*supra*, page 146) apply with even greater force, and it may be questioned whether there is any practical necessity for making a charge for depletion while the unexhausted mineral body exceeds, say, fifty years' supply.

Writing Off Intangibles

By "intangibles" are meant, in accounting, not all assets that are literally intangible but such items as goodwill and relatively high earning power. Reference is here made to "writing off" intangibles, and the word "amortization" is avoided because there is usually no basis for anything in the nature of a process which implies a definite limitation of life capable of reasonably accurate estimation.

Whether intangibles should be written off has until recently not been regarded as an accounting question; but some are suggesting that it is now called for by sound accounting theory, and even that amortization has been recognized as mandatory in the past. The question presents different aspects according as it arises in relation to a regulated or an unregulated industry. In the case of the former, it has an interest for its bearing on regulatory conceptions and policies which goes beyond its intrinsic importance.

The view is sometimes expressed that the existence of regulation negatives the possibility of public utilities having legitimate intangible values. The more logical view would seem to be that regulation, when conducted, for instance, in accordance with the theories of Mr. Justice Brandeis—which are now strongly favored by Commissions—does create a genuine and a relatively permanent though limited intangible value in the case of any successful utility enterprise.

Regulation does not assure a return on investment but only a reasonable opportunity to secure a return, and Mr. Justice Brandeis was at pains to make it clear that, therefore, the rate of return permitted should always be such as would constitute an adequate reward for assuming a risk. Manifestly, if the risk is assumed and the enterprise, in fact, proves successful, the earning capacity which is both permissible and demonstrated can properly be capitalized at a lower rate of yield than that which just regulation would award to the original risk-takers. The result is that the capitalized value of the enterprise as a whole is increased and this increase is a legitimate element of intangible value which regulation should preserve and for which payment may properly be made. An investor might conceivably allow for the hazard that regulation would not, in fact, conform to such a standard even though adopting it in theory, but clearly a commission cannot base an argument for writing off intangibles on the ground that its successors will not respect an obligation imposed on them.[1]

Once it has been conceded that intangible values may properly exist in a regulated enterprise it follows that there is no justification in what may be called the Brandeis theory of regulation for writing them off. Depreciation of tangible assets aims to provide only for exhaustion of life that is inherent in the nature of property. In so far as property may rise or fall in value for other reasons than gradual exhaustion of life, accounting ordinarily makes no attempt to reflect such fluctuations. Accounting does not attempt to provide for a decline in commercial value of an enterprise as a whole that is due solely to a falling off in earning power of the enterprise, and it is probably not desirable that it should attempt to do so.

In these circumstances it is difficult to see why accounting authority should call for or favor writing off intangible assets when earning capacity is unimpaired, as some propose. Any such adjustments are clearly irrelevant to the determination of rates, so that the consumer is not concerned. A requirement of amortization cannot, therefore, be justified as called for in the public interest.

To the investor, the essential questions are whether earning capacity is likely to be maintained, increased, or diminished in the future, and what is the value of the stock that he owns

---

[1] The Brandeis theory raises other questions which are discussed in an appendix to this chapter.

upon the basis of the answer reached. To inject into accounts used in considering these questions a purely arbitrary charge based on a presupposition that the earning capacity will decline in capital value cannot be helpful.

In some cases, at least, it seems clear that the proposal to require amortization or elimination of intangibles has its basis in a conception of social policy rather than in accounting or in concern for the investor. It is therefore pertinent to observe that large amounts of capital investment inevitably disappear from the record annually because of bankruptcy or voluntary liquidation. As a result, the price that the community pays in the form of rate of return on capital for the aggregate service which it derives from corporate enterprise is exaggerated in almost any comparison between capital investment and currently reported income of corporations that survive. If the cost of all intangible values, even where earning capacity is unimpaired, is to be written off; if all permanent declines in earning capacity of any tangible fixed property are to be reflected in write-downs of property, and if no appreciation from any cause whatever is to be allowed to be recorded, the distortion will be increased.

The Federal Power Commission has asserted that good accounting practice demands that intangibles be written off. But these assertions are not supported by either reason or authority. In the case of the St. Croix Falls Power Company the Commission went so far as to say: "In fact, such provision is mandatory under our, and most, if not all, systems of accounts." It added the strange commentary: "In practice, tangible plant assets are generally depreciated, whereas intangible assets are amortized." The significance of this sentence is not apparent, since depreciation, in the Commission's parlance, is amortization.

The Commission refers to G. Preinreich to quote from him the obvious truth that intangible values rest on earning power (which is, of course, true also of tangible capital assets). An examination of authorities cited in that author's careful compilation that appeared in the *Journal of Accountancy* in 1937 (Vol. LXIV, page 28) will show that there is ample authority for the view that it is permissible to write off intangibles; some support for the view that it is wise to write them off; some authority for the view that amortization is called for in special cases, but little if any authority for the view that amortization is generally mandatory.

Paton and Littleton[1] suggest that the cost of intangibles acquired by purchase "should be absorbed by revenue charges —during the period implicit in the computation on which the price paid was based." This statement may be accepted if its application is narrowly limited to cases in which the period of earning capacity was recognized as being limited and the price paid was consciously based on that recognition. But this is the unusual, not the typical case. An argument is offered in support of the view that even if superior earning power in fact endures, the writing off is justified, but this argument lacks the authors' usual persuasiveness. It may be quoted as being one of the few passages which give any measure of support to the contention that amortization is mandatory. The authors say:

> Even if a superior level of income persists beyond the period anticipated, the amortization of the cost of goodwill in terms of the original computation is generally justified on the ground that there is no way of demonstrating that the later earning power is due to factors and conditions present when the business was acquired. It is just as easy and perhaps more reasonable to assume that the success achieved beyond that originally predicted is due to new developments in no way represented by the cost of the goodwill.[2]

---

[1] In their valuable *Introduction to Corporate Accounting Standards* (1940), p. 92.

[2] *Ibid.*, p. 93.

It is difficult to see how the assumptions lead to the conclusion that there should be charged against revenue both a write-off in respect of the old asset and the cost of an exactly similar new asset which has taken its place, as the passage seems to contemplate. A similar reasoning would justify the charge to operating expenses of both depreciation and the cost of replacement in respect of physical property.

In the *Pacific Power & Light Company* case the Commission supplemented its citation of the *St. Croix* case by the quotation of a passage from *A Statement of Accounting Principles*,[1] in which the authors said:

The writing off of such intangible assets as goodwill evokes scarcely any protest, even when it is recognized that substantial goodwill exists. The general distrust of goodwill and the knowledge that it has been widely used to capitalize exaggerated expectations of future earnings leave an almost universal feeling that the balance-sheet looks stronger without it. When actual consideration has been paid for goodwill, it should appear on the company's balance-sheet long enough to create a record of that fact in the history of the company as presented in the series of its annual reports. After that, nobody seems to regret its disappearance when accomplished by methods which fully disclose the circumstances.

It may be observed that the passage quoted is from a discussion of specific examples of the application of the principle of conservatism. The Commission went on to say:

In view of the fact that the $2,741,591.66 represents excess over original cost of acquisitions approximately half of which were made as far back as 1910 and have been carried on Pacific's books all those years without any provision having been made, *as good accounting practice demands*, for writing off any part thereof, we find that an amortization period of 10 years, beginning with 1942, is reasonable. [Emphasis supplied.]

---

[1] By T. H. Sanders, H. R. Hatfield, and U. Moore (1938). Page 14.

Reference has been made in an earlier chapter to an English case in which it was urged that an amount should have been written off and the judge, deciding otherwise, remarked that the contention advanced might be a precept of prudence and yet far removed from the sphere of the categorical imperative. The Commission in its decisions completely ignores this distinction. It cites an opinion that writing off is permissible, and in the next paragraph speaks as though the authority had held the write-off to be mandatory. At no point in either of the opinions mentioned does it cite accounting authorities which support its statements that accounting principles call for amortization of intangibles. The fact is otherwise.

It is important to bear in mind that in many cases intangible assets have been written off because the book values at which they stood were regarded as inadequate. Managements, being equally reluctant to allow the record figures to stand or to record on the books an unrealized appreciation, decided to adjust the asset to a nominal figure, leaving the actual value to be determined if and when the necessity should arise. The impossibility of finding any but a purely arbitrary basis for amortization of intangible assets is itself a strong argument against making amortization compulsory; it does not constitute an objection to voluntary action.

Where, it may be asked, should the amortization charge appear in the accounts if any is to be made? If it is not to be made against revenue in determining net income, the argument for making the charge compulsory falls to the ground. And it is not easy to see how inclusion of such a charge in any computation that results in a figure of net income would make that figure more generally useful or significant for any purpose.

The conclusion upon this whole question that seems to be indicated is that writing off intangibles is permissible but not mandatory. In the past, accountants have favored it solely on the grounds of conservatism. Regulatory bodies have, however, shown a disposition, while extolling conservatism, to treat actions founded solely thereon as if they implied recognition of a mandatory charge, and the exercise of conservatism may therefore be less prudent today than in the past.[1]

Since, in accounting, the fixed assets—tangible and intangible alike—are stated on the basis of cost, not value, and since market prices are based on actual or supposed value, there is little or no correspondence between market prices and the "book *value*" of stocks. What the investor effectively pays for intangible values may be said to be determined by the price he pays for the stock he buys. The figure at which the intangibles are carried on the books is a matter of little or no concern to him. From the balance-sheet standpoint it may be convenient for him to know that nothing is included in the book *value* for intangibles, and adjustments of intangible assets through surplus to nominal figures (or the creation of a reserve equal in amount to the asset), has therefore some usefulness to him. But it can only be inconvenient to him to have intangible assets reflected in the book *value* of the stock from year to year at annually changing and meaningless figures.

There are no doubt some who regard intangible assets as unreal and favor writing them off on this account; but if once the view is accepted that value depends on expectations for the future, the proposal is either invalid or applicable almost equally to tangible assets. Indeed, experience shows that intangible are often more enduring than tangible values.

---

[1] See note, *infra*, p. 265.

APPENDIX TO CHAPTER IX

THE REASONING which led Mr. Justice Brandeis in the *Southwestern Bell Telephone Company* case to the conclusion that prudent investment was the proper measure of the rate base led him naturally to the conclusion that the rate of return to be allowed on the rate base should be fixed on the basis of conditions at the date of investment (a statement on this point in the author's *Twenty-five Years of Accounting Responsibility*, Vol. 1, page 201, is incorrect). If this view be accepted, then if interest rates fall the value of the investment increases. If an enterprise has been financed through an issue of stock, a purchaser of either the stock or the enterprise can properly take the capitalized value of this differential in rates of return into account in determining the price he can afford to pay. The same is true if the enterprise has been financed partly through bonds which are redeemable, except that then the cost of redemption or refinancing of the bonds will be a factor that must be taken into account in the computation.

Going one step further, the theory of Mr. Justice Brandeis really leads to the conclusion that once property is dedicated to the public service the asset of the investor becomes a right to a return, and that the distinction between tangible and intangible property ceases to have special significance, if, indeed, it continues to exist.

These facts are often ignored by Commissioners who appeal to the high authority of Mr. Justice Brandeis but accept only such parts of his views as accord with their own.

FOOTNOTE TO CHAPTER IX

In September, 1943, a committee of the National Association of Railroad and Utilities Commissioners which had been studying the question of depreciation for four years, made its report. The potential effects of such a report on regulation and the whole economy are so great that a brief discussion of it seems desirable, although it has not been approved by the full body of the NARUC.

The NARUC had adopted depreciation accounting in 1936 (as stated in Chapter VIII) and committees had submitted reports favoring straight-line depreciation in 1938 and 1939. It is not, therefore, surprising that the new report should practically assume the acceptability of straight-line depreciation in public utility accounting.

The report is restricted in outlook and takes little cognizance of happenings outside the field of American public utility accounting. The subject is a large one and the Committee had to limit the scope of its study. But the report might have had greater value if more of it had been devoted to laying a broad foundation and less to mathematical ornamentation of a superstructure which is not too securely based. It had been intimated that the report would deal with the subject historically, but the historical discussion might well have been ampler, both in scope and in presentation. It would have been helpful to distinguish between three different senses in which the term "depreciation" has been used in the past and is used in passages cited in the report; viz.: (a) to describe a decline in value from any cause whatever; (b) to describe a decline in value attributable to partial exhaustion of useful life; and (c) to describe a systematic amortization of cost (or other basic value) over useful life without regard to value during that life. A constant regard for these distinctions is essential to an understanding of dicta on the subject contained in court decisions or other statements. The report does not even discuss the reasons which led the NARUC in 1922 to prescribe retirement reserve accounting (as explained above in Chapter VIII).

The report minimizes and, indeed, comes near to denying the importance of the time element in the problem. It presents as all-important the fact that the life of plant units is limited, whereas the length of life is of equal significance. Expenditures on property that has a probable life of only a few years— say five or less—have from the accounting standpoint many points of resemblance to maintenance expenditures. In relation to such property, analogies from the coalpile and from prepayments of rent have considerable validity. In the case of property having an estimated useful life of 150 years, which is presented by the Committee as being governed by the same rules as short-lived property, such analogies are wholly invalid and the governing considerations make straight-line depreciation inappropriate.

The report puts forward a new definition of depreciation as "the expiration or consumption, in whole or in part, of the service life, capacity, or utility of property resulting from the action of one or more of the forces operating to bring about the retirement of such property from service," and says that depreciation "results in a cost of service." As mentioned in Chapter VIII, the Supreme Court has defined depreciation as "the loss, not restored by current maintenance, which is due to all the factors causing the ultimate retirement of the property. These factors embrace wear and tear, decay, inadequacy and obsolescence. Annual depreciation is the loss which takes place in a year."

The Research Department of the Institute has recently invited criticism of a definition of depreciation which emphasizes the fact that it is a charge resulting from the application of one of a number of conventional methods of allocation of the cost of property to accounting periods, and suggests that the essential and common characteristics of acceptable methods of allocation are that they distribute a total actual or estimated cost over an estimated life in a rational and systematic manner and that they provide for any revisions that may be found necessary of estimates initially made.

The differences between the three definitions are of major importance. The NARUC Committee seeks to present annual depreciation as something factual and the adoption of depreciation accounting in public utility regulation as a belated recognition of facts. The Institute sees in that step rather a change of conventions.

A crucial test of the three types of definitions is afforded by considering the meaning of "annual depreciation" in relation to facts noted in the Committee's report. It is there indicated that if interest is taken at 6 per cent, the sinking-fund depreciation on a unit with a life of 50 years is in its first year of use roughly one-sixth of the straight-line depreciation, and that if the estimated life is 150 years, the relation between the two charges is as $9 to $6,666 or as $1 to $741. Under the Committee's definition, therefore, it would be possible for one person to say that the depreciation "cost" for that year is $1 and another, that it is $6 (50 years' life) or $741 (150 years' life) and for both to be right. Similarly, under the Supreme Court's definition, one might properly claim that the loss that takes place in the year is $1, and another, equally properly, that it is $6 in the one case and $741 in the other. It is evident that both definitions fail to meet this simple test.

The major point suggested by the foregoing comparison is of broad significance; it is, that the Committee's definition (and, indeed, its entire report) fails to recognize not only the nature of depreciation accounting but the nature of financial accounting itself. It ignores the fact that accounting is conventional—a fact which the American Institute of Accountants has repeatedly pointed out in recent years, as, for instance, in its letter to the New York Stock Exchange of September 22, 1932, and in its first research bulletin, issued in September, 1939. The outstanding exemplification of the conventional character of the accounting of manufacturing concerns is the rule that the entire profit on manufacture and sale is deemed to arise at the moment when realization takes place. In the public utility field, it is the treatment of plant amortization that affords the most striking illustration of the conventional nature of accounting.

The question may be asked: "Admitting that it is not reasonable to say that a specific cost, or the loss that takes place in a year, can be correctly stated at either $1 or $6, or at $1 or $741 as the case may be—is a choice of conventions acceptable which makes such a difference in the charge against operations possible? The answer is to be found in recognition of the purposive character of accounting, which is stressed in Chapter I.

Depreciation accounting may be required (1) in determining the amount of disposable income; (2) in the measurement of earning capacity; (3) in the determination of income that may fairly be taxed; (4) for the regulation of rates; (5) for the valuation of property, and perhaps for other purposes. For the first of these purposes a high degree of conservatism is justifiable and even desirable, since only prudence and no conflict of interest is involved. For tax purposes, also, conservatism is called for, since the Government shares in profits but not in losses and its participation is continuing. Indeed, Lord Stamp, the greatest modern English authority on taxation, came ultimately to the conclusion that for the purposes of a continuing scheme of income taxation the taxpayer should be given a broad right of election as to the time when he would take any depreciation deductions to which he might be entitled. For valuation as between buyer and seller, conservatism has no proper place; in this instance, the relation between the value of new property and property whose life is partly exhausted is the crucial consideration. The convention that is appropriate for one of these purposes may thus be quite inappropriate for another.

The governing consideration in the choice of a convention for use in accounting, to be employed in the regulation of rates, would seem to be equity—first, as between the investors in the utility and consumers, and secondly, as between the consumers at different times. Convenience, practicability, and the appropriateness of the method for other uses, may all be given some weight. The object should be to combine equity, simplicity, and varied usefulness, but equity should be regarded as paramount.

The case in which the method of allocation between years directly affects rights as between parties is essentially different from one in which the only question at issue is at what time a person with a continuing interest will treat a profit as arising. These considerations are particularly relevant when it is proposed to change a convention with retroactive effect.

It is, perhaps, a defect of the report that it regards depreciation too much as a problem in itself and too little as a part of a larger problem. This is particularly evident in the claim that straight-line depreciation is appropriate because it results in an equal charge for equal service in each year of estimated life. Here, it follows the line adopted by the Interstate Commerce Commission in 1926 in its report discussed in Chapter VIII. In that report (Case No. 15100), the Commission said:

"The principle is fair, however, that the cost resulting from the using up of property in service should be shared equally by the years which have had the benefit of the use."

But as I then pointed out—

" . . . the charges against the traffic are twofold; first, a charge for exhaustion; second, a charge for use, computed as a return on investment, and the truly fair principle is that the combined charges should be the same in each year." [1]

The sinking-fund, or annuity method meets this requirement. It is also the appropriate method for determining residual values on the assumption that the exhaustion of useful life is the only influence causing a change in value that has to be taken into account. These arguments in favor of the annuity method are almost entirely ignored in the Committee's report.

The report, in discussing the extreme case of property with a life of 150 years, says:

"With a 6 per cent interest rate, the depreciation rate under the compound-interest method for a single unit of plant with a 150-year life, would be .000009+ for the first year and .0566+ in the 150th year. On an investment of $1,000,000 this would mean a depreciation charge of $9 in the first year and $56,600 in the 150th year."

This appears to have been regarded as an argument in favor of the straight-line method as against what is there called the "compound-interest method" but what I should prefer to call the "annuity method," since it regards property as representing an "annuity of service" either terminating or perpetual. It seems to indicate, rather, the defects of a straight-line depreciation method when applied to property that has a long life. That the charge in the first year would be only $9 is, of course, due to the fact that an annuity (of service or money) of $60,000 (6 per cent on $1,000,000) for 150 years is worth only $150 less than a perpetuity if interest is taken to be 6 per cent.

It is not suggested that straight-line depreciation should be charged on property the life of which is perpetual, but the illustrative case cited differs so little from that case that if it were possible to extend the life of the $1,000,000 unit

---

[1] See *Twenty-Five Years of Accounting Responsibility*, Vol. I, p. 172.

from 150 years to perpetuity it would be uneconomical to do so at a cost of more than $150 (6 per cent of which is $9.00). If the life were perpetual, the charge against the service in the first year would be a charge for return on investment of $60,000. On the assumption of a life of 150 years, the charge on the annuity basis for return and exhaustion would be $60,009, which is rational. On the straight-line basis it would be no less than $66,666. The annual charge for depreciation would be more than forty times the sum that it would be worth while to spend to secure perpetual life and eliminate depreciation altogether.

The charge on the annuity basis would not amount to as much as $150 a year for nearly half a century. At the end of a half century, the price which a purchaser could afford to pay for the unit on the assumption (1) of a 6 per cent return; (2) of equal usefulness over each of the 150 years; and (3) of a stable price level, would be only $3,000 less than the original investment, but straight-line depreciation would have written the property down by $333,333.

Consideration of this case, chosen by the Committee for illustrative purposes, brings out clearly the point that the real hazard in such a case is one for which depreciation accounting does not provide. The hazard is not that the unit itself will one day become unserviceable, but that the enterprise of which it is a part will be abandoned or become unprofitable. Straight-line depreciation in such a case is an inappropriate arithmetical abstraction with no justification in either theory or utility.

It must be recognized that interest methods are, in principle, superior to straight-line methods for a purpose such as valuation or rate regulation. The arguments in favor of straight-line depreciation are simplicity and conservatism in estimation of profits and in investment. In the case of property of reasonably short life, the difference between the charges on the two bases is moderate and the balance of advantage may be in favor of the straight-line method from the standpoint of both the utility and the consumers—providing always (and the proviso is vitally important) that it is applied from the initiation of the enterprise. In the case of long-lived property, the weight of argument on the Committee's hypothesis is against straight-line depreciation and in favor of either the annuity method or a new method which would take account of the probable life of the enterprise rather than of the life of the individual unit. But even in this case a policy of straight-line depreciation, if initiated with the enterprise, might have been justified. It is the proposal for retroactive adjustment that is both logically and morally indefensible. When life exceeds 100 or even 75 years, there is little or no case for depreciation accounting.

A considerable part of the report and appendices is devoted to the attempt to apply insurance methods to depreciation accounting, to which reference has been made in the preceding chapter of this volume. Here again, cases in which arguments have a certain validity are used to establish a proposition which is then applied to cases in which the arguments have no similar relevance. The often-used illustration of poles (which are of moderately short life, are numerous enough to make application of the law of averages possible, and the causes of retirement of which can be fairly accurately forecast) is used to support an argument which is then applied to a dam that is unique and whose life is wholly uncertain. A so-called "estimate" of 150 years as the useful life of a dam built within thirty years is manifestly a mere conjecture or notional figure. The report ignores the commonplace of the law that though analogies play an important part in the development of rules, the analogies must be chosen with great care and applied only within the limits of their validity, and that points of difference between cases may be more significant than points of resemblance; and the conclusions reached are subject to criticism accordingly.

The Committee does not deal with the point stressed by

Mr. Justice Brandeis (in a passage quoted in an appendix to its report) [1] that despite the relative simplicity of the problem, the margin for error in life insurance premiums based on mortality tables was found to be so wide as to work serious injustice, and that therefore mutual insurance had become almost universal. The general scheme of insurance is to fix a premium that is believed to be rather more than adequate and to make adjusments as time shows them to be justified. Such a policy may be appropriate in the accounting of an industrial company or a new public utility but it does not follow by any means that it can properly be applied retroactively.

It is difficult to understand how the Committee, while recommending straight-line depreciation, can hold the view expressed in Paragraph 29 of the summary that "current charges for depreciation expense should be based upon the best possible estimates of the amount properly applicable to the period covered by an income statement, without modification for excessive or deficient charges in the past." Acceptance of the postulates of continuity and of the necessity for readjustments of depreciation charges to correspond to revisions of estimates of useful life seems an inescapable part of any adequate system of depreciation accounting.

The Committee was, of course, concerned with the major problem of the adjustment of public utility accounting from the retirement reserve basis, which it formerly favored, to the depreciation accounting which it has more recently approved. The first part of its conclusion on this point, that "In principle any necessary correction of depreciation reserves should be made through surplus or a special section of the income account" is highly questionable. The final sentence of the paragraph reads: "Therefore, it is concluded that the

---

[1] See *Pacific Gas and Electric Company* v. *City and County of San Francisco*, 265 U.S. 403 (1924).

objective of correcting inadequate reserves should be approached with appropriate consideration of the practical effects of alternative courses of action," which may mean much or little according to the interpretation that is placed on the ambiguous language employed. As pointed out in Chapter VIII, retroactive adjustments resulting from a change of conventions may easily amount to a denial of substantial justice.

The report discusses the treatment of depreciation in income taxation but leaves untouched the thorny question whether the deduction for depreciation is a necessary charge in determining income within the language of *Doyle* v. *Mitchell* [1] or a deduction from income to arrive at the amount subject to taxation. Inferences that may justly be drawn from practice in that field naturally differ according to the answer given to this question. If, as is probably the common view, the allowance is merely a deduction granted by Congress, the case for the contention that straight-line depreciation is a necessary cost is weakened.

The most persuasive part of the report is that in which the Committee argues that straight-line accounting in the past would have been practically advantageous to the utilities and to consumers because it would have reduced the amount of investment exposed to the hazards of the industry. But this was as true in 1922 as it is today, and it would have added to the value of the report if the Committee had explained why the NARUC did not attach more weight to the consideration at that time. An explanation on this point would seem to be due to the public and to the Committee's predecessors in authority. Some of the possible reasons are suggested in Chapter VIII of this volume.

The report also contains many other useful and interesting contributions to consideration of the subject. It is, however,

---

[1] *Doyle* v. *Mitchell Brothers Co.*, 247 U.S. 179.

to be regretted that no adequate opportunity for the presentation of the points of view herein expressed, or of others that might have been suggested, was afforded before the report was adopted by the Committee. It might then have been possible to secure the presentation of a report that might have been accepted as a comprehensive and unbiased survey.

CHAPTER X

Inventories and Commitments—Accounts Receivable

THE SECOND GREAT DIVISION of the question of the place which cost and value respectively should occupy in accounting relates to the treatment of inventories. This term has come to be used in accounting to describe stocks of raw materials, supplies, work in progress, and finished products, which formerly were brought into account by a process of inventorying. Few people appreciate the diversity of practice in the determination of such figures. No question absorbs a larger part of the interest of those who are continuously concerned with accounts and financial statements. Here, it is not proposed to do more than to indicate the general character of the differences in basic theories that are commonly found and to explain briefly why such differences are permissible and even desirable, at least for some of the purposes for which financial statements are commonly used.

In order to avoid repetition of a cumbersome phrase, in this chapter "*value*" and "*valuation*" will again be used for convenience as describing the process by which the money figures entering into the accounts are determined, and as not necessarily implying either a measurement of worth or the adoption of an appraisal procedure.

One of the five general principles suggested by the Institute committee in its letter to the New York Stock Exchange of September 22, 1932, and at that time generally approved, provided that:

1. Unrealized profit should not be credited to the income account of the corporation either directly or indirectly, through the medium of charging against such unrealized profits amounts which would ordinarily fall to be charged against income account. Profit is deemed to be realized when a sale in the ordinary course of business is effected, unless the circumstances are such that the collection of the sale price is not reasonably assured. An exception to the general rule may be made in respect of inventories in industries (such as the packing-house industry) in which owing to the impossibility of determining costs it is a trade custom to take inventories at net selling prices, which may exceed cost.[1]

It is generally accepted that only in very special cases should inventories be taken at more than cost, and the number of exceptions is steadily being diminished. Packing-houses have now found it possible to arrive at a cost basis that is sufficiently satisfactory to make its use preferable to the old practice of relying on selling prices. The principle described as "cost or market, whichever is lower," has long been established and today continues to occupy the leading position.

There is no uniformity in interpretation of the terms "cost" and "market value." The test of realizability is constantly in the minds of accountants in *valuing* the inventory.

Accountants recognize that joint costs present difficult and sometimes almost insoluble problems of allocation. They agree that it is sometimes necessary to consider the value of the respective products in allocating cost. But almost all cost may be said to be joint in some respect and degree. In one case, goods of different kinds may result from the use of the same facilities and the same raw materials, in the same period. In another case, goods of the same kind may result from the same facilities and the same raw materials, but in different periods, and it may be foreseeable that business conditions in these different periods will differ greatly. A producer of a profitable article may find that his overhead expenses will

---

[1] See appendix in Chapter IV.

be increased only slightly in absolute amount by the addition to production of a secondary line which could not be expected to yield a profit if burdened with a strictly proportionate share of overhead costs. Some favor a degree of uniformity in allocation of costs on purely physical bases, and rely on the alternative of market value to afford protection against resulting occasional overvaluations. Others would prefer to avoid the use of alternative bases of inventory valuation and to allow a greater flexibility in deciding the elements of cost to be included in inventories and in allocating such costs between products.

In practice, the latter school of thought is well represented among controllers and independent auditors. Where no doubt as to realizability exists, a fairly liberal interpretation of the term "cost" may be accepted without demur. If profit margins are slight and uncertain, a narrower definition of costs to be carried forward may be adopted which may exclude some elements of indirect or overhead cost or give them only a slight recognition. The situations presented are so infinite in their variety as to make abstract general rules unsatisfactory and the exercise of judgment indispensable.

Selling costs are not included in the inventory valuations of goods on hand. In an unusual case in which such costs already incurred are deemed to be properly carried forward, they will be classified as deferred charges to operations and not as a part of the inventory. Some accounting opinion disapproves of this rule, but it is almost universally accepted by accountants who are employed to prepare or report on accounts.

The appropriate method of inventory valuation depends to some extent on the way in which business is typically conducted by the corporation. Methods that are appropriate for a company which makes forward contracts for sales and purchases, and maintains a reasonably balanced position between its forward sales contracts and its inventories and commitments, may be quite inappropriate for a company which has no forward sales contracts. Methods that are suitable for a company whose selling prices are infrequently revised and are not affected by moderate changes in prices of raw material, are unsuitable for a company whose selling prices are acutely sensitive to such changes.

The American Institute of Accountants is now engaged on a long-term research program designed to bring about a classification of industries along such lines as are here indicated and to secure substantial uniformity within the several classifications adopted. There is clearly more hope for success in such an endeavor than in an attempt to lay down fixed rules to be observed by all companies regardless of the distinguishing characteristics of their business operations. The objective sought is a *valuation* of inventories that will result in a fair statement of income and a consistent and reasonably conservative treatment of the assets in the balance sheet.

In recent years a method of evaluation known as "last in, first out," or LIFO, has gained favor. It is commonly presented as a cost basis, which assumes that the last goods received are the first taken out. But in any long view such an assumption is clearly in most cases fictional. The reasonable interpretation of the word "cost" in this context is that it means the cost of those goods which by a reasonable convention might be deemed to be those on hand. This does not mean that identification of units is necessary or praiseworthy, or even that valuation on the basis of identity is always justifiable; for to accept this view would obviously facilitate manipulation of operating profits by artificial selection of the units to be delivered on sales contracts. The accepted conventions of first in, first out, or of average cost, guard against this danger. But the LIFO method goes far beyond the limits necessary to prevent manipulation and results in the existing stocks being carried at a figure which represents at best the cost of similar stocks that were purchased and resold or consumed in a period more or less remote.

It is unfortunate that here, again, terminology—adopted for tactical reasons in connection with efforts to change tax practice—is confusing, especially as the method has obvious merits in some cases. It is simple of application where inventories consist of a few commodities which do not vary from year to year; difficulties increase when the effort is made to extend its use to cover cases in which the commodities are only similar from year to year, and over a period of years come to differ greatly. It has no proper application where inventories are in the main intended to be used in producing goods covered by outstanding firm sales contracts.

From an administrative or fiscal standpoint the LIFO method no doubt serves to protect against the illusion of prosperity resulting from a mere general rise in the price level. But it may tend to obscure the dangers of a period of price declines and thus to produce a relaxation of vigilance. Altogether, the method has less usefulness than many of its adherents claim for it, and it is doubtful whether it would have gained its recent popularity but for the prospect of using it to reduce taxes in a period in which prices and tax rates were rising and the law was unjustly insistent on the false concept of each year as an entirely separate taxable unit. Now that the law has been amended so as to recognize the essential continuity of business and of the process of profit earning, and contains provisions for carrying losses forward or backward, the tax appeal of LIFO is greatly reduced and further extension of its use is not so probable as it seemed before those changes were made.

Consideration of the merits of the LIFO method brings out sharply the contrast between the older and the newer uses of accounting. The strongest argument for the method is that the value of a business is determined by its income; that the income is best measured if sales and costs are reflected in terms of the same price level; and that the replacement value of an inventory which must be substantially maintained so long as the business is conducted has little more practical bearing on the value of the business than the replacement value of the plant itself. Critics urge that the balance-sheet figure that results from use of the method is devoid of significance because it is neither a historical cost nor a value figure. They insist that if it is to be adopted there should at least be an appropriate indication of the cost value of similar goods at the date of the balance sheet in a footnote to the accounts.

Historically, the LIFO method is a variant of the base stock method, which has long been employed in a few industries. During the first world war, the acceptability of this method for tax purposes was extensively discussed, both in England and in America. In England, the Inland Revenue accepted the method where it was supported by an established trade practice. It based its decision squarely on court decisions that what is income is to be determined by the best practices of businessmen. In America, the method was rejected after full consideration by an advisory committee which the Commissioner of Internal Revenue had appointed. Even in England, the number of industries in which the method is employed is very limited; and it may be doubted whether the LIFO method has a much wider range of usefulness.

Those who still look on the balance sheet as of substantial if not primary importance will see justice in a demand for some information as to current values where the LIFO method is used. And even those whose interest is mainly in the income account may feel that the information should be given so that those who desire to do so may restate the accounts on substantially a first in, first out basis, which in the past has been the prevailing one.

The variety of concepts concealed in the single word "market" is as great as that which exists in the interpretation of cost. At once the question arises whether the market contemplated in the expression "market value" is that in which the goods would be bought or that in which they would be sold. This in turn suggests the question, What does the term mean in the case of partly finished goods for which there is no market? Today, the term "market value" is, to some extent, an artificial concept based on the notion of a constructive market. This is in part a reflection of the influence of taxation on accounting practice.

In earlier years, the alternative form of *valuation*—"cost or market"—was regarded as requiring no more than that raw materials should not be carried at more than their current value in the markets in which they would normally be purchased, nor finished goods at a figure exceeding the net realization that might be expected therefrom on the basis of conditions existing at the date of the financial statement in which the asset was included. For finished goods selling price in the market in which the goods would normally be sold, less an allowance for selling expenses, was the measure of the market value, to be compared with cost and adopted if the lower of the two. The value of goods in process might be computed by working forward from the base figure for raw materials or backward from the inventory valuations of finished goods by allowing for costs of completion.

A special situation which arose as the result of the conclusion of the armistice, near the end of the calendar year 1918, was largely responsible for an extension of the concept of market value for finished goods beyond the limits previously in force. At the end of 1918, the price situation was confused and the effect of applying the cost or market principle in the old form was difficult to appraise and certainly gave inadequate protection against taxation at high rates of apparent profits that would not, in practice, ever be realized. To meet this situation, under a law which recognized only two alternatives of inventory *valuation*—cost, or the lower of cost or market value—the Treasury undertook to extend the meaning of the latter term. It permitted taxpayers to compute a market value for both goods in process and finished goods on the basis of the cost of replacement at current prices for raw material. This was accomplished by the introduction into a definition of "market," contained in Article 1584 of Regulation 45, of a statement that "market" was "applicable to goods purchased and on hand and to basic materials in goods in process of manufacture and in finished goods on hand." This extension, coupled with the natural conservatism of accountants, has led to a situation in which market value is conceived by some as the lower of two measures—one, the probable net selling price less a margin of profit, and the other, the cost of replacement by purchase or manufacture under conditions existing at the date of the statement. Such methods are disapproved by some practitioners and perhaps more teachers of accounting.

There are those who hold that, even if it is clear that inventories will be sold for a net yield that will fall short of cost, the loss should not be anticipated in the inventory *valuation*. Paton and Littleton, for instance, would make the purely recording function supreme in formal accounts and would require that recording to be a severely consistent and logical application of certain basic concepts, such as matching revenues against cost. They would reserve the interpretive function for explanatory notes. This, however, seems to me to ignore the reasonable expectations of the unlearned stockholder. He is not interested in the symmetry or logic of the financial statement, but in its practical significance. The management owes him a duty of interpretation as well as of disclosure, and that duty is best discharged in the accounts themselves. Footnotes may still be called for as a matter of disclosure, and in order that the stockholder may be able to make his own adjustments if his interpretation differs from that of the management.

In *Accounting Principles Underlying Corporate Financial Statements* the American Accounting Association deals with the question in a manner that is not free from ambiguity. It stresses cost as the basis of *valuation* and lays down the rule that *values* other than cost applicable to future periods should not appear on balance sheets except as footnotes. However, it does not specify how the costs fairly applicable to future periods are to be determined. In the absence of any explicit statement which negatives such a view it may, perhaps, be argued that costs are not fairly applicable to a future period if there is no reasonable present ground for believing that the amounts thereof will be recovered in the future in the normal course of business. Along such lines the statement might be held to approve a method of inventory *valuation* that would be, in substance, the same as cost or market, whichever is lower. But it is at least doubtful whether the Committee contemplated such a result.

In recent years there has been a natural disposition to restate the rule in a form which would avert the objection that it is illogical. The majority of accountants are, however, content to regard the demonstrated practical wisdom of the rule as outweighing any supposed illogicality.

A decision as to the relative merits of this basis and the alternative of cost (whether above or below market) might turn, perhaps more than any other accounting question, on the relative importance attached to the various uses of accounts. The conflict also presents a phase of the broad question of continuity in accounting—of how far it is practical or desirable to determine profits in terms of current conditions without regard to inheritances from the past. For instance, it is said that inventories should not be charged against the new accounting period at more than the current cost of replacement at the beginning thereof, because if they had not then existed they could have been secured at the current cost. But the argument overlooks the continuous and historical character of accounting. It is also in many cases of doubtful validity, in that it ignores the time element in replacement, which may be important.

The cost or market rule is well suited to the older uses of accounts, since it guards against overstatement of assets and of disposable profits. It is less clearly appropriate for any purpose "which glorifies the annual period of reckoning" as income taxation and computations of earnings per share do. Thus controversies over the question are largely between those who emphasize coherence of doctrine and those who look more to practical consequences, and between the new and the old uses of accounts.

Opinion among practicing accountants is perhaps predominantly influenced by consideration of the older uses. The problem is one which affects all manufacturing and trading companies, large or small, so that the unlisted corporations, whose number greatly exceeds that of listed corporations, are vitally concerned. To such companies the use of accounts as a guide to earning capacity is not as significant as is their usefulness for credit purposes and as a basis for prudent fiscal policy. The demonstrated value of conservatism in inventory *valuation* and its beneficial effects on credit, are sufficient to account for the enduring authority of the cost or market rule.

Since the last in, first out basis is accepted as a cost basis, it is permissible for tax purposes and in general accounting practice to use the alternative of "market" in connection therewith. By convention, a market price applied to the goods in the inventory at a closing date is treated thereafter as if it were a cost determined at that time; hence the "last in, first out cost or market" basis has, in times when prices are fluctuating with a general upward trend, the two merits (to those who so judge merit) of producing the most conservative balance sheet and also the most conservative income statement during the upswing of prices.

An illustration may be helpful in bringing out both the

arguments that support the various methods and the importance of the bearing of the method employed on the significance of profits reported at the different stages of the price cycle.

Let me take, as I have taken before, the simple case of one of the unemployed who joined the apple-selling rush in the winter of 1931. The first day he bought two crates of apples at $2.00 each and sold the contents of one for $5. Apples were quoted at the close of the day at $2.25 per crate. The second day he bought a crate at $2.25 and sold one for $5.50. The market price remained at $2.25. The third day he bought a crate for $2.00, sold one for $4.50, and the closing price was $1.75. On the fourth day he sold the contents of his last crate at $4.00. Over the four days it was clear that he had bought four crates of apples at a total cost of $8.25 and had sold the contents for a total of $19.00, and thus had made a total profit of $10.75. But the only day in which the amount of the profit was clear to him was the first. The following table shows the distribution of profit between days on four different theories corresponding to those just described:

	FIRST DAY	SECOND DAY	THIRD DAY	FOURTH DAY	TOTAL
On the basis of cost, first in, first out, the profit was	$3.00	$3.50	$2.25	$2.00	$10.75
On the basis of cost, last in, first out, the profit was	3.00	3.25	2.50	2.00	10.75
On the basis of cost, FIFO or market, the profit was	3.00	3.50	2.00	2.25	10.75
On the basis of cost, LIFO or market, the profit was ...	3.00	3.25	2.25	2.25	10.75

If we assume four men each having exactly the same experience but each using a different inventory method and reporting his profits accordingly, then if we were to appraise the value of the respective businesses by multiplying the profits shown in any period by a uniform multiple, we should conclude on the basis of the fourth day's experience that the businesses of the two men who had used the cost or market basis at the end of the third day were more valuable than those of the other two. Of course, in the illustrative case assumed such a conclusion is fantastically absurd; but enlarge the scale of the operation in volume, time, and complexity, so that it will deal with years and millions of dollars instead of days and dollars, and the situation is one in which similar conclusions have repeatedly been drawn by those who worship blindly at the shrine of "earnings per share."

Whether a high degree of uniformity in inventory valuation is attainable, or is even an objective worthy of a great effort, is doubtful. Similarities of circumstances are seldom more than partial, and the gain from enforced uniformity may therefore be illusory. Moreover, it can be achieved only at the cost of a relaxation of managerial responsibility. So long as a management is free to choose within limits its inventory basis it can properly be held responsible for selecting one that is appropriate and applying it in a manner that produces a fair result. Once a prescribed method is established, the management and the company's auditors can be held responsible only for seeing that it is followed.

Accounting rules should preferably not only be sound but seem reasonable to the intelligent though not expert user of accounts. It is desirable that the idea underlying the cost or market rule should be expressed in terms that will meet this requirement and be capable of application in a reasonably consistent manner on the basis of observable business facts. These considerations point to a restatement of the rule as requiring only a measurement of the cost that may properly be carried forward. Various suggestions looking towards this goal have been made, and a solution of the problem seems necessary to the attainment of agreement between theoretical and practical authorities.

A cost that is not likely to be recovered or even one that will be exactly recovered is scarcely useful. The cost of an article which is intended for sale cannot be said to possess normal usefulness unless it can be expected to produce on sale at least a minimum normal profit. A rule that, in allocating costs between the past and the future, only costs having a normal usefulness in the future should be carried forward would seem to cover all the legitimate uses of the cost or market rule. This would avert the embodiment of the two rival concepts of cost and value as alternatives in a single rule. It would have the positive virtue that it would suggest the vital features of the process of inventory *valuation*—that it is primarily a process of allocation of costs between the past and the future and that apportionment cannot be purely mechanical but always involves judgment.[1]

Contracts for future purchases, often referred to as purchase commitments, may in one sense be regarded as constituting both an asset and a liability. They are not so recorded on the books because the corporation may never secure the delivery of the goods, and in that case it will have no liability. However, there are times when such contracts and the corresponding contracts for future sales are among the most material facts affecting the financial position of a corporation. Therefore, they always require consideration in the preparation of a balance sheet.

Clearly, if binding sales contracts with responsible customers at prices which will insure a profit are in existence in respect of any stock on hand, the fact that the current market price of that stock is lower than cost does not make it necessary to write down inventories from cost to market. On the other hand, the existence of binding contracts to purchase at a price in excess of market in the absence of firm sale contracts might be said to call for a reserve in the amount of the difference as much as if the goods were already on hand.

---

[1] Cf. "Problems of Inventory Pricing," George Bailey, *Journal of Accountancy*, Aug., 1941.

Where forward contracts for both purchases and sales have been made at prices above the current market the position may require careful analysis. In the crisis of 1921 (which was an "inventory crisis" and permanently influenced accounting practice), many merchants who had such a balanced position were compelled to perform their purchase contracts but found that on many of their sales contracts the only choice open to them was to agree to a cancellation or to incur a bad debt. Manufacturers who had future commitments for purchases but not for sales found themselves in an equally serious position. In a balance sheet of the Goodyear Tire & Rubber Company of May 1, 1921, a reserve of $24,000,000 was made for losses on commitments in addition to one of $18,000,000 to reduce inventories from cost to market value, and even these reserves were not unduly conservative.[1]

Commitments for future sales are less likely to prove seriously burdensome to a manufacturing concern because it will usually have covered its material purchase requirements at least to a sufficient extent to make the probable loss of relatively minor importance.

Those who favor taking inventories at cost and allowing losses on subsequent sale thereof to be reflected in the period in which the sale is consummated, naturally disapprove of the creation of reserves for prospective losses on commitments. The Institute has taken the position that such reserves are not mandatory, though desirable, and that fair disclosure of the material facts is all that is absolutely requisite. A reserve for commitments is not allowed for tax purposes—indeed, a *reserve* for the difference between cost and market value of inventories is not allowable; the inventories must actually be *valued* on the lower basis if the reduction is to enter into the measurement of taxable income for the period at the close of which the inventory is taken.

---

[1] A discussion of this case will be found in *Twenty-five Years*, Vol. I, pp. 292–95.

In 1936, a combination of a profitable year, an undistributed profits tax, and falling prices at the close of the year led to corporations paying substantial sums to cancel commitments for future purchases and making new contracts at correspondingly lower prices. In this way, they accomplished the purpose (which they could not have achieved by making commitment reserves), of reducing the taxable profits for the year and the amounts required to be distributed in order to avoid the undistributed profits tax.

UNCOMPLETED CONTRACTS

In the same general category with inventories falls the asset represented by partial completion of large contracts, such as those for shipbuilding. In earlier days, when less emphasis was placed on the profits for single years, it was the almost universal custom to carry such contracts at not more than cost, until the contracts were so near completion that the amount of profit thereon could be determined with reasonable certainty. At that point a profit could usually be said to have been realized in the same sense in which goods sold are deemed to be realized when a valid accounts receivable is created in respect thereof. The increasing emphasis on annual profits and the desire to avoid the fluctuations in reported profits which would have resulted from adherence to the old methods by corporations whose business consisted of a few large contracts, have led to a steady relaxation of the rule against taking credit for profits in advance of substantial completion. However, accountants are, in general, still cautious in doing so and are much more ready to recognize the probability of a loss on a contract than to be convinced that a profit is reasonably assured. This is clearly a problem on which no specific rules can be made, but which must be dealt with by the exercise of judgment within the limits of a rather broad rule.

A similar tendency is to be found in the history of valuation of completed pictures in the motion-picture industry. In the early days, the simple rule was adopted that all receipts from pictures were applied against the cost until that cost had been recovered; thereafter all rentals were profit. Obviously such a method was conservative, but not scientific. If the picture as a whole produced a profit, some part of each dollar of rental received should more properly be deemed to be profit. Extensive research led to the discovery that the earnings of the ordinary picture followed a more or less well defined curve, being naturally greatest in the early days of presentation and gradually tapering off at the end of perhaps two years. As a result, the practice became general, and has been recognized by the Bureau of Internal Revenue, of computing income by writing off the cost of the picture against rentals on the basis of such curves. Clearly there is great need for the exercise of judgment in determining the precise shape of the curves to be used from time to time, and naturally when this has been done the experience of every picture will not conform closely to the curve, so that constant watchfulness and the exercise of judgment are necessary to insure the proper computation of the residual asset and income.

ACCOUNTS RECEIVABLE

When goods in the inventory are exchanged through a process of sale for an account receivable, cost ceases to be the determining factor in accounting. It is not practicable to carry the concept of cost through to what might be its logical extreme and to defer recognition of gain until actual cash is received. The language of the Corporation Excise Tax Law of 1909, which was discussed in Chapter IV, might be regarded as adopting the extreme view—indeed, it has been suggested that the form of that law was in part, at least, inspired by a desire to avoid any constitutional questions and a fear that the constitutionality of taxing income not received in cash might be questioned. However, the proposition that gain or loss should be measured when property is received which is either cash or the equivalent of cash, had so many practical advantages that it has hardly been seriously questioned.

It follows that in measuring the gain, what is received should be stated at its equivalent in cash, which is not necessarily the face value of the account receivable. This point has not always been adequately recognized in general accounting or tax practice, partly because it is obscured by the way in which provision for the difference between face value of an account receivable and its cash equivalent is customarily made. It is convenient to record the account receivable at its full amount and to provide through separate accounts for such items as discount and the possibility of the debt being irrecoverable— hence these deductions are sometimes treated as losses sustained after gain has been measured, whereas they are more properly regarded as entering into the measurement of gain in the first instance.

In relation to discount, the point is obvious. Certainly an account receivable cannot be regarded as the equivalent of cash in an amount larger than the sum in cash which would discharge the debt if it were tendered immediately. Any further sum that may be collected eventually is a penalty paid by the debtor for delay in discharging the debt and is income to the recipient for the period covered by the delay.

The argument for a deduction of an allowance for the hazard that the debt may not be collected is in theory equally clear, for no purchaser would pay the face amount of all debts without making such a deduction; and therefore the deduction is necessary in determining the equivalent in cash of the receivable created. Recognition of the validity of this reasoning no doubt accounted for the early departure from the rule that reserves were not permissible deductions for tax purposes, and the making of an exception in the case of a reserve for bad debts based on experience and honest judgment.

A rule or principle cited by the Institute Committee in its letter of September 22, 1932 (Appendix to Chap. IV), declared that "profit is deemed to be realized when a sale in the ordinary course of business is effected, unless the circumstances are such that the collection of the sale price is not reasonably assured." This statement implicitly applies the rule of cash equivalence but recognizes that there are cases in which the creation of an account receivable is not a reasonable equivalent of a receipt in cash. The outstanding case in this category is that of sale on the instalment basis, and an elaborate special method of accounting has been developed for the allocation of gain on such sales according to the time when collections are made. In practice, the application of the deferred profit method involves so many assumptions and apportionments in respect of expenses more or less closely related to the gross profit deferred, that the system does not produce a satisfactory result.

There is much to be said for approaching the problem from the point of view of estimating the fair cash equivalent of sales collectively on the basis of experience tables and taking credit at the time of the sale on the basis of the equivalent so determined. Some corporations have adopted this practice in their own accounting but, in the hope of saving or at least deferring the payment of taxes, have adopted, for tax purposes the deferred profit concept sanctioned by the Revenue Act. As a result, they have brought into their corporate income account profits the taxes on which are deferred to future years. The proper treatment of taxes in such circumstances is a question of great difficulty, upon which there is much difference of opinion. Many if not most companies engaged in instalment selling have in the past made reserves in respect of the taxes deferred; but as tax rates have risen and war conditions have supervened, the estimation of future taxes has become an almost insoluble problem. This is one of the most important phases of the general problem of the treatment of taxes where a corporation employs different methods in its own corporate financial accounting from those employed in making tax returns, which will be considered in a future chapter.

Another element in the determination of the cash equivalent of an account receivable may be a guarantee covering a period of months or years which is sometimes given in respect of goods sold. The cash equivalent doctrine would seem clearly to justify and require the establishment of a reasonable reserve for the cost of making good on such guarantees, both for general accounting purposes and in the determination of taxable income arising at the time of sale.

CHAPTER XI

Liabilities

IN THIS CHAPTER heading, "Liabilities" is used in the same sense in which it is used at the head of one side of a balance sheet. Once more it is necessary to explain that the accounting and colloquial uses of a word are not the same. The Institute, as it faced the problem of defining the word "liabilities" when used as a balance-sheet heading was forced to the conclusion that it connoted those balances which would be properly carried forward on the closing of books of account kept by double-entry methods—excluding, of course, credit balances, which are deductions from assets. Balances so carried include not only items which constitute liabilities in the popular sense of debts or obligations (including provision for those that are unascertained), but also credit balances to be accounted for which do not involve the debtor and creditor relation. For example, capital stock, deferred credits to income, and surplus are balance-sheet "liabilities" in that they represent balances to be accounted for by the company, though these are not liabilities in the ordinary sense of debts owed to legal creditors. On the other hand, there are contingent "liabilities" which are not ordinarily carried on books of account, and which appear on balance sheets only in notes if at all.

In discussing this side of the balance sheet it will be convenient to consider, first, long-term bonds and similar obligations, leaving other liabilities and capital stock and surplus for later consideration.

Nothing better illustrates what has been called the cohesiveness of accounting than the fact that many of the considerations which arise in the accounting for fixed property are found to have a bearing, also, on the accounting for long-term borrowings. This fact is not always immediately recognized because, particularly in American thought, discussion of such borrowings is apt to center on their character as debt. But this characteristic, although the simplest and most obvious, offers only a minor problem in the performance of the recording function of accounting. From the standpoint of theory, and of the relation of accounting to the economy, it is more significant that an issue of bonds provides capital than that it creates debt; and as a long-term contract for the use of money it presents even more important and interesting problems.

In studying this as well as other problems already considered, light can be gained from historical review, from comparison with British practice, and from consideration of the subject in relation to three types of enterprises—railroads, other public utilities, and manufacturing and trading concerns.

By far the largest proportion of long-term corporate debt in America is the creation of railroads and public utilities. In England, the corresponding capital is largely represented by irredeemable debentures. There, the double-account system of accounting is in force for such companies. Under that system, capital obligations and fixed property accounts do not appear in what is called the balance sheet but in a "Statement of receipts and expenditures on account of capital," only the balance of which is carried to the balance sheet. This system of accounting rests on the assumption that the enterprises in relation to which it is employed are permanent in character. As a result of the acceptance of this premise, and of the fact that the debt capital is ordinarily not redeemable at a fixed date, the English system does not present the same accounting problems as our railroads and public utilities face.

Another difference between British and American practice which has far-reaching effect is that in England no difference exists between interest and dividends as factors in computing the income-tax liabilities either of corporations or of individuals.[1] Under our income tax law, interest is allowed as a deduction and is therefore taxed only to the holder of the obligation, whereas income which is distributed by way of dividends is the remainder of a gross sum from which tax has been deducted—yet the dividends are again taxed to stockholders on precisely the same basis as interest is to bondholders. This distinction has become of crucial importance as tax rates have risen. It is satisfactory to note that there is growing appreciation on the part of economists of widely different schools of thought of the unwisdom of provisions which place equity capital in so much more unfavorable a position than debt capital. The war has accentuated the importance of the point—not only because of the increase in tax rates that have become necessary but because the desirability of encouraging investment in equity capital in the postwar period is manifest.

It is noteworthy that although total interest deductions claimed by corporations in 1939 were, roughly, equal to those claimed in 1922, the deductions by all manufacturing and trading corporations fell during the period from over $800 millions to less than $500 millions. Many companies took advantage of the prosperity of the 1920's to retire debt, and the depression of the 1930's caused many reorganizations which resulted in a reduction of debt. The fall in interest rates during the 1930's led to the refunding of a large amount of debt at lower rates of interest. Doubtless other factors affect the comparison. Withdrawal of the privilege of making consolidated returns means that in 1939 a certain amount of intercompany interest appeared in the returns for that year, the figures corresponding to which were canceled out in the tax returns of 1922.

When everything is taken into consideration it may be said

---

[1] *Vide infra,* p. 219.

that, with the taxation policy putting such a premium on debt financing, it is a tribute to the financial management of manufacturing and trading corporations in general that debt and interest deductions are today as small as they are. It would seem that by and large, managements have realized that the savings, including saving in taxation, in the cost of financing through bonds may be too dearly purchased at the price of the risks which are entailed and which can be avoided by stock financing.

However, with tax rates as high as they are today and seem likely to be in the postwar period, a modification of the law which will reduce the incentive to debt financing and afford encouragement to equity capital seems imperative in the postwar tax planning. In the 1942 Act, important new provisions were enacted which encourage the reduction of railroad debt, both through reorganizations and through repurchase of outstanding bonds by continuing corporations. Thus there seems likely to be such a reduction on a large scale, the desirability of which is manifest. A recent synopsis of reorganization schemes approved by the Interstate Commerce Commission shows that under twenty-one plans, roughly $3,000 millions of debt is to be reduced to approximately $1,600 millions, of which less than half is to be fixed-interest-bearing debt. Fixed charges are to be reduced by approximately 70 per cent.[1]

Important questions in American accounting for long-term borrowings arise from three causes. First, there is frequently a difference between the sum borrowed and the sum required to be paid at maturity; in other words, bonds are issued at a discount or, less frequently, at a premium. Secondly, changes in current interest rates may result in borrowing contracts becoming highly disadvantageous, so that refunding is under-

---

[1] "Railroad Reorganizations Under the Bankruptcy Act," W. H. Stevens, *Journal of Business,* Vol. XV, pp. 205–61.

taken. Thirdly, an impairment of the value of enterprises may make possible redemption of debt at large discounts.

When bonds are issued at a discount it is the common practice to record the par value among the liabilities and to deal with the discount on the asset side of the balance sheet. Some accountants argue that just as accounting for assets is conducted on the basis of cost, so only the amount received by way of loan should be recorded on the books of account when the loan is made, and that the par value should appear merely in an explanatory note on the balance sheet. The existing practice is, however, so well established that today more inconvenience than advantage would result from the adoption of these views, even if there were general acceptance of them within the profession, which there certainly is not.

At the same time it may be well to point out that so long as accounting is based, as corporate accounting normally is, on an implicit assumption of continued solvency, the principal sum that has to be paid at some future date may be the least significant element of the contract. The amount of the annual payments (or coupon interest) called for, the rights of the lender in case of default and the extent of the borrower's privilege to terminate the contract in advance of maturity, may all be more practically important than the obligation to pay a sum of money at maturity, and this is more likely to be true the longer the term of the bond. In the early part of the century it was common for railroads to issue bonds with a maturity of one hundred years. If we assume a bond, such as the Louisville & Nashville Railroad Company 5 per cent bonds of 1903, due in 2003, to be sold at par, so that the true interest rate is 5 per cent, then according to the actuarial tables, the value that attaches to the right to receive 2½ per cent of par semiannually accounts for more than 99¼ per cent of the value of the contract to the lender, and the right to receive 100 per cent of par at maturity has a present value of less than ¾ of one per cent.

Fifty years ago it was the common practice if bonds were sold at a discount below the par value to record them as liabilities at par and to charge the discount to a capital asset account. Discussions preceding the adoption of the first Interstate Commerce Commission classification of accounts (1906) brought recognition of the fact that discount is a part of the cost of the use of money during the term of the bond and is as properly chargeable against income as the nominal interest coupons.

This view, however, was regarded by many as somewhat academic, and it was generally accepted as a permissible, and, indeed a praiseworthy course, to charge the discount immediately to surplus account, leaving only the nominal interest to be charged annually in the measurement of income. As the emphasis in accounting shifted from the older uses to the newer use of measuring earning capacity, it became recognized that this procedure might be seriously misleading. Certainly it was so in cases in which repeated refinancings were effected, and in each case discounts were incurred which were charged directly to profit and loss (surplus) and never reflected in the income account. Today, it is the generally accepted view that the entire cost of money should be shown in the income account and that therefore discounts should be amortized by charges against income account rather than written off in lump sums to surplus account. However, the Interstate Commerce Commission classification still sanctions the latter course.

A theoretical question of great interest, often ignored, is the proper treatment of bonds issued for property or assumed in connection with purchases of property. Accounting generally has proceeded on the assumption that all these bonds are issued at par, although in some cases the surrounding circumstances, such as the issue of similar bonds for cash at a substantial discount, may suggest that the assumption is unwarranted.

Despite the drastic reduction in fixed charges contemplated

in railroad reorganizations already referred to, many of the new issues will undoubtedly sell on the market at the time of their issue at substantially less than par. They will, however, under the Interstate Commerce Commission rules and classifications, be treated as having been issued at par—an assumption supported by the findings of the Commission that the value of property received is equal to the capitalization authorized. If accounting is to be utilitarian and realistic, this procedure is appropriate. It is difficult to see what practical purpose would be served by treating bonds issued in the reorganizations as having been issued at a discount which must be amortized over the term thereof.

It is difficult to reconcile theory and practical common sense if the view is insisted upon that for all purposes value is to be determined by discounting the yield estimated to be received in the future. But reconciliation is made easier by acceptance of the view adopted by the Supreme Court in its decisions approving some of the plans,[1] that value may have different meanings and be differently determined for different purposes. The practical difficulties encountered in applying the discount theory of value have been discussed in Chapter V and in the appendix thereto.

A second major accounting question in relation to long-term debt arises when the borrowing contract becomes disadvantageous. Such a situation presents points of resemblance to the case discussed in Chapter IX of fixed property which has become obsolete or obsolescent.

Obviously changing conditions may make extremely burdensome a long-term contract which confers a right and creates an obligation. It was in this way that the depression most seriously affected chain-store companies which had entered into long-term leases at high rentals. This will happen to an

---

[1] Cf. *Chicago, Milwaukee & St. Paul Railroad Company* reorganization case, decided Mar. 15, 1943.

issue of long-term bonds if interest rates decline greatly. Frequently, a corporation borrows at a high rate, either because the going rate of interest is high or because its own credit is not such as to enable it to secure a favorable rate. Some years later, a fall in interest rates or an improvement in its credit may bring about a situation in which it would be able to secure a new and much more advantageous contract if free to do so. The position at such a time has, from an accounting standpoint, strong points of resemblance to the case in which a company could replace an existing machine with a more efficient one.

We have seen that in the case of a machine it is customary to anticipate a somewhat similar possibility and to provide for obsolescence even before it has become manifest. It is not, however, customary to give accounting recognition to the fact that a contract for the use of money has become burdensome except as that fact is evidenced by positive action to terminate the contract. Corporations normally provide in any long-term borrowing contract for a right to terminate the arrangement in advance of the nominal maturity upon specified terms. The proper accounting treatment where this right is availed of and a contract that has become burdensome is displaced by a new and more advantageous contract, has been the subject of much accounting discussion, particularly in view of the fact that such transactions on a large scale have taken place in the last decade. At first sight, it would seem clear that the cost of terminating a contract that has become burdensome should be written off immediately, just as the loss due to the retirement of an obsolete piece of machinery is written off.

But whereas in the case of the physical unit it is customary to anticipate obsolescence, it is not the practice (as already noted) to anticipate the loss that may result from a borrowing contract becoming not merely worthless but burdensome. Hence the plausible argument has been presented that if refunding is not undertaken there is no necessary charge to income or surplus; that refunding in itself is advantageous, and that it is irrational to make a transaction which is admittedly advantageous the cause of a charge to income or surplus which would not otherwise be called for. It is also argued that if the bondholder consented to a modification of the contract by a reduction of the coupon, all other provisions being unaltered, no charge against surplus would be called for, and that none should be necessary if the same result is achieved by refunding instead of by a readjustment of the existing contract.

For these and other reasons, some specious and others more or less plausible, it has become the practice in recent years to recognize that it is permissible on a refunding to deal with the cost thereof (a) as an immediate charge to income or surplus at the date of refunding; or (b) by amortization over a term of years subsequent to the refunding not exceeding the term of the original issue. Whether, if the first alternative is adopted, the charge should be made to the current income account or surplus is a question on which differences of opinion have existed. The American Accounting Association has taken the view that an immediate charge to income is the only correct treatment; the Interstate Commerce Commission has sanctioned the charge to surplus. In general, the Institute has favored the charge to income, though regarding a charge to surplus as permissible if the charge to income would be so great as to produce a distorted impression in the minds of investors as to the results of the corporation's operations for the year.

For income-tax purposes there is no distinction between a charge to income and a charge to surplus, and the tax law recognizes a deduction for a loss on refunding only in the year in which the refunding takes place. Since the effect of a refunding in reducing income tax will be reflected in the income account, and at the present tax levels may be a major fraction of that cost, distortion is today more likely to result from a charge to surplus than from a charge to income. Recognition of this fact, and of the further fact that refundings may be undertaken mainly to secure the benefit of tax reductions, has led the Institute recently to lay new stress on the presumption in favor of a charge to income, and to suggest special safeguards in the case in which a charge to surplus is made without regard to the major saving in income taxes effected. It has expressed the seemingly reasonable view that such happenings should not be so reported as to result in materially larger net income for the year being shown than if the cost of refunding had not been incurred.

The Institute has recognized as permissible the practice of spreading the amortization over the unexpired term of the original issue that has been refunded, provided that nothing should be carried forward beyond the time when the debt is finally extinguished. Others would sanction, and indeed prefer, spreading the charge over the term of the new issue. I am unable to share this view, but the point does not seem to me to be of sufficient importance to warrant an extensive technical discussion. I believe that the time is ripe for limiting the permissible period of amortization to the term in which it can be effected by application of savings resulting from refunding. In the public utility field some further extension of the period may be justifiable if, but only if, the idea of quasi-contract between the utility and the customer is accepted. The case then presented is substantially similar to that discussed in relation to obsolescence of fixed property of utilities (see page 148).

An even more interesting accounting question is presented when long-term bonds are acquired at a price which is less than par, or more exactly speaking, at less than the net balance carried in the financial statement in respect of them (which normally is par less unamortized discount, if any). The proper treatment of this difference, which for convenience may be called the discount on repurchase, should, it would seem, vary according to the circumstances which make reacquisition at a discount possible.

The essential fact is, that reacquisition of a corporation's bonds at a discount may be possible as the result of causes which possess quite different accounting significances. As contracts for the use of money, bonds are dealt in on the exchanges and those of even the most solvent makers fluctuate in price with variations in the going rate of interest and with changes in general financial conditions. When such fluctuations enable an individual or a corporation to derive a net amount from a purchase and sale, in whatever order effected, that sum is in the nature of a gain from a trading transaction. Such a gain is a proper credit to the income, profit and loss, or surplus account of a corporation.

However, it may be possible for a corporation to acquire its bonds at a discount because the value of its enterprise has become impaired. And if no recognition has been given on the books to that impairment, it may be questioned whether it is proper to treat as a credit to either income or surplus the discount on reacquisition that is directly attributable to the impairment. There is not always a precise method by which the discount on reacquisition can be attributed to one or the other of these causes, but this merely means that a problem is presented of the same type that is commonly found in accounting, and that examination of the facts and the exercise of judgment is necessary to determine into which category a particular transaction falls. To say that in the absence of an exact rule for making such allocations the discount should always be treated in one way would be to confess the impotence of accountancy.

A comparison of bond yields at the date of the original issue and at the time of redemption will usually show whether the discounts reflect a change in the yield demanded by investors. In recent years, interest rates have been falling, and the prices of well-secured bonds have therefore been rising.

If in spite of this general condition it has been possible for certain corporations to acquire at substantial discounts, bonds issued prior to the depression, the presumption is almost conclusive that the possibility is attributable to a decline in the value of the enterprise which presumably has not been recorded on the books. In such circumstances, discounts on reacquisition should, it would seem, be carried to a capital adjustment account which should not be classified with surplus.

When write-ups of fixed property were regarded as permissible and even desirable in some cases, the credit arising therefrom was often carried to a capital surplus account. However, the better view came to be that it should go to a capital asset adjustment account, not designated as surplus. There would seem to be even more reason for such a disposition of a discount on the redemption of either bonds or stock which is not attributable to a rise in interest rates. Such an adjustment account should preferably be shown as a deduction from assets rather than as a part of the proprietorship section of the balance sheet. If any intangible assets are carried the credit might properly be applied thereagainst—if not, it could be treated as a deduction from the historical investment figure of fixed property.

The view expressed derives some support from the history of the problem under the tax law and from an English decision which brought the two questions of reacquisition discount and the value of the enterprise together. In *Wall* v. *London and Provincial Trust* [1] it was held that a discount on redemption of debentures could not be made the basis of a dividend if, in fact, the value of the enterprise had fallen to an equal or greater extent. The history of the problem under our tax law affords a number of cases, the decisions in which are not altogether easy to reconcile. Ultimately it was recognized that

---

[1] 2 Ch. 582–1920.

to tax the reacquisition discount as income might be a logical corollary of our system of treating borrowed capital as debt and allowing interest thereon as a tax deduction, but was nevertheless unwise. The taxpayer is, in general, given the alternative of reporting the amount as income or treating it as a reduction from the tax basis of property for the purpose of measuring subsequent profit or loss on sale.

Capital, Surplus and Undivided Profits

"Capital" and "surplus" are both words of ambiguous meaning, and when the two are combined in the expression "capital surplus," a high degree of uncertainty of significance is attained. However, all three expressions are firmly embedded in accounting literature and even in laws, so that it is, perhaps, easier to clarify than to change usage.

This area of accounting is one in which the lawyer, the economist, and the accountant all feel that they have a point of view and a terminology which demand recognition; and few accountants would regard present accounting procedures within it as satisfactory. These procedures suffer from conflicts of laws and legal concepts; from legal fictions, and from legal devices which, if convenient for business purposes, are out of harmony with accounting and economic ideas. They are affected also by the conflict between value and cost as basic accounting concepts and by uncertainties of valuation. With the growth of legal interest in accounting there has come a disposition in some quarters to take advantage of the fact that there cannot be forty-eight sets of accounting rules as there are forty-eight different codes of corporation law. Attempts are being made to call on accounting to unify and reform where legal rules are diverse and unsatisfactory, but difficult to change.

Since accounting is now recognized as utilitarian, writers are apt to postulate rather than demonstrate a usefulness and advance from that point to the conclusion which they favor.

One group proceeds from the assumption that usefulness calls for a careful segregation of values paid in from values created by operations and not distributed. Another finds usefulness in differentiating between amounts legally divisible and those not distributable except in dissolution. A third group regards segregation of contributions by individual classes of stockholders as indispensable. Still another holds that here, as elsewhere, matching transactions in an appropriate manner is the essence of sound accounting, and insists that the choice of transactions to be matched against one another should be based on realities.

The Institute has not yet taken a definite stand on these questions. It has raised the preliminary question whether the word "surplus" has any proper place in accounting, and if so, within what limitations. Following the procedure of comparison with English practice and historical retrospect we may note, first, that the expression "surplus" is unknown to English accounting, and that the general use in American accounting of "earned surplus" as a substitute for the older one of "undivided profits" is a comparatively recent and regrettable change. Paradoxically, it came at a time when the value basis of accounting, which afforded some justification for its use, was giving way to the cost basis, the acceptance of which makes its use inappropriate. A surplus in terms of value is a readily understandable concept; in a cost-profit calculation it has no logical place.

The American Accounting Association in its statement [1] issued in 1941 stressed as a primary objective "an effective distinction between contributed capital and capital accumulated as a result of earnings." As a secondary objective it proposed that where corporation laws permit the payment of dividends from paid-in capital, the extent to which paid-in

---

[1] *Supra*, p. 12.

capital is available for that purpose should be indicated on financial statements. It did not propose to make mandatory the disclosure of the amount of legal capital. Professor Hatfield, in his Dickinson Lectures of 1942, spoke of the segregation of capital accumulated as the result of earnings as "mildly interesting information," and expressed the view that the importance of showing the legal capital could not be over-stressed.

A difficulty in attaining the Association's first objective arises whenever earnings have been capitalized either through a declaration of stock dividends or through other formal actions of directors. In such cases the fact that the sums involved now represent capital which cannot be legally distributed is more significant than the fact that at one time they were undistributed earnings which might legally have been distributed in cash. The minor objective of the Association is not, in practice, attainable, since in most of the jurisdictions in which paid-in capital is available for distribution the amount so available is determinable by a process of valuation and not by a system of accounting based in the main on cost.

Undoubtedly legal capital, originally designed as a substantial safeguard to creditors, has now become in many states little more than a legal fiction. Protection for creditors and senior securityholders is provided, not through this device but through other means, such as restrictions on distributions contained in the sections of the corporate charter relating to preferred stocks, in trust deeds, or in other forms of contract. Despite this fact, the legal capital is in many cases a fact of major significance, and it would seem to be undesirable for accountants to undertake to decide in what cases it should be ignored. It would seem to be preferable to clarify what is sometimes called the proprietorship section of the balance sheet so as to show separately (a) capital legally restricted as to distribution; (b) paid-in capital not so restricted; and

(c) the amount of profits retained in the business without having been formally capitalized or permanently dedicated to capital uses.

One difficulty that stands in the way of securing the use of appropriate designations for such classifications is the fact that the dividend laws of many states have been revised so as to prohibit distributions; particularly distributions to common stockholders, except out of "earned surplus," and it is convenient in the case of companies incorporated in these states to use classifications which are significant in relation to the terms used in the law.

The term "capital surplus" has in the past been used to describe two materially different accounting concepts: first, the excess of capital values paid into a company on an issue of capital stock over the legal capital created by the issue; and, second, unrealized appreciation in the value of the fixed properties or, as they are sometimes called, the capital assets of a corporation.

In the first case, the term is used to describe what is, from an economic standpoint, capital; in the second case, it is applied to an unrealized gain which some economists would regard as a part of income. Since the distinction between capital and income is of great importance in accounting, this dual use has led to much confusion and error. In the decade following the first world war, capital surpluses created through revaluation of properties were used to absorb losses and charges of a special character which would otherwise have gone into the income account. Towards the end of the decade, however, this practice was generally questioned. When the Committee of the Institute in 1932 undertook to set forth accounting principles then generally accepted, it included among the number the rule:

Capital surplus, however created, should not be used to relieve the income account of the current or future years of charges which would otherwise fall to be made thereagainst.

The Committee recognized that losses and shrinkages of capital were frequent, and that reorganizations in order to make a new start were expensive and troublesome. With this thought in mind it suggested that the rule laid down should be subject to an exception; that where, upon reorganization, a reorganized company would be relieved of charges which would require to be made against income if the existing corporation were continued, it might be regarded as permissible to accomplish the same result through what has come to be called "quasi-reorganization." This proposal was conditioned on the facts being as fully revealed to and the action being as formally approved by the shareholders as in a formal reorganization. For a time it was thought by some that a corporation might go through a process of quasi-reorganization and still carry forward an earned surplus; but it is clear that this was not contemplated by the Committee in 1932, and the point was expressly covered in Accounting Research Bulletin No. 3 of the Institute, issued in September, 1939.

A legal procedure, by which a part of the capital values paid in is available for distribution to stockholders, has only a very limited justification. Some such arrangement may be desirable to permit dividends to be paid, particularly on preferred stocks during the early days of a corporation, before the first formal determination of profits has been made. A wider use of the capital surplus so created is sometimes defended on the ground that stockholders need current distributions on their holdings, and that their needs should be met, if this is possible, without injustice to creditors.

Such an argument implies a very different concept of the nature of a dividend from that formerly entertained. It is probably not practicable to limit the existing legal rights to make distributions, granted under the corporate laws of the various states. The alternative seems to be to require a clear declaration of the source from which dividends are paid in the case of all corporations whose securities are offered on the markets. Such a requirement seems to be called for on two grounds. In the first place, in the present circumstances there is, as stated in an earlier chapter, no conclusive presumption that a dividend is a proper credit to the income account of the recipient; and stockholders, particularly corporate stockholders, should receive sufficient information in regard to dividends to enable them to determine the proper accounting treatment thereof in the light of the circumstances attending their own ownership. In the second place, dividends are important for the implications to which they give rise as well as for other reasons, and sufficient information regarding a dividend should be given to avoid erroneous inferences being drawn from the fact of its declaration, at least by those who take advantage of the information that is available.

The legal rule which permits the treatment of only a part (possibly an insignificant part) of the capital paid in for stock, as legal capital, presents problems and is open to the gravest abuses where stock is issued as a so-called stock dividend. Perhaps no single practice which developed during the Stock Exchange boom of the 1920's was more far-reaching in its ill effects than that of declaring stock dividends, which involved the capitalization of an amount of earnings that was small in proportion to the market value of the shares of capital stock distributed. Through the pyramiding of holding companies and the practice of treating such stock dividends as income to the full extent of the market value of the shares distributed, spirals of so-called earnings and market values were generated which reached fantastic proportions. A "stock dividend of 10 per cent" in respect of which a dollar of earnings was capitalized, might bring to the investor stock which he could sell (at $20 per share) for $2. On the theory that this was income yielded by the original stock outstanding, the market price per share of the stock might rise to $25. In that case, by a parity of reasoning the next "10 per cent" dividend would be worth $2.50, and a further rise to $31.25 per share thus be deemed warranted, and so on.

Before the break in the stock market in 1929, a special committee of the New York Stock Exchange, though "finding no certain guide in generally accepted accounting principles," concluded that the procedure was indefensible. In a report dated September 4, which was adopted by the Committee on September 11, 1929, the Committee made a specific recommendation requiring that companies having listing agreements with the Stock Exchange, which treated stock dividends as income, should be required to include in their income account in respect thereof sums not exceeding the dollar value per share at which such dividends had been charged to the income account or earned surplus account of the paying companies. Many companies not subject to the jurisdiction of the Exchange continued the unsound practice of treating the dividends as income to the full market value of the shares received until the collapse of values in the depression demonstrated the unsoundness of the practice. Today, periodical stock dividends are relatively uncommon. However, it is desirable to emphasize the unsoundness of the procedure discussed, since in a recent dissenting opinion of the Supreme Court [1] at least some degree of approval was given to the view that market value of stock received by way of stock dividends was a measure of income that could fairly be subjected to tax.

It is now the settled accounting view that transactions in a company's own stock do not result in a proper credit to income or earned surplus. The opposite view was long held by accountants and lawyers, whose opinions were entitled to respect. In England, the question may be said to be answered before it arises, since a purchase by a company of its own capital stock with a view to resale is there held to be a reduction of capital that is not effected in conformity with law

---

[1] *Griffiths* v. *Helvering*, 308 U.S. 355.

and is therefore illegal. The American rule that a purchase may be made only out of surplus accepts the same underlying concept that the purchase results in a reduction of capital—not in the creation of an asset. It would seem to follow that the subsequent sale must be regarded as a new creation of capital—not as the realization of an asset.

Acceptance of the view that accounting is utilitarian, and that usefulness must be judged from a broad social and economic point of view as well as in relation to legal and accounting concepts, lends support to the proposition that trading by a corporation in its own stock does not produce income. It seems doubtful whether such trading should not be prohibited, in justice to individual traders in the market. Except in the case of Investment Trust companies, to which the prohibition is applied, the New York Stock Exchange has contented itself with urging corporations not to trade in their own shares and requiring prompt reports of any transactions, with an implication that if the reports indicated that the practice was resulting in abuse, the Exchange might take further steps. If trading in its own stock could result in income, a practice that is socially undesirable would be encouraged, especially as in many cases a corporation finds itself in a position to purchase its own stock at such a price that if resale at a profit proves impossible, retirement can be effected and produce a credit to capital surplus.

The accounting treatment of premiums and discounts on redemption of stock presents a number of points of general interest. As has been pointed out in the discussion of the redemption of long-term bonds, the considerations applicable differ according to the circumstances of the transaction. It cannot be lightly assumed that the credit resulting from a purchase at a discount should go to the same account as a charge in respect of a redemption at a premium.

The treatment of premium on redemption of a preferred stock has been under consideration by the Securities and

Exchange Commission and the Committee on Accounting Procedure of the Institute, but no release or bulletin has been issued by either. In the discussion of the problem, the Commission has suggested that accounting "calls for recognition of the classification of shares in respect of the . . . contributions in excess of legal capital." Professor Frank P. Smith, at one time associated with the Commission, in an article published in the *Journal of Accountancy* of August, 1941, stated the proposition as being that "each class of stockholders can fairly expect that the equity accounts which represent their contributions will remain intact except as liquidating payments may be charged against such accounts," and that "the corporation is bound by the tenets of accounting theory to maintain a careful distinction between equity balances originating from the different classes of stock issues."

The contentions so advanced raise the question how far accounting theory can be regarded as possessing an authority superior to rules established by law. It must be admitted that accounting is a utilitarian art and not a science, the laws of which are necessarily controlling—like the law of gravity. Therefore, while proven utility should be at least persuasive if not determinative in the general area of the measurement of profits, the authority of accounting can hardly be claimed to extend into the area in which the rights of persons are established by legal contracts under general laws. Within this area accounting should not claim an authority to lay down mandatory rules that go beyond the terms of the contracts and the provisions of any overriding law, though it may properly plead for and encourage desirable practices. However, there is no evidence to show that such a rule as Professor Smith suggests would produce useful results or operate in the best interests of stockholders. It would not seem, therefore, that there should be any tenet of accounting that would impose on the corporation the obligation suggested by him, and certainly no such tenet is now generally accepted.

In support of Professor Smith's view, an analogy is sometimes sought from partnership accounting.[1] This analogy fails to give the support desired. For, suppose that a special partner in a firm has a capital of $1,000,000 on which he is entitled to draw 7 per cent annually, and that the active partners have the right to pay off this capital at 110 per cent of par. They find someone willing to provide the funds to buy out the special partner and step into his position except that the newcomer will be content with 5½ per cent on the capital of $1,000,000 instead of 7 per cent. They offer the existing partner the choice of changing the contract so that he will receive only 5½ per cent, or of having his capital replaced. It can scarcely be argued that the undivided profits of the firm are affected, whichever election the special partner makes.

Practicing members of the Institute's Committee on Accounting Procedure have rejected the proposition advanced by Professor Smith without a dissenting voice. I believe it is the general view that where, for instance, a preferred stock is retired at a premium through the issue of a new preferred stock at the same premium, made for the purpose, there is and should be no accounting requirement which would compel the premium paid to be charged to earned surplus and the premium received to be credited to a capital surplus account. Such a rule would be particularly inappropriate where the corporation is formed under laws which permit dividends to be paid out of capital surplus. If, for instance, it be assumed that the corporation has no earned surplus brought forward from an earlier year but earns in the current year $100,000, receives a premium of $100,000 and pays a premium of the same amount, and also pays a dividend of $50,000—all as permitted by law—what could justify the accountant in insisting that the premium paid must be deemed to have been paid out of earnings, and the dividend out of the premium received?

---

[1] Cf. H. T. Scovill, *Accounting Review*, Vol. XII, p. 265 (1940).

Where a preferred stock is retired by an issue of common stock made for the purpose, at a premium equal to or exceeding that paid on the redemption of the preferred stock, there would seem to be no reason to require the latter to be charged against earned surplus at any time.

While it is difficult to find either in reason or in authority support for a rule that all premiums paid should be charged either against premiums received on the same class of stock or against earned surplus, there are many cases in which the premium should be so charged as a matter of sound business practice. Indeed, many accountants would probably be willing to approve a rule that the presumption is in favor of the charge being made to earned surplus, provided that the presumption is regarded as rebuttable by evidence that the premium was in fact, and with the approval of stockholders, paid out of available capital surplus, and that to require it to be charged to earned surplus would produce an unwarranted hardship to stockholders, or cause other inequities.[1]

The treatment of contingent obligations in balance sheets may conveniently be discussed in this chapter. Since such obligations are frequently spoken of as contingent liabilities and one side of the balance sheet is usually headed "Liabilities," the criticism is sometimes offered that accounts are defective unless all contingent liabilities are shown on the balance sheet. But as has been pointed out, the word "liabilities," used as a balance-sheet heading, is a word of art. It is used to describe not only items which constitute liabilities in a popular sense, but also credit balances which do not involve the debtor-creditor relation. On the other hand it excludes, and rightly excludes, most of those obligations which are commonly referred to as "contingent liabilities." In many

---

[1] While this volume has been in the press, SEC Accounting Release No. 45 has been issued in which the subject is dealt with along the lines anticipated. A subcommittee of the Institute's Committee on Accounting Procedure has indicated that it is not in agreement with the conclusions reached in that release.

cases, if a contingent liability became enforceable an asset would be simultaneously created. If, therefore, the contingent liability were recorded it would be necessary, also, to record the asset, and the result would be to inflate the balance sheet with potential liabilities on the one side and potential assets on the other, to such an extent as to impair its meaning. Indeed, these considerations afford another indication of the technical character and limited significance of the balance sheet and of the impossibility of presenting all the elements of the financial position of a corporation which is conducting a complex enterprise, in a single financial statement.

Certain contingent liabilities are, however, properly recorded in notes on balance sheets or in schedules supplementary thereto. These include what may be called "contingent capital liabilities," such as long-term leases and guarantees, and also current contingent obligations to the extent that they appear to be burdensome—as, for instance, the commitments discussed in Chapter X. The amount of bills receivable discounted is commonly shown on balance sheets even though recourse to the discounter is regarded as improbable. It is an element in the relation between current assets and current liabilities to which importance is generally attached.

Cases in which it is uncertain whether a liability exists or not require individual consideration in the light of the principle that those to whom accounts are furnished are entitled to be advised of material financial facts in relation to the corporation.

CHAPTER XII

Income

THE GROWTH OF INTEREST in accounts as a guide to the value of securities has resulted in increased importance being attached to the income account, but it has not led to as extended and careful a study of the form and content of that account as might have been expected. It has brought recognition of the importance of the allocation of credits and charges as between income and surplus, but other questions in this area have received relatively little consideration.

Once the view is accepted that the most important statement is that which discloses the amount and sources of income, the next step is to recognize that all kinds of income do not possess the same significance. It becomes necessary to analyze the elements of income, positive and negative, and to allocate them to categories with greater care and refinement than in the past.

In Chapter II it was explained that under a double entry bookkeeping system income may be measured either by a comparison of successive balance sheets or by an analysis of transactions, one method being used as a check on the other. Problems which affect the measurement and allocation of primary income have been discussed in earlier chapters in relation to various balance-sheet items. Here, the accounting for investment income will be considered, and also some more general questions in relation to income.

There is a vital distinction between primary income, such as that which is derived from trade, manufacture, or services, and investment income, such as interest and dividends, which represents a transfer of income from one corporation to another. The growth of intercorporate security holdings during the present century has increased the practical importance of this distinction. Further, what is transferred may represent income from a first charge, like interest on a bond, or income from an equity, like a dividend on common stock. The relation between the amount of the income stream and its capital value may vary widely according as it is one or the other.

Still another distinction is that between investment income —which represents a transfer of primary income earned by another corporation—and gains or losses which reflect changes in the capital value of rights to income. The process of multiplying income per share in order to arrive at a capital value is obviously not applicable to income which itself represents a change in the capital value of an income stream. Corporate securities are often if not, indeed, generally held with a dual purpose or expectation. The first is that transfers of income will be received in the form of dividend or interest; the second is that a gain on sale may be realized. This gain may arise from retentions of profit by the corporation whose stock is sold, or it may represent profits of quite another nature and significance.

The Investment Company Act of 1940 makes a distinction between income from interest and dividends, and capital gains. However, the problem of differentiation is much more difficult than a mere separation of this kind. There is need for a penetrating analysis and classification of investment income similar to that which has been undertaken in the field of cost accounting.

The foundation for a study lies in recognition of a few simple truths. The first is, that the source of real investment income is the earning of a profit by the corporation in which the investment is held. A second is that there is no medium for passing losses on to the stockholder comparable to the dividend by which profits are passed on. A third is, that a classification, to be really useful, must be based on essential characteristics and not on mere names. Interest and dividends are not homogeneous classifications, especially in view of the variety of dividend laws of our states and the infinite variations of dividend practice and of types of interest-bearing securities. And capital gains may have widely different significances according to the causes that give rise to them.

The nature of a payment to its corporate payor is not necessarily decisive as to its proper treatment by the payee. This point is particularly important where the investor has acquired his securities at a large premium or discount, as compared with the price at which they were issued by the corporation and enter into its accounting.

A dividend is not always, though it is normally a proper credit to the income account of a corporate investor. It may have been paid not out of profits but out of capital in excess of legal capital. Even if it has been paid out of profits, those profits may have arisen before the corporate recipient acquired any stock. In the latter case, it will be taxable income to the corporation, and reasonably so because the law manifestly cannot undertake to discriminate between stockholders, and a purchaser may fairly be regarded as stepping into the shoes of his predecessor in respect of taxation as in other respects. But each stockholder can and a corporate stockholder, at least, should deal with dividends in its own accounts according to the special circumstances of its own investment.

A sound general rule is that, in order to justify a credit to income in respect of dividends, it must appear that the paying corporation has both earned and paid during the investing corporation's ownership of the stock sums equal to the rate of dividend for which credit is proposed to be taken. Of course, this rule is not to be enforced rigorously in respect of normal dividends on relatively small holdings, but where either the dividend is extraordinary or the holding is large, reasonably conservative accounting seems to call for application of such a test.

Where an investor corporation has paid a premium for capital stock, sound accounting may call for amortization of that premium out of the gross income received in the form of dividends.

A corporation in which stock is held may not distribute all its profits, or it may make a loss. If the corporation makes a loss, no part thereof is passed on to the stockholders as profits are passed on. Some recognition of losses would, however, seem to be called for in the accounting for current income of the investor corporation unless they are inconsiderable. Where an investor corporation holds a number of stocks the share of undistributed profits attributable to the stocks held in some companies may exceed the share of losses attributable to stocks in others. In such a case, an offset may properly be recognized. If this is not the case, and if the share of losses is substantial, a reserve therefor should be charged against current income account of the corporate stockholder. The corporations which have made losses may later earn profits which will offset them. In that event, the reserve made by the corporate stockholder will become unnecessary and the amount thereof may be retransferred to income. The credit is properly made to income rather than to surplus because it is the current earning of profit by the corporation in which stock is held that justifies the transfer.

It is not customary to treat income from dividends as accruing from day to day, even on preferred stocks. They are governed by the rule that income is realized gain. The treatment of interest and rents as an exception to this rule is of doubtful wisdom but has a legal justification and a long historical record to support it. In England, interest appears to have accrued from day to day at common law and therefore to have been apportionable in respect of time. Rent was placed on the same basis by statute in 1738, and it was nearly one hundred years thereafter before any additions were made to the list. In English estate practice the procedure today is regulated by the Apportionment Act of 1870, which provides that all rents, annuities, dividends, and other periodical payments in the nature of income shall, "like interest on money lent," be considered as accruing from day to day and shall be apportionable in respect of time accordingly.

In American estate accounting, also, interest is, but dividends are not, in general, apportionable; and, under the income-tax regulations, where returns are made on an accrual basis interest may be treated as accruing from day to day but dividends do not become income until after they have been formally declared by directors.

It is true that interest and rents differ from dividends in that they are legally due and payable whether the debtor has or has not income out of which to pay them, and that no action by the debtor is necessary to create the creditor's right to receive them. But when interest and rents are paid currently it is almost immaterial whether they are treated by corporations as income when they accrue or when they are received. Once default has occurred the latter course is preferable. Today, there is much to be said for removing the exception to the rule of corporate accounting that income is realized gain that now exists with respect to interest and rents. The distinction between interest and dividends is at times unsubstantial. An extreme case is presented by an issue of debentures which has been listed on the New York Stock Exchange for nearly fifty years, the holders of which are entitled as a class to receive by way of interest the corporation's earnings in excess of 5 per cent on its capital stock. When this issue was originally listed, the chairman of the Exchange committee inquired why the security was called a debenture, and was told by counsel for the corporation that the designation had been chosen because it was one term used in corporate finance which did not seem to have a very definite significance, so that any holder of the security would have to refer to the instrument itself to ascertain his rights. While this case is exceptional, there are many issues of income bonds which are comparable to preferred stocks and the number of such issues will be increased as railroad reorganization plans now in progress are finally consummated.[1]

An interesting phase of accounting for interest and dividends has been presented in relation to the determination of income from defaulted bonds of railroads in receivership. In recent years it has been possible to purchase such bonds with large arrears of interest accrued upon them, at small fractions of their par value. In some instances improved earnings due to war conditions have brought substantial interest payment on these bonds. In November, 1942, the Securities and Exchange Commission issued a release dealing with a case in which bonds with defaulted coupons attached, amounting to 25 per cent of par, had been bought at 26 per cent of the par value and shortly thereafter the purchaser had received an interest payment equal to 4 per cent of par on account of defaulted interest coupons covering a period prior to its purchase of the bonds.

The Chief Accountant of the Commission held that the interest received in the case mentioned should be treated as a reduction of the cost of the investment; that further collections in respect of either the principal or the defaulted interest at the date of purchase should be applied against the purchase price, and that if and when they should exceed this price the excess should be treated as a capital gain on securities and not as interest. On the other hand, he held that interest covering the period subsequent to the purchase might be treated as interest income unless the circumstances of the particular case should be such as to indicate that recovery of the cost

---

[1] See, also, refunding of preferred stock with interest bonds of Armour & Company, May, 1943.

of the investment was so uncertain as to make it necessary to treat the payment as a reduction of the investment.

This release was not discussed in advance with any committee of the Institute, and while probably accountants would agree with the decision as to the treatment of the specific receipt which led to the release, it may be doubted whether this is true of the more general application of the views expressed.

The question here raised is worth discussion, not only on its own account but because it involves a fundamental issue which is the converse of one discussed in the preceding chapter. There it was suggested that often the difference between transactions to which the same name is given may be more significant for accounting purposes than their points of resemblance; here the question is raised whether the points of resemblance between the case of a defaulted bond and a stock are not more significant than the difference in name and precise legal rights in the two cases.

The case which has been discussed may be usefully considered in comparison with one in which a year's dividends are received annually on a preferred stock on which large arrears have accrued or one in which several years' arrears of dividends are received by a recent purchaser.

The release, except as to its final proviso, follows the rule that is adopted under the tax law. Under that law, preferred stock dividends are treated as income whenever received and it would not be safe to assume that the Commission would follow the tax rule in that case, also. As already suggested, the tax rule on dividends seems justifiable on the theory that a purchaser steps into the shoes of his predecessor for tax purposes. And while in the case of a bond not in default the vendor, not the purchaser, pays tax on the interest accrued at the date of transfer, this is not so in the case of defaulted bonds. It might therefore be logical in taxation to apply the dividend rule to interest received by the purchaser in such cases.

It seems a legalistic rather than an accounting approach to make the period covered by the coupon required to be surrendered determinative of an accounting disposition of an amount received, without regard to the time when the income was earned which made the payment possible, or to the amount of interest accrued during the period of ownership. The suggestion advanced earlier in this chapter in relation to dividends might well be applied to interest in the case under consideration. This would mean that to the extent that an amount of interest had accrued, had been earned, and had been paid during the ownership of the bond, it would be a proper credit to income account in the category in which dividends and interest are included, and not a capital gain.

Conservatism similar to that reflected in the release might conceivably call for the additional proviso that the credit should only be made to income if the recovery of the principal of the investment seemed reasonably assured at the time it was taken. But the appropriateness of such a rule might be questioned unless it were given much wider application—as, for instance, to cases of bonds not in default but selling at large discounts, such as a 5 per cent bond selling at 50 per cent of par value. Moreover, there is something incongruous about the application of rules founded in conservatism to the accounting for operations which are of a consciously speculative character.

Ultimately, the concept of investment income is a highly subjective one. In general, neither accounting practice nor the tax law takes account of the speculative and possibly short-lived character of income or of the probable ultimate fate of the investment. The release seems to be open to the criticism that it strives to give speculation the character of investment and thus, perhaps, encourages what might better be discouraged.

In cases involving the question whether the same persons were in control of a corporation before and after reorganization the Supreme Court has accepted the view that in certain circumstances bondholders may be in control before the transaction and virtually occupy the position of stockholders. This ruling may evidence some relaxation of the rigid legal distinction between bonds and stocks. The provision of the 1942 tax law that dividends on certain preferred stocks of utility companies shall be allowed as a deduction from surtax income tends in the same direction. There would seem, therefore, to be strong arguments for assimilating the treatment of dividends and interest in the accounting for investment income.

Capital gains and losses present a difficult accounting problem because of the diversity of the causes which produce them. Four principal causes must be recognized in the case of holdings of capital stock: first, retention of profits by the corporation whose stock is held; second, appreciation in the value of the enterprise of the corporation whose stock is held, either as the result of increased earning capacity or otherwise; third, a lowering in the rate of return on the basis of which the capital value of the stock is fixed by the market; fourth, an increase in monetary value due to depreciation in the monetary unit in which the value of the stock is expressed.

Capital losses may result from causes which are the opposite of those which produce gain; however, the important point already mentioned requires recognition in respect of the first of such items. If a corporation makes profits, a portion—probably a major fraction—of those profits will be received by the investor in the form of dividends and only a residue will be left to be reflected, perhaps in the form of a capital gain on sale of the stock. On the other hand, if the corporation makes a loss, no part of that loss is passed on to the stockholder currently—instead, it is left to be offset perhaps by later profits or perhaps realized as a capital loss. Recognition of this difference is essential to a just appreciation of the significance of income accounts in which dividends are treated as income, but in which capital gains and losses are not included and the undistributed profits and losses of the corporations whose stocks are held are ignored.

The importance of this point becomes apparent upon an examination of the accounting of some of our large railroad companies. In January, 1940, a single railroad company made a reserve of $150,000,000 to cover prospective losses that had been accumulating on investments and advances over a period of years.

The practice of submitting consolidated accounts possesses, amongst other advantages, the merit that it resolves investment income into its constituent elements and automatically brings losses of subsidiary companies into account. Where railroads have followed this policy the inaccurate reflection of investment income in the parent company's accounts is of less significance than where only the parent company or partially consolidated accounts are presented, as in the case of some of our important systems.

Whether capital gains and losses should enter into the determination of income at all is a question which has been much debated, and on which English and American opinions differ. The answer is, perhaps, that no universal rule can be laid down because of the variety of causes which give rise to such gains and losses and because, also, of the difference in uses for which accounts are required. My own preference would be, as the foregoing discussion has indicated, for a rule which would exclude gains and losses from income accounts except where they could be shown or fairly be presumed to result from causes the effects of which it is generally regarded as desirable to reflect in concepts of income. Capital gains which might be deemed to have their origin in accumulation of undistributed profits, excessive charges for depreciation, and the like would be recognized as income. Similarly, losses which might appear to be due to accumulations of operating losses by a corporation whose stock is held, or to inadequate depreciation, would be reflected as charges to the income account. Gains or losses which might be attributable to changes in interest rates or in the amount of an income stream would be excluded. Gains or losses due to a change in price level would probably also be excluded. Gains in terms of money which reflect nothing more than a change in the price level are at times reflected in operating income to a very considerable extent; but this is recognized as a regrettable necessity, and efforts are constantly being made to minimize the extent of such inclusions, a striking illustration being the use of the base stock, or LIFO, method of inventorying discussed in Chapter X.

Difficulties in applying the theory outlined would arise especially where different forces might be operating in opposite directions; but whenever the distinction might be important it should not be impossible to formulate reasonable working rules to attain results that would be preferable to treating all capital gains and losses as if they were homogeneous.

A further problem in dealing with this question is, that the significance of the distinction between realized and unrealized gains and losses is not always substantial. If it is desired in effect to maintain the existing position and yet to realize a gain or loss, one security may be sold and a substantially similar one bought in its place. The security sold may even be a bond of one series, and that which is purchased a bond of another series of the same issue. Some have suggested that no loss or gain should be recognized in such cases; but adoption of this suggestion would create more problems than it would solve, and a line would have to be drawn which would have its own defects. As a matter of practical wisdom, the traditional rule that realization is necessary to the recognition of a gain but not of a loss has much to commend it.

In corporate accounting, as in taxation, capital gains and losses constitute a difficult problem, and where they are relatively important, no single figure of income, however computed, is very significant—only an intelligent survey of the accounts as a whole can make it possible to reach a valuable conclusion.

INCOME AND THE COMPENSATION OF MANAGEMENT

The Supreme Court has defined income as the gain derived from capital, from labor, or from both combined. Management is sometimes regarded as a separate source of gain. In a corporation organized on a broad, profit-sharing basis, management and labor may receive a substantial part of their compensation in the form of a share of the gains of the enterprise in excess of a certain minimum reward to those who contribute labor, management, or capital. In the case of management, the principle is applied extensively and in a variety of ways.

When the industrious apprentice achieved final success by becoming a partner, his whole compensation became a share of profits. The position was in law, as in fact, that a new group of enterprisers was formed, and that profits thereafter were measured from the standpoint of that new group. In the private corporation that later developed as the typical form of business organization, he might be given, or allowed to acquire, capital stock which might or might not be a new issue. In either case, the profits thereafter included a new element which had previously been regarded as a cost. No change of enterprisers was recognized, though in fact one might have occurred that was as definite as that resulting from the admission of a new member into a group of partners. In many private concerns the distinction between the compensation of the stockholders for their services in contributions of capital, and their compensation for the contribution of management, was imperfect or not attempted at all.

When the excise tax on corporate income was enacted in 1909, there being no tax on individual income, stockholders in such companies in some cases increased their salaries and drew as compensation for services (which was a charge against revenue), a part of what they had formerly received as dividends. When the effective tax on salaries became more burdensome than the tax on corporate profits, the tendency was reversed. When management and beneficial ownership became separated the problem assumed a new form. It became a common practice, particularly in England, if a private company was converted into a public one, for the new company to make contracts with former stockholder-managers under which they became entitled to compensation for their services on a higher scale than they had received when they had been owners just as much as they were managers. In prospectuses of new companies, past profits were commonly adjusted to reflect the resulting changes in management compensation.

The development of a personal income tax steeply graduated in scale and applied without substantial differentiation to fluctuating income from services and regular income from capital, tended to produce arrangements which further obscured the true distribution of gains between management and capital. Advantageous opportunities to make immediate purchases of capital stock, options to make purchases in the future, and pension schemes, are the most important forms of indirect or postponed compensation, and difficult accounting questions have arisen in relation to each.

If an executive is given $20,000 as additional compensation for the year, and is allowed at the same time to buy 1,000 shares of the corporation's stock of a par value of $10,000, for $30,000, income is reduced by $20,000; capital stock or capital surplus is increased by $30,000. If, instead, he is allowed merely to buy the stock at par, the result to him is the same (except tax-wise); but according to established practice, the earned surplus of the corporation is unaffected and capital stock is increased by only $10,000. Thus, after the transaction has been effected, earned surplus is greater and capital, or capital surplus, less than if the arrangement had taken the other form.

The question may be and, indeed, has been asked whether if the result of the second form of transaction is the same as that of the first, and if accounting is based on substance— not on form—the accounting result reached in the first case should not also be reached in the second. Before attempting to answer this question it is desirable to consider some more complex cases.

Suppose the transaction to relate to a contract for employment over a term of years in the future. Then, if it takes the first form, it would produce not an immediate charge to surplus but a deferred charge to income. An accountant will look with unconcern on a credit to capital surplus offset by a charge to earned surplus, since a transfer from earned to capital surplus can be made at the discretion of the directors even without any reason for it being assigned. He is not so ready to approve a credit to any form of surplus offset by a deferred charge.

A more common form of arrangement involves the grant of an option to buy stock at any time during a prescribed but considerable period at a fixed price that is usually higher than the current market quotation. The underlying idea may be that if the management is successful the capital value as well as the earnings of the corporation will increase, and that the management is entitled to a share of that increment. It may be argued that all the corporation gives up is a share of an increment, and that as the gross increment is not recorded on its books there is no reason why the part of it surrendered ought to receive accounting recognition. It might perhaps be argued, further, that the dual object of the arrangement should be recognized, and that it would be erroneous to charge to income that part of the compensation which was motivated by a desire to bring about an appreciation in capital value, and which involved no cost or sacrifice to the company except in the event that an appreciation should take place.

In general, it is a rule of accounting that no profit is derived from buying, even in cases in which this is obviously not literally true. Therefore, a credit to surplus resulting from a contract for the purchase of future services is one which is not readily acceptable to accountants. From a practical standpoint, the problem of valuing an option which is not transferable is difficult and may be almost insoluble.

It has been shown that the cost of management is not reflected with any precision in the accounts of partnerships and private corporations a point illustrated by comparison between Ford Motor Company and General Motors Corporation. It would seem that the present practice of not attempting to make highly technical adjustments—based, perhaps, on uncertain assumptions and estimates—is warranted. But there may be cases in which the rights granted to management are so substantial, the facts so clear, and the point of such great importance as to require departure from the usual practice.

Another view is taken by some. Professor Paton, in his *Advanced Accounting*, suggests that when an option is granted to an employee, the value of the services rendered should be estimated, a charge to expense of that amount made, and a credit to the option account—the latter to be ultimately transferred to capital stock account if the option is exercised, and if not, to capital surplus. It may be doubted whether this course has been widely, if ever, followed. It avoids the problem of valuing the option but only by creating the probably more difficult one of evaluating the services. Professor Paton makes no distinction between the case in which the option price exceeds the market price of the stock at the date of the grant, and the case where the relation is reversed. In the latter case there is at least the same argument for a charge to income account and a credit to capital surplus, as where stock is sold outright for less than its market value.

Professor Paton's desire to measure the profits to the corporation accurately, is natural, and, as already noted, there will no doubt be cases in which the rights granted to executives, which are not represented by direct cash outlays of the corporation, will be so material that they ought to be reflected in some way in operating expenses, especially for the purposes of a prospectus. The growth of a management class and increased rates of tax on personal income undoubtedly create an incentive to resort to such procedures. However, the principle involved is far-reaching. There have been and still are many corporations whose securities are listed which enjoy the services of stockholder executives for compensation that is but a small fraction of their value. Professor Paton's line of reasoning might lead to the conclusion that in such cases the so-called income of a corporation consists partly of gifts from the executives, and that the point is of major importance where there is a probability that services on such a basis will not be long continued.

The concept of the corporation as an entity different from its stockholders and unaffected by changes in its capital stock or in the ownership thereof, is artificial; and accounting is conventional. There is danger in attempting to refine corporate accounting too highly. The cost rule, which is a vital part of accounting today, is rough and ready but practically useful. Only in exceptional cases is it desirable to introduce into accounts charges against income which represent no actual cost, especially if there is no sacrifice of money or money's worth.

Another form of compensation is the grant of a right to a future pension. The change of social outlook in recent years has had a profound effect on the practice in accounting for pension benefits—an effect that has been stimulated by special provisions written into the Federal income-tax laws. Schemes that constitute binding contracts have been substituted for plans that were in form only voluntary, and there has been a growing acceptance of the view that even voluntary plans are often virtually compulsory, since the consequences of abandonment would be more adverse than those of adherence to them. Accounting should be based on reasonable expectations rather than on theoretical possibilities. Even under a voluntary scheme, therefore, the charges against current income should, it would seem, preferably be based on the assumption that the scheme will be continued in force unless there is evidence to negative such an assumption.

Marked changes in interest rates may create problems in pension accounting similar to those occasioned by pronounced fluctuations in rates of exchange in the accounting for foreign enterprises. The charge against the year should normally be the estimated present value of the future payments incurred. If the protection is not secured through a contract with an insurance company, this involves an assumption as to the future rate of yield on the fund created. A rate may be fixed and may seemingly be made effective by treating the fund as invested in the enterprise and crediting the fund and charging income with interest at the assumed rate. In that case, questions arise how the rate should be determined, and whether it should change with fluctuations in current yields on loans and enterprise investments. The higher the rate of yield that is assumed, the lower becomes the present value of the future obligation. Assumption of a higher rate of yield than is warranted is, therefore, equivalent to throwing forward a part of the pension burden that should be borne by the present.

The question arises what adjustment should be made if the current rate of yield falls. Should the pension computations be revised on the assumption of a lower rate of yield in respect of current and future contributions only, or should that assumption be applied, also, to the fund already accumulated?

It would seem reasonable to treat the fund already accumulated as having been invested at the rate appropriate when the accumulation took place. At this point the problem approaches that of long-time borrowings at rates which have become disadvantageous, which is discussed in Chapter XI. As was there pointed out, it is not customary to give accounting recognition to the view that such contracts have become burdensome; and while it may be suggested that such a policy lacks conservatism, it must be recognized that it is impossible to disassociate the computation of profits and losses, today, from actions taken and obligations assumed in the past.

The same considerations do not apply to the question whether it is permissible to continue to charge currently and assume for the future an interest rate as between the fund and the enterprise which, though reasonable when it was originally established, is higher than present conditions would justify. It seems doubtful whether such a procedure is warranted.

If the amount of pension ultimately payable is a fraction of the compensation received during the last years of service rather than based on the average for the entire term of employment, a rise in the price level reflected in rates of compensation may render accumulated provisions inadequate and the charges necessary to bring them up to a proper level may be burdensome. Considerations such as these have led in recent years to greater care in formulating pension schemes and to a disposition to resort to outside insurance to a greater extent. Liberal provisions in the tax law have encouraged such tendencies and have conduced to the establishment of pension funds on a more satisfactory basis by grants of tax relief in respect of the burdens caused by readjustment.

Income and Income Taxes

The treatment of income taxes in statements of income has become a question of major importance in recent years. Since

1936, the Federal corporate income tax has been completely divorced from the personal income tax, since payment of it affords no relief from taxation to individual stockholders. It is now purely an excise tax. The rates of tax are so high that, today, few transactions outside the regular routine of business are undertaken without prior consideration of their effect on tax liability. This being so, and in view of the importance of a clear presentation of the results of routine business operations, there is a strong case for an allocation of income taxes that will follow the treatment of any unusual charges and credits which affect the amount of tax payable.

The argument is sometimes advanced that although the tax is an excise tax, it is levied in respect of the right to carry on business in corporate form and therefore should be treated as a final deduction in arriving at corporate income. The making of a gain attracts the tax and the making of an offsettable loss will reduce the tax. It should therefore be the treatment of the gains and losses in the corporation's accounting that should govern the treatment of the tax, itself.

Three different phases of the question may be recognized; the first is that in which a subdivision of income is made—as, for instance, between capital gains and losses and other income; the second, that in which credits and charges entering into the determination of the tax are reflected partly in the income account and partly in the surplus account; and the third, that in which charges or credits are reflected in the income account in one period and in tax returns in another.

If the question related to credits or gains only, it would probably give rise to little controversy. Difficulty arises from the cases in which gains in one category are set off for tax purposes against losses or charges in another—as where a capital loss reduces the tax that would be payable on current income from other sources.

Where the question is one of subdivision between categories in the same statement, there would seem to be little objection to allocation of the tax even if it results in a credit against a loss in one category and a charge exceeding the actual tax in another. The income account as a whole will still bear a charge equal to the actual tax paid, and the allocation between categories may result in a statement that is more informative than if the tax were treated as a single deduction.

Such facts as that the tax may be graduated, and that interest may be an allowable deduction, may complicate the apportionment, but the problem thus presented is not essentially different from many encountered and solved in matching costs against revenues. Similar difficulties are met, for instance, in allocating overhead costs and in dealing with cases in which the unit cost of a commodity or service purchased diminishes as the volume of purchases increases.

Most accountants would probably be willing to approve a subdivision of the tax between income account and surplus where gains which give rise to the tax are credited in part to one account and in part to the other. There is, however, evidence of considerable reluctance to take the further step of approving the introduction into the formal income statement of a constructive charge against income for taxes offset by an equivalent credit to surplus where the actual tax has been affected by losses which are charged not against income but against surplus. However, this procedure has been approved by accountants of high standing, and there seems to be a growing recognition that the alternative solution of a footnote is not always an adequate form of disclosure if the amounts involved are substantial.

The reluctance is natural and in harmony with traditional accounting attitudes; but it should yield to the clear demands for the most illuminating presentation, and it should be possible to overcome any objections by careful use of language. If this is deemed impracticable, a change in the form of statement would be justified by the importance of the point in many instances.

In an extreme case, for the purposes of an income tax, which makes no distinction between losses relating to the current and past years, a charge growing out of the past may offset the profits of the present so that no tax is payable. In such a case a figure of net income for the year without any deduction for tax is almost bound to be misleading. It is not an adequate answer to say that the danger of misunderstanding may be mitigated by an explanatory note. Footnotes are, at best, unsatisfactory, and in this instance whatever can be done in a note can be done in a way that will be more helpful to the inexpert reader in the presentation of the statement itself. If there is any justification for making charges to surplus there is an equal justification for taking income tax into account in making the charge. With tax rates as high as they are now, the better course is no doubt to limit severely the charges to surplus account and obviate any such questions as are here under discussion. The same high rates of tax make charging the gross loss to surplus and the reflection of the tax benefit in the income account the less defensible.

In considering the third class of cases a distinction may, perhaps, be drawn between recurrent and exceptional transactions. Such a distinction is realistic, for often the exceptional transaction is actuated either wholly or in part by a desire to effect a reduction in the taxes immediately payable. Where this is so, the treatment of the tax reduction should be closely related to that of the transaction itself.

These considerations seem to be clearly applicable to the case in which discounts and redemption premiums on bonds are carried forward in the corporation's own accounts but taken as an immediate deduction for tax purposes. If the unamortized discount and redemption premium are charged off to income, no problem arises. If they are charged off immediately to surplus, a case in the category just considered is presented, and the net charge to surplus should be no more than the excess of the unamortized discount and premiums over the immediate tax reduction resulting from their being incurred. If any amount is to be carried forward in respect of unamortized discounts and redemption premiums (by an exception to the general rule that ascertained losses should be written off immediately), this amount should likewise not exceed the excess of the discounts and premiums over the tax reduction secured on account thereof.[1]

Turning now to routine transactions and considering, first, cases in which the method used for tax purposes produces the lower immediate tax, it may be proper in determining the treatment to inquire (a) whether the alternative method is acceptable for taxes, (b) whether the choice may fairly be deemed to be determined by a desire to reduce presently payable taxes, and (c) whether there is reasonable ground to expect that the present reduction of taxable income will be offset by equivalent increases in future taxable income.

All three conditions may be said to exist in the case in which a new company takes credit for the full estimated profit on instalment sales in its own accounts but defers a part thereof for tax purposes. Such a case seems to call for the application of the principle that future costs arising out of income-producing transactions should be provided for at the time when the revenue is brought into account. The amount to be provided can fairly be estimated on the basis of the tax law which is in force when the revenue is brought into account, and it should be held to be applied towards the tax in the year in which the deferred profit is reported for tax purposes. In the interim tax rates may have increased greatly, as they have in recent years. In that event, conservatism may call for an increase in the reserve; but it may be doubted whether accounting makes such an increase mandatory.

A case presenting quite different aspects, at one time much discussed, is that of public utilities which adhered to retire-

---

[1] Cf. Bulletin No. 18, American Institute of Accountants.

ment reserve accounting in their own statements but took depreciation deductions for tax purposes. Here, the method employed by the company was in accordance with prescribed accounting classifications but not with tax regulations. There was no reason to suppose that the current allowance of depreciation deductions correspondingly increased taxable income of a future year because the essential difference in the two systems of accounting was that depreciation accounting called for the creation of cumulative reserves greatly exceeding those required under a retirement accounting policy. In this case, therefore, it was generally held that no reserve for a future tax was called for.

Percentage depletion presents, perhaps, an even clearer instance of the same kind, since no difference in accounting theory is involved, the tax allowance being a reflection of a policy that does not have its foundations in accounting.

If a corporation anticipates a charge which for tax purposes is not a current deduction, it is not customary to take into account a possible or even probable reduction in future taxes as an offset to the charge. However, the creation since the outbreak of war of reserves which are not deductible under the tax regulations, for costs or losses which if actually incurred later will be allowable, has lent a new importance to this question. Uncertainty whether there will be otherwise taxable income against which to take the deductions is a part of the problem. The question merges into that of dealing with taxes in cases in which the right to carry losses forward or backward for tax purposes arises and is exercised.

The broad grant of these rights in the Revenue Act of 1942 may be interpreted as a recognition by the Congress of the impracticability of measuring profits annually during the war period with any substantial degree of accuracy. It might be wise for corporations engaged mainly in war activities to accept this view and frankly to abandon the attempt to effect such a measurement. By so doing they would avoid all questions of adjustments between income and surplus in future years. The desired result could be accomplished by presenting annually cumulative totals for the war period and showing the amounts taken into account in earlier years as deductions. The remaining figures would represent the corporation's best estimate for the year, plus or minus revisions of estimates made in earlier years.

The strength of tradition probably makes the extensive adoption of any such procedure improbable. It is more likely that statements in the standard form will be given—accompanied, perhaps, by explanations of the lack of the validity which such statements ordinarily possess.

Efforts to distinguish the results of operations for the year from adjustments arising out of earlier operations have already presented difficulties and given rise to sharp differences of opinion.[1] If the attempt to show income for the year is to be made, and if the tax payable in respect of the year is greatly reduced because of a loss sustained in another year, it would seem that the underlying purpose of financial statements would be best achieved by charging against the income for the year the tax that would have been payable but for the "loss credit" and carrying to surplus account the tax reduction due to that credit.

It may be argued that suffering a loss does not create a right to refund of tax, and that it is the making of a profit that gives effectiveness to the relief provision. And as already noted, there is considerable accounting objection to the charging against income of tax that has not actually been paid. But these arguments do not seem to weigh heavily in the scale against the consideration that to charge only the net tax against income would give a false impression of the result of the year's operation and also of the relation between the corporation's

---

[1] Cf. Annual Report for 1942, Gillette Safety Razor Company.

profits and its financial contribution to the war effort in the form of taxes.

It must be recognized that it is impracticable to deal with every case in which tax practice recognizes charges or credits to income in part or in whole in other periods than those in which they are reflected in the income statements of corporations. In general, corporate statements are likely to be more conservative than tax returns, so that there is no strong ground for a rigid insistence on such adjustments or allocations. However, where the amounts involved are relatively important and the corporate practice is the less conservative, they should be encouraged.

CHAPTER XIII

Forms of Statements

THE PRESENT STANDARD forms of financial statements are the
unsatisfactory outcome of a series of compromises between
conflicting aims and modes of thought; the balance sheet, as
the oldest and long the principal or only statement issued,
displays these characteristics most clearly. It is a compromise
between the modes of thought of those who prepare it and
those for whom it is designed. Originally, it was recognized
as a statement of balances and a product of accounting technique, as the symbols—"Dr" and "Cr"—by which its two
sides were headed indicated.[1] Later, an effort was made to give
it a more authoritative character; the inexact, but less esoteric
headings "Assets" and "Liabilities" were substituted, and the
document was described as a statement of assets and liabilities, or of financial position or as showing the state of the
company's affairs. Such descriptions gave rise to the belief
that it was photographic in character. In time its character as
historic rather than photographic became generally recognized; but in America, at least, the new headings were by then
in almost universal use. The Institute found it necessary to
define "assets" and "liabilities," when used as balance-sheet
headings, as connoting only balances that are or should be
carried forward when books kept by double entry in accordance with generally accepted accounting practices, are
closed.[2] Corporations began to omit headings entirely; regulatory bodies resorted to such expressions as "assets and other

---

[1] Cf. Table A, Companies Act of 1862 (Eng.).
[2] Accounting Research Bulletin No. 9, 1941.

240

debits" and "liabilities and other credits," which conveyed no more than the early "Dr" and "Cr."

The cycle thus completed is matched in the history of the income account or statement. Fifty years ago the charges to the trading or profit and loss account were usually classified according to the nature of what was purchased or consumed —raw materials, supplies, wages, etc. Analysis of expenditures according to the purposes for which they were made became general with the development of cost accounting as an integral part of the general bookkeeping system. New categories then came into general use in the income account (which had superseded the profit and loss account) and the charges were classified as "manufacturing costs," "selling costs," etc.

Gradually the analysis for administrative purposes became more intensive and the results less suited for the purpose of general financial statements. The social aspects of corporate operations assumed increasing importance. As a result, the classification of charges against revenue is beginning to be presented once more in terms of the character of the consideration received for expenditures. The latest statement of the United States Steel Corporation—which since 1902 has been a pioneer in informative financial reporting—shows charges against gross sales and revenues under such headings as "Employment Costs," "Purchased Products and Services," and "Taxes." Instead of the ladder which in the case of some companies led down by successive steps from "Sales and Revenue" to "Manufacturing Profit," "Profit Before Depreciation, Interest, and Income Taxes," "Profit Before Interest and Income Taxes," "Profit Before Income Taxes," to the final "Profit," the Steel Company's statement treats all deductions on a parity and shows only a single figure of gain described as "Income."

The preceding chapters have emphasized the facts that accounting is predominantly historical and based on cost, not value, and that the light thrown on value by accounts is to be found mainly in the income statement, since value—unless the enterprise is decadent—is measured primarily by earning capacity.

It used to be said that assets were carried in the balance sheet at their value, but that the criterion was their value to a going concern. The foregoing chapters should have made it clear that this is not, today, an accurate statement, and it is doubtful whether it was ever significant, even when true. At best, it meant that the balance sheet reflected and added together values that were values only so long as no attempt was made to realize them all as separate items at the same time. The modern view is that assets reflect (a) costs, the usefulness of which is indefinite; (b) the part of costs of limited usefulness that may upon an allocation between the past and the future fairly be attributed to the future; and (c) cash, and values received in the course of business transactions and stated at their fair cash equivalent.

The significant classification of assets suggested by these considerations is one between those which are necessary to the maintenance of the earning capacity of the enterprise, and those which are not thus essential. The value of the first group of assets is collective, not individual.

Another logical subdivision would be into "Fixed Assets Not Depreciable," "Fixed Assets Depreciable," "Working Assets" including inventories and "Assets Equivalent to Cash."

The standard classification of current assets and liabilities has no great significance, especially if inventories are carried on such bases as last in, first out on the theory that the investment in them is as permanent as that in plant. The balance-sheet classifications of today are too largely based on conditions and needs that either have ceased to exist or are no longer of major importance. However, established usage and acquired familiarity are considerations not lightly to be disregarded. The practical course is, perhaps, to present supplementary statements which, as their value becomes recognized, will gradually make the older forms of presentation superfluous. The balance sheet of a complex business today is a statement of balances or residuals. In its entirety, it is of little value, but parts of it are highly significant. Emphasis on classification in the balance sheet is a recognition of this fact, but it is questionable whether classification within a single statement can ever be a satisfactory method of presentation of items so varied both in their nature and in the way in which monetary expression is given to them.

The double account system has long been employed in England by companies whose assets are predominantly of a capital nature. Mr. J. M. B. Hoxsey, as a result of his experience with the New York Stock Exchange, strongly advocated some such form of statement for similar companies in America. If the amounts expended by a corporation on construction and equipment of a railroad, for instance, are shown as under that system only in an account entitled "Receipts and Expenditures on Account of Capital," no one can be misled into false assumptions as to the value or net worth attaching to each share of capital stock of the corporation.

The objective in presenting the income statement might be to bring together the elements which determine the earning capacity of the enterprise under the conditions existing during the period covered by the statement. These should be distinguished as sharply as possible from income or losses arising from other sources and from changes in the capital value of the assets of the enterprise due to causes other than exhaustion of their useful life.

Faith in a single figure of "net worth" to be derived from the balance sheet has fortunately been dispelled except for certain traditional legal purposes, but there are still many who attach great if unwarranted importance to a figure of net earnings or net income per share to be derived from the income statement. The wide use of such computations is the cause of much concern to conscientious executives and independent accountants. They know that the term "net earnings" or "net income" is often misunderstood; that the assumptions implicit in the use made of the expression may be unfounded; and that the results of operations of a complex business cannot be satisfactorily expressed in any single figure. Yet, being aware of the great importance attached to such figures (and, indeed, to multiplication of them as indicating capital value) they feel an obligation to make the figure likely to be so described as significant as possible in the case of the corporations for which they are responsible.

A paragraph in which the expression "earnings per share" is discussed is perhaps the least satisfactory portion of the American Accounting Association's statement of principles, to which reference has been made herein. The authors first say that the emphasis given to computations of earnings per share and to other measures of corporate performance makes necessary a common yardstick. They thus imply that a yardstick which will serve as a satisfactory measure of corporate performance within the year is attainable. But they go on to stress the importance of bringing into a single statement "not only the best possible measure of income from ordinary operations but also gains and losses not always associated with the transactions of a single year." Little more than this is necessary to show that a satisfactory yardstick in the form of a single figure of earnings per share is merely an objective of wishful thinking.

The war has emphasized the inadequacy of a single figure for the purpose to which it is commonly put, and the time would seem to be opportune for the accounting profession, with the cooperation of the Securities and Exchange Commission, to make a drive against the use of "earnings per share" as they have successfully done against the use of "net worth." This campaign would doubtless be long and arduous, and until it has been successfully conducted the problem of indicating in the statement of income and surplus the figure to be adopted as the net income per share will have to be faced.

How, then, should income per share be conceived? If the older uses of accounting are regarded as controlling, it will be as connoting the increase during the year in the cumulative disposable income. This concept would be acceptable to theorists and to economic statisticians. Traders would probably prefer a figure more indicative of earning capacity and more closely related to the operations of the year itself. Inconsistency has resulted from shifts of emphasis from one concept to the other.

The added uncertainties due to war led the Institute to suggest that the dangers of attaching great importance to a single figure, such as "net income per share," might in many cases be so great as to make undesirable the presentation of any figure designated, without qualification, as "net income." [1] However, this suggestion has not been generally adopted. The tendency seems to have been, rather, to set aside reserves—not, perhaps, supported by evidence which indicated even approximately a probable need—in an effort to avoid the danger of an exaggerated impression of earning capacity being formed.

Probably the wisest course in peace or in war is in general to adhere to the objective presented by the older uses, but to set forth the accounts in such a way that those who care to do so will be able to make the adjustments necessary to reach a figure that conforms more closely to the uses with which they are concerned.

In any case, those who rely on financial statements should realize that computations of past income are based on present knowledge that is often imperfect and on implicit assumptions as to the course of events in the future. They are not statements of fact but are conclusions that result from applying a body of conventions to the events and transactions during

---

[1] Accounting Research Bulletin No. 13.

the period which they cover. They cannot safely be used as a guide to action by any who have not at least a reasonable understanding of their nature. Moreover, such statements are in part a reflection of the temperament and modes of thought of those responsible for their presentation, and no rules can change this fact.

The objection is sometimes made by those whose goal is uniformity that acceptance of this view makes the investor too dependent on management. The answer is, first, that since business success depends largely on management, it is illogical for the investor to strain at the gnat and swallow the camel; and, secondly, that a requirement of fair disclosure, and the exercise of an honest and informed judgment by independent accountants, provide the best means yet devised for affording to the investor such protection as is practicable. The definition and extension of the responsibilities imposed on the management and the profession in this respect by the legislation of the last decade have proved helpful both to the profession and to the investor.

The problem of distinguishing those charges and credits that relate to the current production of income from other items has long been the subject of discussion. Surplus charges and nonrecurrent charges are familiar terms which at times have been employed in questionable ways.

There are differences among accountants today on the question whether the income account and the surplus account for the year should be regarded as separate accounts, as two sections of a single account, or as an indivisible whole. If the two are regarded as separate, the question whether corrections of estimates and other charges and credits arising out of past operations, and not related to the production of income during the year, should be reflected in one or the other, becomes a matter of substance rather than form. If they are considered to be an indivisible whole the question takes the form of how the figure to be used as income per share should be indicated and described. A related problem is presented by charges, of which the Federal income taxes are the most important, that are payable on the basis of computations in which current income and corrections of past estimates are combined without any distinction being made between them.

It used to be common to exclude corrections of estimates and similar charges and credits arising out of past years' operations from the current income account and to show them as charges or credits to surplus. This practice is even today common in classifications such as that of the Interstate Commerce Commission. However, experience has shown, and an examination of the accounts of the railroads will confirm, the dangers attendant upon the adoption of such a course. The better view today is that within wide limits it is preferable to act on the assumption that such corrections and adjustments are inevitable; that some, though not the same, abnormalities are likely to occur in almost every year, and that any distortion resulting from inclusion of the items in the income account of the year will not be significant in relation to the inevitable uncertainties that attach to even the best computations of income. The Institute has therefore discouraged charges and credits to surplus. The wise policy is for managements to display moderate caution in making estimates at the close of any year, so that normally the result of subsequent adjustments to the ascertained facts will be credits rather than charges to income.

However, cases occur in which the inclusion of charges or credits growing out of the past, in the current income statement, would by reason of their relative magnitude be likely to result in a distorted impression as to the results of operations for the year. In such cases, charges or credits to surplus are and probably should be regarded as permissible.

An illustration of the legitimate use of surplus is afforded by a retroactive change from retirement accounting to cost amortization, discussed in Chapter VIII. Such a change involves the creation of an additional reserve representing the depreciation which under the new system is deemed to have accrued prior to the date of the change. If the new system had been put into effect with the initiation of the enterprise, the additional reserve would have been created out of revenues and the surplus would have been correspondingly lower. If the retirement accounting method had been continued, the charge involved in the adjustment would never have been required to be made against revenues of the future. From either standpoint, therefore, the charge if it is to be made at all should go to earned surplus rather than against current or future income.

An interesting case is presented when a corporation adopts or greatly extends a pension scheme which is binding and not voluntary. Cases of this kind have been frequent as the result of changes in the social outlook in recent years. It is customary in such cases to confer on employees benefits in respect of services rendered prior to the initiation of the plan, and the cost of these benefits is regarded as a proper charge to surplus. It might be argued that though the cost is measured by services in the past, it results from action which has been taken and perhaps has become necessary or expedient only in the present, and that therefore the cost is a present cost which should be reflected in the income account. However, a cost that results from a great social change may fairly be regarded as so unusual as properly to be made against the portion of past earnings that was reserved to provide for contingencies, rooted in the past, that might develop in the future. However this case presents clearly the question discussed in the preceding chapter of the proper treatment of income taxes, where a distinction not made in the tax law between charges to income and charges to surplus is made in the company's own accounting. The net amount carried to surplus should, therefore, be only the excess of the cost of the benefits attributable to past services over the tax saving corresponding thereto.

In concluding this chapter it may be desirable to discuss briefly the question of uniformity.

The demand for uniformity in financial accounting is as natural as the demand for certainty—and as incapable of being met. Accounts are historical records, but they cannot rise higher in the scale of certainty than the knowledge which they reflect. Nor is it always possible when uniformity is sought to say whether the resemblances or the differences between transactions are the more significant.

Uniformity in the treatment of routine transactions is undoubtedly practicable and of great value for a number of administrative purposes. However, this uniformity relates largely to subdivisions of general classifications which are dealt with in totals in financial statements. The complaints which are heard of lack of uniformity in corporate accounts relate sometimes to the treatment of inventories, but more frequently are concerned either with charges and credits which cannot be allocated to the years to which they strictly apply because not then ascertained or ascertainable, or with charges and credits arising from major changes in conditions or policies.

It will be apparent that the questions so raised are of an entirely different character from those involved in preparing a uniform classification of operating expenses. No invariable rules for their treatment are laid down in what are commonly called "uniform classifications," such as those of the Interstate Commerce Commission. Failure to appreciate these facts is responsible for much unwarranted criticism of an alleged lack in industrial accounts of a uniformity which is supposed to be, but is not, attained in regulated fields of activity. There is today, at least, as close an approach to uniformity in the published accounts of the large steel companies as in those of the large railroads, though the former are not and the latter are subject to a uniform classification.

The income-tax law has long frankly recognized that complete uniformity of accounting is neither desirable nor attainable. Our present income tax was first levied in 1913, and a provision which was written into the law of 1918 and which has remained substantially unchanged until the present time is very significant:

The net income shall be computed . . . in accordance with the method of accounting regularly employed in keeping the books of such taxpayer; but if no such method of accounting has been so employed, or if the method employed does not clearly reflect the income, the computation shall be made in accordance with such method as in the opinion of the Commissioner does clearly reflect the income.

It is true that the Bureau of Internal Revenue has established uniform rules to govern certain classes of transactions, but it is equally true that in other cases it has specifically allowed optional procedures.

The income-tax law has always recognized as a deduction from gross income in determining taxable income "a reasonable allowance for the exhaustion, wear and tear of property used in the trade or business, including a reasonable allowance for obsolescence." The present regulations lay down no rigid rule but provide that "the capital sum to be recovered shall be charged off over the useful life of the property, *either in equal annual installments or in accordance with any other recognized trade practice*, such as apportionment of the capital sum over units of production" (emphasis supplied).

In relation to inventories they have said:

In order clearly to reflect income, the inventory practice of a taxpayer should be consistent from year to year, and greater weight is to be given to consistency than to any particular method of inventorying or basis of valuation so long as the method or basis used is substantially in accord with these regulations.

As indicated in Chapter X, it is doubtful whether we are nearer uniformity in inventory methods than we were in

1918, and no one has suggested a satisfactory uniform basis. For income-tax purposes, the distinction between charges directly related to the year and charges attributable to past operations is irrelevant. This, of course, is logical, since the taxing authority takes annually its full share of the income of the year, as determined under its rules, and leaves in respect of its share of the income nothing corresponding to the undistributed profits which are left by stockholders to provide for just such contingencies as are under discussion. This fact is sometimes overlooked by persons who regard as vicious any treatment of a loss or expense in the annual accounts of the corporation which is different from the treatment given to it in the corporation's income tax return.

Both reason and experience indicate the unwisdom of any attempt to enforce rigid uniformity in accounting for other than routine transactions. Routine transactions offer no difficulty, but transactions which are out of the ordinary will often require exceptional treatment. Any system which provides for absolute uniformity tends to put an end to progress and to exalt form at the expense of substance. In the case of corporations engaged in rendering service under a scheme of regulation, the problems are much less complex than in the general industrial world. This consideration, together with the paramount public interest, might justify the creation of a uniform system in relation to these corporations, but even in those cases regulatory bodies have found it necessary to sanction departures from uniformity. Obviously, where there is no paramount public interest involved, and where accounts are required for a variety of purposes, the case for latitude is far stronger.

Admittedly, any current determination of corporate income for a year, or shorter period, is at best an approximation; but the further question—an approximation to what?—would be answered somewhat differently by different classes of persons, such as executives, investors, stock speculators, financial statisticians or investment counselors, bank creditors or bondholders, economists, accounting theorists, etc. No account will serve equally well the purposes of each of these classes, so that the practical question to be faced is how far the form is to be determined by their respective needs or desires. The accounting theorist would probably urge uniformity of treatment and suggest that, if for any particular purpose an exceptional transaction may call for special treatment, the party interested should make his own adjustment if he deems it worth while. This, however, seems to me an extremely theoretical solution of what is an intensely practical question.

It is apparent, first, that the interest of some groups is more direct and substantial than that of others, and, secondly, that some groups are better able than others to adjust accounts to fit their own requirements. In general, the individual stockholder has the most direct interest and is least qualified to make adjustments. He is entitled to the benefit of the judgment of the executive and the auditor on the question how, in all the circumstances, the special situation should be dealt with. True, the judgment of the executive may not always be entirely objective, nor the auditor always as independent in fact as in theory; but these are merely phases of the risks which the investor must always run when he entrusts his investment to a management or relies upon an audit. A special treatment should always be fully disclosed so that those who think the risk of dishonesty in the judgment outweighs the advantage of fuller knowledge in its adoption, and prefer to adhere to immutable rules, may make necessary adjustments for themselves.

The view should not be accepted that disclosure is all-sufficient, and that no criticism can justly be made where the facts are disclosed, even though the form of disclosure is unsatisfactory. Investors are entitled not only to an honest judgment by the executives upon both form and substance, but also to demand that auditors shall use their influence to make effective the views which they honestly hold on either point and shall be frank and explicit in expressing any material dissent from the form or content of an income account prepared by the executives.

CHAPTER XIV

Accounting and Regulation

The committee regards corporation accounting as one phase of the working of the corporate organization of business, which in turn it views as a machinery created by the people in the belief that, broadly speaking, it will serve a useful social purpose. The test of the corporate system and of the special phase of it represented by corporate accounting ultimately lies in the results which are produced. These results must be judged from the standpoint of society as a whole—not from that of any one group of interested parties. (Accounting Research Bulletin No. 1, issued September, 1939.)

IN THE FOREGOING CHAPTERS, the history of financial accounting during the first third of this century has been presented as influenced very largely by the increased recognition of the claims of those who buy and sell securities, which found its ultimate expression in the Securities Exchange Act of 1934. Whether the creation of that interest was in itself desirable, it would be idle to inquire, because it was an inevitable accompaniment of broad economic and social movements. A. A. Berle, Jr., in *The Modern Corporation and Private Property*, has pictured the rise of great corporations with managements virtually independent of the beneficial owners, as the growth of a new monopolistic and financial feudalism, in a way that demonstrated his breadth of vision and his skill at delineation as well as his ability to penetrate to the heart of legal doctrines, devices, and fictions. The statistical background provided for his text by Gardiner C. Means was drawn too largely from railroads and other natural monopolies or quasi-monopolies to carry conviction to the competent critic, but undoubtedly added to the popular appeal of the picture.[1]

But the causes of the development lay deeper; and while the desire to restrict competition and the activities of issuing houses may have stimulated the movement and determined to some extent its form, they do not account adequately for the movement itself. Acceptance of the philosophy of mass production as a means of increasing the material welfare of the people in general, and efforts to secure a more even distribution of wealth are, however, sufficient to account for the existence of such corporations and all that they imply. While the United States Steel Corporation and the General Motors Corporation may have been the result of a policy of consolidation, the Carnegie Steel Company might well have grown to its present magnitude under the direct guidance of men like Mr. Carnegie, just as the Ford Motor Company has grown.

A comparison between the year 1930, which marked the end of a period, and fifty years earlier, throws a clear light on the extent of industrial development. Statistics expressed in terms of wealth or even of income are so affected by the disturbing influence of the monetary unit as to be less significant than figures such as those of mechanical horse power in use per person employed. These show a rise from 0.6 H.P. in 1880 to 3.0 H.P. in 1910 and 4.9 H.P. in 1930.

The enormous investment in capital goods which was necessary to secure mass production had to be paid for. To a large extent, the financing was effected in the first instance through the plowing back of earnings of corporations which were under the control of the beneficial owners. The appeal of the opportunity to secure capital gains through participation in mergers or through the conversion of ownership of enterprises into securities of listed corporations was often strong; but

---

[1] See W. L. Crum, *American Economic Review*, Vol. XXIV, p. 69.

death and taxes were the forces that made conversion inevitable in a large proportion of cases at or before the death of the original entrepreneurs.

In the early years of the century consolidation was, perhaps, the major factor in the conversion of private companies into corporations whose securities were widely distributed. Imposition of high Federal and State death taxes, and later of gift taxes, resulted in a need for liquidity and in refinancing becoming the more important factor in increasing the number of corporations whose securities were listed during the third decade of the century. Examination of the stock lists indicates that conversion from privately to publicly owned corporations has been the principal cause of the increase in the number of manufacturing and trading companies whose securities have been on the New York Stock Exchange's list—from 37 at the beginning of 1897 to 677 at the end of 1942. There has, of course, been a great increase in the number of securities listed on other exchanges.

Whatever may have been their causes, conversions of interests in enterprises into securities designed to be readily marketable, and the broadening of the markets in which these could be bought and sold, made necessary the dissemination of a reasonable amount of current information in regard to the progress and financial position of the various companies.

The interests of the potential trader, though not in all respects opposed to those of long-term investors, are by no means identical with them. In particular, the trader may desire disclosure of information which the long-term investor would prefer to be kept from the public. He is interested not so much in values as in changes in value. But when a corporation seeks the advantage of marketability for its securities it may fairly be required to disclose information which has a material bearing on the value of those securities, though in a privately owned concern that information might be treated as confidential.

Until 1933, the stock exchanges were the arbiters on the question of what constituted reasonable disclosure, exercising this authority through their ability to attach conditions to the listing of securities. The Securities Exchange Act of 1934 transferred this jurisdiction to a commission, which shortly thereafter was given authority to deal with various other factors of corporate life—not in the interest of traders or investors, but from the standpoint of a broad public interest. In recent years, other commissions have been created or have been given additional powers, and have thus acquired jurisdiction over accounting matters. Accounting has come to be recognized as more largely affected with a public interest. Today, the interests of the long-term investor and the trader alike are subordinated to other interests in a large part of the corporate field. Even the policy of the Securities and Exchange Commission under the Act of 1934 is inevitably affected by its actions taken under other laws. The current and prospective effects of these developments are matters of great importance to accountants and to those who rely on accounts.

Already we see commissions which are vested with policy-making, regulatory and quasi-judicial functions seeking freedom from legal restraints by asserting the higher authority of accounting principles, old or new, laid down by them and based supposedly on considerations of equity or economic reality. They next undertake to relax the application of such principles as a matter of regulatory expediency or administrative policy. Thus with the aid of legal presumptions of administrative expertness and impartiality, accounting may be made superior to law but still remain the not too rigid implement of policy. Acceptance of some postulates of accounting, such as those of its utilitarian character and the stability of the monetary unit, and disregard of others, such as those of continuity and consistency, have resulted in the development of concepts of accounting new in the field in which they are applied, of which original cost and straight-line depreciation in the utility field, discussed in earlier chapters, are perhaps the most notable. If the procedure is challenged in the early stages the defense is that only methods of recording and no substantive rights are involved. But once the record is established it is made the basis of orders which affect rights but are in practice almost irreversible. In the Telephone case,[1] the Supreme Court insisted on a stipulation designed to protect the utility from the practical effects of what was claimed and held to be only an order for classification of accounts. Later events have created doubts as to the effectiveness of such protection.[2]

The grant to a regulatory commission of power over accounting in unregulated industries was not and could not have been supported by a claim that abuses had developed in that field which did not exist where accounting was regulated. On the contrary, the practices which had become discredited were more general in the regulated industries (and among the utility holding companies) and had spread from those fields to unregulated industry to only a minor extent if at all. This is true of the nonacceptance of the cost amortization concept of depreciation; of questionable reappraisals and improper charges against capital surpluses arising therefrom; of pyramiding of holding companies; of periodical stock dividends improperly accounted for; and of the practice of charging to surplus items which more properly belonged in the income account. These together constitute the major defects of accounting that had developed in the prosperous period that ended in 1929 and in the depression that followed.

Control over accounting has been advocated in the past for the purpose, among others, of securing uniformity. It has been emphasized in earlier chapters that uniformity in the

---

[1] *Supra,* page 35.
[2] *In re* Northwestern Electric Company, *infra,* page 261.

treatment of other than routine transactions is not always attainable because there may be a question whether resemblance or difference between transactions is the more significant from an accounting standpoint. Quite apart from this fact, however, it would be erroneous for the investor to assume that control by commissions and similar bodies is likely to produce a maximum of uniformity. Examination of decisions and classifications will disclose a disturbing number of cases in which disposition is to be "as directed by the commission" or to be determined in some similar way.

Departures from principles on the grounds of expediency have long been an incident of regulatory practice. Three types of cases may be considered. First come those in which authorities have been vested with the duty of enforcing statutes which required securities to be stated in accounts at their "market value." On more than one occasion such bodies have authorized the use of "values" for securities which no accountant would have felt justified in accepting as conforming to the standard in the absence of such regulations. A second type of case is illustrated by the authorization given to the carriers by the Interstate Commerce Commission to charge repairs and losses from retirement to profit and loss (surplus) and not to operating expenses, to which reference has been made in Chapter VIII. A third class of cases includes those in which commissions have expressly authorized departures from accounting principles on the ground of regulatory expediency.

To raise questions about departures from principles is not necessarily to doubt their practical wisdom. In the first class of cases, rigid adherence to the statutes would no doubt in some cases, at least, have produced consequences that would have been disastrous to those whom the statutes were designed to protect. Moreover value, and even fair market value, are unquestionably vague concepts. The rules made were of universal application and were not discriminatory. In such cases the question that suggests itself is, perhaps, whether the statutes were well conceived or whether they should not have anticipated the situations which gave rise to the special rules, especially as there was nothing novel about those situations.

In the second class the same considerations may have existed, though it is difficult for any accountant to accept the view that ordinary current repairs could be properly charged to surplus accumulated in the past, without a fundamental change in accounting concepts.

The deferment of depreciation accounting by the Interstate Commerce Commission for eleven years after it had been decided upon does not present quite the same question. Here, there was a choice between two methods of accounting, and the balance of argument in favor of the new method was narrow if, indeed, it existed.

Some of the cases arising in the third class present still other questions. Decisions under which costs and losses incurred in the past were carried forward to be charged against the future, might be wholly acceptable if related to the doctrine of quasi-contract between utilities and consumers even though they might otherwise be disapproved by independent accounting opinion (see Chapter XII). These considerations are inapplicable to other instances, such as decisions which relate to intangible assets, capital structures or fiscal policies and lie outside the area in which the doctrine of quasi-contract has any application.

One such case has elicited vigorous criticism by the Institute and has produced extended discussion; it presented many questions of current importance besides that of the relation between law, accounting principles and regulatory policy, but only that aspect of it will be considered here. The original transaction which gave rise to the question to be decided was, according to the Commission's findings of fact, a flagrant example of a form of corporate abuse which, common and tolerated when it occurred a generation ago, is now discredited. But while this may avert sympathy it makes consideration of the implications of the decision even more desirable.

The order of the Federal Power Commission in question was made in the case of the Northwestern Electric Company in April, 1942. It raised technical accounting questions and also the much broader issue of the proper function of accounting.

The facts as found by the Commission were very simple. The Company had outstanding common capital stock with a par value of $3,500,000. The original issue of stock had been made in or before 1915, and the Commission had found that no consideration had been received therefor. The stock had been acquired by its present holders in 1925 at a cost of over $5,000,000. The Company had a surplus derived from earnings [1] of approximately $1,000,000. Its annual earnings in excess of preferred dividends were between $150,000 and $200,-000 a year. The Commission had called upon the Company to submit a proposal for disposing of the debit balance of $3,500,000 created in respect of the stock issued. On the Company's failure to submit a plan the Commission, after a hearing, ordered that the Company should apply against the balance a sum equal to its net income "less its preferred stock dividend appropriations for each such calendar year until the amount of $3,500,000 shall have been entirely extinguished."

In directing the disposition the Commission said, first, ". . . we find that it is in the interest of consumers, investors and the public to direct the disposition," and second, "This disposition, assuming adequate earnings, is the equivalent of obtaining ultimately from the holders of the common stock (the holding company) a consideration of $3,500,000 for the stock." A brief filed later on its behalf states that the Commission "was extremely anxious to protect the interests of Northwestern's preferred stockholders."

---

[1] This surplus was apparently restricted as to distribution by an order of the Securities and Exchange Commission.

The Chief Accountant of the Commission had testified that as far as accounting principles were concerned the amount should be removed from the books of the Company at once—adding, however, "A policy and not an accounting principle may call for spreading the amount over a reasonable period of years in the future." He expressed the view that the period "should not be more than ten years, five years being a much more desirable period." He restated his position as being that, "in other words, the amount does not belong on the books of account at all, hence the period of amortization, if amortization is approved, should be as short as possible."

The matter under consideration was thus, how a debit balance carried in respect of capital stock issued without consideration should be disposed of. The question could obviously be regarded from the standpoint of legal or equitable rights or from that of wise financial policy; but the Commission was exercising a purely accounting authority, so that only the strictly accounting aspects of the question need to be considered.

Theory might lead to the conclusion that if the law permits stock to be issued without consideration and no right against the holders of the stock is created by such an issue, then the stock issued should be carried at or adjusted to a purely nominal figure for record purposes only, with a corresponding nominal debit balance. Such a disposition would meet the requirements suggested by the Chief Accountant of the Commission.

On the other hand, practice, as illustrated by the classification of the Interstate Commerce Commission for carriers, both before and since its revision as of January 1, 1942, has contemplated that, where a stock is issued at a discount from its par value, the par value should be shown on the credit side and a "discount on capital stock" account set up which is not required to be amortized or disposed of in any way.

A charge of discount on stock to a surplus representing a

demonstrated appreciation in value would have been regarded until quite recently as permissible, but would not now be approved. A charge to a surplus created either by a reduction of legal capital or out of earnings would clearly be permissible, and the Commission has authorized such dispositions in other cases. Whether a charge against surplus earnings over a period in the future would conform to accepted accounting practice—assuming that no existing surplus was available—is highly doubtful. That such a disposition is unacceptable when a surplus already exists and is left undisturbed seems clear beyond question.

In so far as the Commission ignored the existing surplus, its action is without support in accounting theory or in the testimony of its own accountants. It is open to the obvious and serious objection that it permits what the Commission has decided to be a nonexistent asset to be carried for a period of years and a surplus to be carried at the same time without apparent reason.

The Commission's action in requiring the write-off to be made to the extent of approximately $1,000,000 out of future surplus instead of existing surplus is irreconcilable with its objective and unnecessary for the purposes which it regarded as determinative of the proper disposition of the amount. Even, therefore, if it were assumed that the Commission had the broadest power to determine what was equitable rather than what was called for by good accounting, it would be impossible to justify the order in this respect.

The case thus raises far more than a technical accounting question regarding the proper disposition of a particular balance. It presents the question whether it is a function of accounting to prescribe what a corporation shall do with its net income after that net income has been determined in accordance with accounting principles. That this is what the Commission undertook to do is clear, since the order calls for a disposition of net income and, indeed, of balances of net income after the payment of certain dividends. It also raises the question whether it is a function of accounting to supplement corporation law, as by making an order which "is the equivalent of obtaining ultimately from the holders of the common stock (the holding company) a consideration of $3,500,000 for the stock." It raises the questions whether accounting principles are subordinate to regulatory expediency and whether a commission can depart from accounting principles as laid down by its own witnesses and still justify its orders on the ground that it is adhering to those principles.

Finally, the issue of discrimination and punitive intent is presented by the facts that the Commission's order goes beyond what is necessary for even the purpose asserted; is contrary to the opinion of its own accountant and all accounting theory, and is at variance with its orders in other cases.

On appeal, the Circuit Court of Appeals for the Ninth Circuit upheld the order, dismissing the point made in regard to the ignoring of the existing surplus with the curiously irrelevant comment that this contention was "not pertinent because it has no bearing on the 'original cost' theory of the system of accounts." It is apparent that the Court either was unwilling to review the order or completely failed to apprehend the accounting point involved.

As the case stands, it illustrates the dangers to which Mr. (now Assistant Secretary of State) Berle drew attention in the article quoted in Chapter IV and the problem he foresaw of deciding what the accounting profession should do in such situations.

There would seem to be an opportunity for accountants to render a public service and to regain professional ground lost through grants of power over accounting rules to other bodies in and since 1933. The courts are not expert in accounting, and our methods of informing them on technical matters are deficient, as anyone who has had experience as an expert witness must realize. Decisions on important general issues should not be allowed to depend upon the skill and knowledge displayed by counsel and witnesses for the parties or upon fortuitous aspects of the cases in which the issues are first raised. The alternative is for the profession to follow events closely and to intervene through its Institute in an expert and disinterested manner and in whatever way may be appropriate when issues of sufficient general importance appear to be at stake. Such a policy will tend towards consistency in the decisions of various regulatory bodies and also between regulated and unregulated accounting.

No doubt there are those who prefer the freedom from responsibility that comes from unquestioning conformity to regulation. But the profession cannot render its full service to the community by adopting such a policy. It can do so by a policy which will combine with a willingness to cooperate with regulatory bodies to the fullest possible extent, acceptance of a responsibility for the maintenance and wise development of accounting rules and principles in the broad public interest. In addition to the long-recognized obligation of accountants to maintain their complete individual independence in relation to their clients, there should be accepted a collective obligation to be independent in their relations to commissions. In each case, proper exposition and persuasion should in the great majority of instances achieve the desired objects; but when a public disagreement unfortunately becomes necessary, it should be frankly and effectively made known.[1]

---

[1] The Federal Power Commission in the case of Pennsylvania Electric Company (Opinion 102, decided in August, 1943) approved the acquisition of property for cash upon the condition that about one-third of the cost should be written off immediately against a capital surplus to be artificially created. It added: "This is in accord with sound accounting principles." Now, one of the best established of accounting principles is that capital surplus shall not be used to absorb charges which otherwise would require to be made against income. Whether the dictum above quoted is or is not acceptable, it is irreconcilable with the dicta of the Commission about amortization of intangibles, discussed at pages 153 to 157 above.

General Index

(See also Table of Cases Cited)

CASES CITED

UNITED STATES COURTS